Deep Gardening:
Soul Lessons from 17 Gardens
Biodynamic Memories

Woody Wodraska

Aurora Farm Press

2010

*Our mission is to efficiently provide the world's finest, most comprehensive book publishing
service, enabling every author to experience success. To find out how to publish your book, your
way, and have it available worldwide, visit us online at www.trafford.com*

Trafford rev. 01/13/2010

 www.trafford.com

North America & international
toll-free: 1 888 232 4444 (USA & Canada)
phone: 250 383 6864 ♦ fax: 812 355 4082

Contents

Excerpt from the Author's Last Will and Testament

This is how I want you to dispose of my meat body. I'm assuming I have died on the farm without benefit of outside experts, and that we can keep it that way. No doctors, undertakers, EMTs or others who will try to make an emergency out of the whole thing. Do what you have to do to get my death officially noted, but don't let them take my "remains" away. No no no. For the most part my body has been built up of the produce of Aurora Farm, and now it's time to give back. Compost me.

Please have someone turn the most recent cow stall compost pile over onto the space next to it. This will leave a nice, damp, wormy place at grade level where you are to dig my grave. Not too deep. This grave is to be built UP, not dug down. Now bring what's left of me down there to the compost yard. Should be easy, for I never have weighed much and a lot less now. No box. No concrete "vault" for goodness sake. Just a shroud of some sort, or maybe my barn coveralls, which are probably on their way to being compost anyway. Lay me down, there among my friends the worms and say a few words, play a little music, then cover me lightly with soil and all hands grab a pitchfork and rebuild the compost pile over me. Add the Biodynamic preparations.

A year or so later go ahead and use the compost on the gardens. Whatever good energies I've managed to bestow on it will spread and diffuse into the landscape. Don't scrape past the grade level now. My bones will still be there and we don't want to startle anyone. Build another pile on top of me. And so on. Dust to dust, ashes to ashes, meat to worm to compost to garden. And so on.

Thank you.

Preface - A Deep Map

I aim to convey what William Least Heat Moon called in his wonderful book *PrairyErth* a deep map of my 40-year career, the personal terrain underlying 17 gardens in almost as many states. I'll tell you as honestly as I can of the triumphs and failures that were there and what they meant to me. Each garden is a node in a web of stewardship. My energy is in it still, and its energy in me.

How the deep map works

Picture our deep map with me. Layers upon layers. Unlike paper road maps, our garden maps come in 3-D. Each layer is etched with words and mind pictures in a thick sheet of clearest glass and each positioned on top of another until we have a three-dimensional vision of shimmering, interpenetrating, shifting *meaning*. What does the garden mean…to me and through our common humanity to you? To the workers and the eaters. What does the garden mean in the landscape, in the multi-generational scheme of time? What does it mean that we have changed the energy here in this place, and been changed by it?

First layer is the topography of the garden and the watershed in which it lies, for flowing water informs a place and if I tell you there is a stream rushing next to the garden you should see energy moving there in your mind's eye, an edge of wild motion where anything can happen. What other features are there? Which trees and wild plantings are there and what wildflowers and berries? Its slopes and shady spots, outcrops, boundaries and secret places are there to be treasured. How does the garden fit in with its surroundings: a village, a farm or ranch, a backyard? How does the energy flow?

Second is the social context: a family or perhaps a community supporting the garden and in turn being sustained by it; what other market does it serve, what are the economics of the situation? This can be as stark as a gardener working alone to pull a ton of carrots for a distant market, or as rich as cutting lettuce to feed a dozen folks joining your farm family at dinner. Every garden exists in a culture: does the culture nourish and sustain the garden and the gardeners? Or does it exploit and isolate them, failing to honor uniqueness and integrity? Terrence McKenna said, "The culture is not your friend," but he was talking of the large culture. Can we create small cultures for our gardens that nurture people and biome? Yes we can. I've seen it done, not often, but even one such culture is a model that radiates its influence forever.

Then there is the garden in time, the rich layering of seasons, how it was in winter and how it will be in high summer; in the upwelling growth of spring and the slow fading of light in fall. The budding and flowering and gathering; the annuals and perennials in their separate and complementary rhythms. The trees over all, how are they there on the edge next to the garden, or within, bearing fruit and offering shade. Over decades, as boundaries and purposes and personnel evolve, how is it with the garden's being.

Come now the layers comprising the gardener's observations in varying scales, from inspecting the underside of a single leaf or delving under a compost pile to see wormlings and bug eggs, examining mosses and insect wings—to scanning the wider landscape, seeking the visual and energetic harmony of the whole. And even wider afield, to judge weather coming up the valley or off the mountain slopes at the horizon. Shifts in scale, shifts in perception and consciousness are the among the gardener's highest functions, for s/he is the eye and mind of God on the scene. I can lose myself in a square inch of mosses or a flower structure that draws me in like a pollen-laden honeybee…there and back again for the sheer joy of it, and curiosity, to try to imagine what the world of the mosses or flowers means to the tiniest white spider or gnat I find there. And listen! There is a shift in awareness possible when we stop, close eyes, and listen…to the hum of bees, and birdsong, and murmuring growth. Be quiet and hear the corn grow and the worms digesting. Can we be the ears of the Goddess?

Yet another layer: the garden in its atmospheric and planetary surroundings, the influence of the moon and the other planets and, of course, the sun. Its place in the wider biosphere, the etheric web. What energies come to the garden with moon shadow and dew and frost? What forces traverse the solar system to form my spinach and let it express itself. How do air and fragrance and warmth flow through beds and hedges. Rain…ah rain. Why should I come in out of the rain when the plants don't?

Add color to the layers: the infinite shadings of green manifesting there; the bright yellows and oranges of daffodils and winter squash blossoms; the scarlet of runner bean flowers, tomato reds, the pink of dogwood blossoms; black and white and every hue between. Swirl and spin the colors throughout like an artisan glass blower.

The soil with its own layers, the basis of it all. The mulch with its cooling effect on top, and the moisture just there in the zone where worms work and transform mulch into soil, even bringing stems and leaves far down in their burrows. The compost-rich top inches where the first plant roots take hold and proliferate; and deeper roots penetrating further into the less-rich but differently-nourishing middle layers where there is less organic matter and more minerals; tap roots going even further into the untilled hardpan. Let us honor soil as a rich and nurturing map of life itself.

The people of the garden, the workers: how they find themselves here and what motivates them. How do they respond to the tasks imposed by the garden? How much do they perceive of what is here for them? Can they get out of themselves long enough, far enough, to see and smell, hear and taste this place? Can they climb out of mind and inhabit their fingers for a while?

More people of the garden, the eaters: how they are nourished and how the energy of the garden, packaged as lettuce or cabbage or strawberries, moves in them. How it disperses and evolves in the wider context.

Layers inside the gardeners: our journey toward competence and stewardship; inner training and insights on the personal level. Virtues won and lost. How the garden shapes human-ness and helps us approach the spirit.

And the writer. There is only this question: can I write truly?

Introduction - Garden as Guru

When I was a child my mother watched one of those 1950s television shows, locally produced in Cincinnati across the Ohio River from our home in Kentucky. The hostess would greet folks in the studio audience asking how they made their living and they would sometimes answer "Oh, we're just farmers..." That *just* annoyed me, even as a kid. City bred, I'd only experienced a couple of farms—my uncle's in Missouri, a friend's closer by—but to me a farmer was a hero engaged in mighty deeds. In the sweep of a vast landscape of fields and woods and barnyards, my farmer milked huge horned cows, slopped feed to snorting monster pigs, commanded regiments of exhaust-belching implements doing mysterious things. And these heroes of mine brought forth plenty. On the farm we had fresh berries, vegetables straight from the garden, home-grown meat, rich, aromatic, frothing milk like none I'd ever experienced; ears of sweet corn as long as my arm, dripping with home-made butter; piglets, calves, chicks and puppies. On the farm were legions of pettable (and not so pettable) creatures, while at home in the city I had no pets at all. As for that wonderful raw milk fresh from the home cow, when I came home from one of those infrequent farm visits I refused to drink the homogenized, pasteurized, stale, lifeless version served up by our milkman. (I was bribed with chocolate milk and I relented.)

In the city, for the most part I learned things from books. Life was ordered and tame. In the country it was all intense and direct experience—smells, sights, sounds, terror, tumbles, and total abandon. I was intoxicated by the smell of the hay mow, the horse's stall, even the pigsty. The view of the land stretching out in front of me always beckoned to more adventures. The vibration and clangor of the tractor, with me aboard standing exactly as Uncle Elmer told me and holding on for my life, exalted and terrified. I got hung up in barbed wire sliding under the fence, got upended by a sow 10 times my bulk, held my ears as uncle pounded hammer on anvil in the workshop and blasted a stump in the pasture with dynamite. We fired .22s and .410 shotguns and tin cans toppled off fence posts. We rode ponies and fell, hard, in the stubble. I got sunburned, blackberry-scratched, chigger- infested, and half-drowned, and at the end of every day except the last I celebrated the thought of more of the same coming tomorrow. When the farm visit came to an end and what I had to look forward to was going home, my spirits were bereft.

Mom said, "Why on the farm that boy has more fun rolling an old tire into a ditch than when we go to Coney Island!"

My mother's mother, Madeline Simon, lived with us for a few months at a time while I was growing up. Grandma was tiny and quiet, but there were always things we did differently when she resided with us: No baked goods came into the house from outside; she was in the kitchen all day Saturday, baking; and we said the rosary after dinner, every day. In blackberry time we went as a family to pick and came home to make jam with Grandma, covering the jam with melted paraffin from a tiny tea kettle reserved for the purpose. We ate potato pancakes for supper on meatless Fridays and sometimes what she called "Himmel und Erd," a surprisingly tasty mix of mashed turnip, potato and apple. Grandma was from Alsace Lorraine, that region along the Rhine that has switched hands several times between France and Germany in recent centuries. She spoke German often, and English with a heavy accent. She was born about 1875, immigrated as a child and raised 10 children in St. Louis. My Mom, Kathryn, was the oldest girl. We heard many times the story of how, when meat was scarce (most of the time?), the elder brothers, who were working, presumably as teenagers, to support the family, were served the meat while the younger children did without. Grandma came from peasant stock, I know, but did not share stories of her country childhood. It may have been her unhappy recollections of hungry times then that colored my parents' view of farming as a lower calling than, say, engineering or doctoring.

Grandma was remote and somewhat severe. Many of my childish concerns and enthusiasms were met with her dismissive, "Humbug!" At one point, I couldn't have been more that six or eight years old, I came to her in tears with a tragically hurt finger. There was a splinter under the nail and I could tolerate no amount of probing with a needle, the usual splinter removal procedure at our house. Grandma had a peasant trick up her sleeve, however. She sent me into the back yard for a couple of dandelion leaves and when I brought them back had me chew on them, macerating them a bit. Then she smoothed the wet gob over the end of my finger and carefully wrapped it in a strip of old sheet. By evening the drawing power of the dandelion had extracted that ugly, jagged splinter. By rights I should have been astonished but I don't remember that. This was Grandma at her mysterious, all-knowing best, taking care of business. Almost as mysterious was her profound friendship with Sister Celestina. The hospital cattycorner from our house in Covington was St. Elizabeth's Hospital, in the days I'm talking of, the late 1940s, a small hospital run by nuns. It was a single, multi-winged brick structure fitted neatly into the neighborhood, parking available on the street and a small lot at the Emergency Room for doctors. The grounds were more landscape than structure and Sister Celestina, tiny as Grandma and also from Alsace Lorraine, was gardener. There were benches set in trellised grottoes entwined with clematis and honeysuckle, these for grieving, bewildered family members awaiting the outcome of a relative's surgery or an imminent death. She had charge of hedges and flower beds, mature trees, little fountains and bird feeders. We would sometimes go with Grandma to find the Sister in her voluminous habit and headdress and her vast pinstriped apron, rake in hand, tidying up her little empire. She and Grandmother would chatter in German and both would work in the flower beds, bottoms up and knees locked, wrist deep in the soil, exactly like those kitschy plywood decorations you see in people's yards. We children, blessed in the hush of the hospital garden, would be very well behaved on these occasions.

The rest of the time I was growing up, the lovely serene landscape gave way to parking lots and therapy buildings, a nursing school behind and expanded facilities of every sort, including the name, now St. Elizabeth's Medical Center. I don't know if, broken-hearted, Sister Celestina watched from her spare cell in the sisters' quarters as her gardens were obliterated and paved over, or whether she, like Grandma, died at the century's halfway point.

As I grew up I was gradually co-opted by the rewards the culture had to offer… seduced away from my childhood agrarian tendencies by jobs, cities, college, marriage. It wasn't until I was 23, in graduate school at the University of Kentucky, when the pull towards the country overtook me. An ad appeared in the "Houses for Rent" classified for a home in the country about halfway between Frankfort, where my wife worked, and Lexington where I was attending classes The rent was $50 per month. This is 1965. I got directions and drove out into Woodford County to find the place… drove further and further on progressively narrowing roads, then gravel, down into the Kentucky River valley. Over a cattle guard at Roy Thompson's farmyard, down a two-rut road and take a right at the fork by the sinkhole, down even more steeply, to a gate. The rental place was there, literally at the end of the road, the Watts Ferry road.

When I realized that I could have the proprietorship of 100 acres of rough fields and woods a kind of land greed seized me, and after renting the place for a year or so, when I found out the owner was willing to sell, I bought it. $14,700. This was in the mid-1960s.

To buy the land at that price I needed to assure the county Agricultural Stabilization Board that I did not want the tobacco allotment, that is, I would not seek to grow tobacco on the land. In their mind, and the owner, that was about all the land was good for—the government-allocated permission to grow 3 acres of tobacco. I was neither competent nor interested in that, so giving up the allotment was not a problem.

There seemed little difference to me between proprietorship and ownership. I related to the farm pretty much as I had before I bought it: mostly I walked, inspecting every feature of the place with my dog and my gun. I "possessed" the land. I marked my territory, but I was no kind of steward.

I was there four years and a little more when I lost the farm in a relatively amicable divorce settlement. Having owned and had the use of land, but not having taken it under stewardship in any productive way, it was fairly easy for me to leave the farm and begin a career as a wandering writer and finally a wandering farmer. From Kentucky, then, to New Brunswick, to New York, to West Virginia…west to Nevada and Oregon and on…

In each of these places I lived in the country and almost always I gardened. Each of these gardens was a guru; each taught me lessons, subtle or dazzling. Many times the lessons were not apparent to me until much later and most of the time I characteristically resisted them anyway.

So the plan of this book is to navigate through this oddball career of mine, unsettled farmer and gypsy peasant, and see what these lessons have been for me and whether we can make any sense of them at all, and live the lessons when they fit.

Later is time enough to detail these gardens and farms, but it might help to have a bird's eye view of the itinerary of my adult life. Don't ask me why I hopped around like a flea on the hide of North America. Each move seemed to be a good one at the time, and most were accomplished with little more than a van or pickup load of stuff. I learned early on to travel lightly on the Planet.

From central Kentucky with its bluegrass and the Kentucky River to

→ Hopkinton, New York (not much of a garden there), to

→ Fallon, Nevada (multiple gardens there, and my first undertaken with a family to feed,) to

→ Charles Town, West Virginia and my introduction to Biodynamic alchemy, back to

→ Fallon, and then to

→ Fossil, Oregon, (two gardens, both instructive, plus a sunflower patch, just for the birds), to

→ Charles Town West Virginia again (swineherding), to

→ Lake Jem, Florida (tropicals), to

→ East Eden, New York (goats) where I once again was faced with how little I knew, to

→ Blacksburg, Virginia and a backyard salad garden and a nurseryman's training, to

→ Kimberton, Pennsylvania where I finally got to experience Biodynamics and learn it from the ground up and the planets down. This is a long interlude, from spring 1981 through the 1984 growing season, and the seminal experience of my career, in large-scale gardening, greenhouse work, time management, volunteer direction, crew care, compost making, chickens on a large scale and pigs aplenty.

Leading, in late 1985, to

→ Camphill Village Minnesota, in Sauk Center for my formal introduction to cows, the basis of compost making in the biodynamic way. On to

→ Fowler, Illinois and a smallholding that included major gardens, greenhouse building, pigs and chickens, and Lynda, a Guernsey cow. Here I undertook to feed 27 families, CSA style, in 1988, then to

→ Temple, New Hampshire and the heart of the CSA movement, and a three or four year hiatus from gardening. Westward to

→ the Tom Miner Basin, Montana just north of Yellowstone, and a challenging but very nicely underwritten garden at 7,000 feet...enough supplies, enough help, a chance to grow 39 varieties of lettuce and flowers forever. Now the dry country at

→ Patagonia, Arizona to garden in high desert, without cow manure. This lasted less than a season. On to

→ Honeoye Falls, New York where the challenge of gardening never-before cultivated land and feeding, ultimately, 100 families was matched by the social challenges which I either met or didn't meet, depending on how you read the story.

In 1998 to 2005

→ Aurora Farm, which felt at the time like the last, best place, on a hilltop overlooking the Kootenay River and the Creston Valley in southeastern British Columbia. Here came the ultimate lesson, surrender. Then to

→ The Big Wood River in Idaho, just south of Sun Valley, where ever finer nuances of surrender may be required. To

→ New Hampshire and finally to

→ the Azores.

* * *

Missing persons

I have pledged to spare the reader an account of my non-gardening life which, be assured, is fully as idiosyncratic as the gardening part. In consequence, I appear to have plowed, sown, cultivated and harvested these many gardens all by my lonesome, which is not true at all. Others shared the work and what glory there was to be had, and sometimes these others were wives and lovers.

Except for my current-and-forever wife and garden partner Barbara Mary Victoria Scott, founder and guiding light of Aurora Farm, they remain nameless and unacknowledged here, for to detail the relationships and how they impacted on my life and career would smack of self-inflicted gossip. Not to my taste at all.

You may imagine then, if you wish, that there was a domestic scene with all of the complexities and joys and missteps that implies, adjacent to each of the garden landscapes I write about, a domestic scene seething (or not) with drama; refulgent (or not) with high purpose.

Woody on that old Farmall tractor, 1965.

Chapter 1 – I had a farm in Kentucky 1965-69
Ownership/Proprietorship

I have to tell you about this farm. One hundred acres, shaped like a slice of pie, with the point to the northeast and two fence lines running straight downhill to the Kentucky River. The crust of the pie slice is a half-mile of river frontage, mostly with a steep bank. Across the river is a sheer, wooded bluff with no floodplain, just rocky cliffs diving straight into the river, relieved only by one creek coming out of a steep-sided hollow. No one overlooks my Kentucky River farm, and the nearest neighbors, save Roy Thompson, are a mile away, up or down the river.

A private spot, made to order for a hermit like me.

The terrain is pretty rough. From the long-vacant tenant house at the high point of the farm and the tip of the pie slice, the landscape drops in elevation irregularly, with humps and pocket watersheds, in open, depleted-looking pasture and woods. The closer to the river, the more lush and the bigger the trees, until on the river bank itself there are huge tulip poplars, oaks and black walnuts. Further uphill, on the other side of the two bottomland fields the woods are less dramatic, but still impressive, with eastern red cedar and other conifers, hickory, ash, oak, maple. Toward the river the watercourses are gullied where thunderstorm events carved them out. There are three of these cutbank gullies on the land, with sandy outwashes into the river. Further away from the river and the terrain rising, the gullies become charming creeks in the spring. The rest of the year they are just damp. The only surface water on the farm is the overflow from the spring house, below the main dwelling.

The creek banks and low spots on the land are the most interesting places on the farm, and the half-mile of riverbank is the most interesting of all. Many trees on this edge of the land are larger than I can put my arms around. The woods are special, more so than the more open and dryer scrub-pasture, with its briers and broom sedge.

In addition to the houses—the vacant and dilapidated tenant house and the serviceable two bedroom house we rented—there was a 100 foot long tobacco barn, a rundown garage with no doors, a couple of more or less intact outbuildings. At the high side of one of the bottomland fields was a large open fronted sheet metal shed for hay storage. With the exception of the first year we were there, the fields were not cultivated. This was not a bad thing, for the dozens of bags of Muriate of Potash abandoned in the hay shed were evidence that the 25 acres of bottom land fields had been pushed to the limit of production, corn and oats, I would think, chemically fertilized and depleted of organic matter. They needed a rest, and if the woods encroached on my watch, then that was not such a bad thing either.

The tobacco barn we rented out to neighboring growers for the fall and winter curing and stripping season. In September suddenly there would appear tractors pulling flat bed trailers piled high with wilted tobacco plants skewered on 5-foot-long hickory sticks, sharpened at one end and thrust through the base of the plants, which had been cut off close to the ground. The crews would drive to the barn, which was constructed on a completely open plan, with a bay down the middle for the wagons to drive through. On either side and going all the way up to the ridgepole, 30 feet off the ground, were wooden rails, making a giant jungle gym with rails spaced just far apart enough to support a tobacco stick with its hanging plants. Starting at the top the harvesters hung the tobacco, still green and moist from the field, each stick separated by a foot or so to allow for air circulation. Within days the barn was full and the atmosphere around it was fragrant with curing tobacco.

Much later, in the winter, smaller crews, often a neighboring farmer and his wife, would come to the barn, stoke up the stove in the stripping room (this is the same room I used to shelter baby chicks and their moms in the spring), and take down the hanging curtains of now cured plants. They stripped the leaves from the stalks, graded, and bound into "hands", consisting of a pound or so of leaves, all of a specified quality, from the broad, thick ones found at the bottom of the plant to the narrower, more spindly ones near the flower head.

There was no thought in those days before the brouhaha about smoking and the killer weed tobacco, that there was anything disreputable about growing tobacco for the market. Indeed, for many of my neighbors, the tobacco crop represented their entire cash income for the year, and considering the work involved in growing harvesting, curing, stripping, grading, transporting, and selling it…little enough income.

* * *

This was the domain I was called upon to steward, with nothing to go on but dim memories of the farms I visited in childhood. I was not up to the task.

Mostly I walked. Every day almost I walked, first with Tippy, a nondescript mongrel we inherited, then with Ol' Bob, a German Shorthaired Pointer given to me by a friend. Down along the river we walked and we'd sit there on the bank, letting the river take our thoughts away on the current. My dad had taught me about that, sitting with me on the bank of the Ohio. Up into the higher ground the dog and I walked, looking at stuff, inspecting, making our marks on our territory.

I looked, but I didn't see. The maxim is that the farmer's footsteps are the best fertilizer, that knowing attention and observation of what's needed are the prerequisites for stewardship. These didn't apply in my case. I wasn't a bad farmer…I was no kind of farmer at all. I did no harm, most of the time, but I didn't do any good either. Mainly the farm was an unwinding place for me, a place to be, not a place to do. My work was elsewhere at the time, at school and later for the State of Kentucky. The farm was a place to retreat from the world.

POSTED
NO

TRESSPASSING

SHOOTING

HUNTING

KRS (Kentucky Revised Statute)
39-321 provides
severe penalties for trespassers and
effective remedies for landowners

I had 50 of these signs printed in black and red on white sheet steel, 16"x24", unmistakable assertions of ownership and territorial rights. All this happened within a week after I confronted a shotgun-toting gent breaking out of the riverbank brush and trees into the open bottomland field, deep in MY property. We had words with each other, no-nonsense words but civil enough, I thought, ending with him heading south, down river toward my fence line, shotgun shouldered. I watched him go, letting my blood pressure and heart rate ease, a trickle of sweat running down my ribs under my shirt. I'm not good when it comes to confrontations. As the intruder entered the strip of woods at the fence line, without turning to see if I was there, he let off a shot, echoed immediately by the cliff on the other side of the river. My anger and resentment soared and my resolution to post the land, simmering for a while, grew urgent and puissant.

The fellow at the sign shop was impressed enough with the wording on my proposed signs to offer me an extra 10 of them in exchange for the rights to print up another batch of them to sell ready made.

I hung them on fences, nailed them to scantlings in turn nailed to big trees…every 500 feet or so along the property lines, including the unfenced riverbank. In places where visibility was limited by brush and undergrowth I put them closer together. Never again would anyone be able to claim they'd inadvertently crossed onto private land. It was the work of a couple of days and I completed the job by screwing the last sign to the metal gate that closed our yard fence at the end of the gravel track through Roy Thompson's pasture.

Bird Watts would have taught me a thing or three about stewardship if I'd been listening. This old boy showed up at the house yard one Saturday morning, leaning heavily on his tobacco stick cane, shiny with the use of years and worn down at the business end. Bird was tall and skinny, bent and old and—I blush to admit it—no more welcome than I had to make him. I wasn't happy to be spending more than a few minutes with this neighbor from the next farm over. Up against my callow post-adolescent self-importance and ignorance, Bird's country manners and country dress, his self-effacement and patent need to talk and find out something about "The Doctor," as I'd come to be known in the neighborhood, failed utterly to make an impression. (The distinction between studying to be a doctor of psychology and being a doctor was lost on the folks hereabouts.)

I knew the last portion of the road to my farm, from the mailboxes onward to the fork in Roy's pasture, was known as Watt's Ferry road. What stories Bird could have told me about the days when his—what? grandfather, great-grandfather?—ferried folks over to the mouth of that unknown creek (Bird would have known the name) on the other side. Did they take teams and wagons or just foot passengers? Bird could have told me too about floods and crop failures and the days when fields of hemp (for sailcloth and rope and cordage during the Civil and the World Wars) were grown in these bottoms. He'd have had stories about droughts and crop failures and hard times. Now, I am close in age to Bird at that time, and I have a deep remorse that I didn't ask to hear Bird's stories, that I didn't beg the man to share his life's memories and all he'd been told as a boy and all he'd learned as a man. I should have sat at his feet as long as he would allow and walked with him back home. Even when he offered me a bandana full of sassafras root he'd dug so as not to show up at a neighbor's empty handed, my self as I was then discounted this inconvenient visitor, disregarded and diminished him. I can see and feel that puerile twenty-something's impatience and fatuous self importance and reflect on how things might have been different in my own farming education if I'd treated Bird as respectfully as he deserved. But I didn't, and he left after a little while saying "Y'all come and see us over home…" I did accept the sassafras root and did actually sample the tea, which was pleasant enough. This was the first Spring we were on the land, 1965, and I was just 23, if that's an excuse.

Most of my waking hours were spent commuting and at the University, later at work. What I had during my five years there was weekends on the farm. Vacations I went elsewhere, often to New Mexico. As always, I walked, but there were certain things—guy things—I did do. Fencing. Cutting some firewood. Trying to hold back the Osage orange hedge. I had to have a tractor. Not that I did much with it beyond mowing rough edges around the house and, once attempting to plow, but I had to have it. Those adventures hanging on to Uncle Elmer's tractor seat were well engraved in memory and I knew that I needed a tractor if I was going to be a farmer.

I kept an eye out for a cheap used tractor, and pretty soon struck a deal with a guy who ran a Standard Oil station just outside Frankfort. He sold me a pre-war Farmall, with big rear tires and small front ones. No battery. It started with a crank and some mumbo jumbo. No hydraulics. Exhaust pressure got shunted from the manifold to a large cylinder just at your left knee, and pushed a piston and connecting arm lever at the back of the machine, to lift your implement. Theoretically. It was an ingenious apparatus, one I've never seen or heard of since, but the tractor never ran well enough while I had it that the back pressure didn't threaten to shut it down when I lifted the plow. Never mind. For the occasional mowing I had to do, or pulling up a fence post, that $400 Farmall was about as much as I needed.

I cranked it and cussed it and filled up the tires with a hand pump, probably about the same as any farmer would, but it didn't make me a farmer to have a tractor.

Walnut Trees. I mentioned the black walnut trees that graced the river bank. The lumber from these magnificent trees was and is much prized for furniture, gunstocks, and when a trunk is reasonably straight and more than eight feet from ground to first limb it's a veneer log to be shipped to Germany where precision milling equipment was in place to shave micro-thin veneer—thin as a magazine page—miles of it, like paper towels coming off a roll.

Toward the end of my time on the farm, with a marriage breaking down and my wanderlust beginning to assert, I confess I eyed those trees with dollar signs in my mind. The proceeds from selling those veneer logs would help pay the mortgage down and make the whole situation more escapable. I shudder to admit my greed and self-centeredness, but there it is. Now, however, three or four years into my lame stewardship of the land, Nature stirred conscience in me and, while guilt and remorse were close to the surface, a plan for redemption came to me. For every tree I allowed to be cut down, profiting from the demise of an older, weightier, altogether more honorable and wiser creature than myself, I would plant 20 seedlings of the same. If I was to succumb to greed, I could at least make a stab at replacing the trees I have destroyed. No telling how many of those trees survived, but I spent most of my spare time that last spring on the river bank digging holes for black walnut seedlings I acquired from the Kentucky Department of Fish and Wildlife. Almost 40 years later, I think about those hundreds of seedlings…saplings…trees. Hardwood nut trees grow slowly. Those planted 8 or 10 years ago at Aurora Farm are now head high, and almost as broad as they are tall, beautifully shaped, stable and well supported by sturdy root systems. In Kentucky, the natural habitat of these trees, on and near a river bank with unlimited water, the Landscape Angels helped just the right number of those seedlings I started to survive and thrive. At 40 years their trunks could be about eight inches in diameter at breast height and their crowns shading an area big enough for a picnic.

The other thing, besides a tractor, that made a farm a farm in my mind, even then, was animals. I was on the right track, but maybe a little askew in my reasoning. For the first few months of our stay on the farm, while we were still renting, the owner kept a small herd of beef cattle on the place. These animals, all steers of about the same age as far as I could tell, interested me not at all. If there had been cows and birthings and calves and bulls, that would have been a different thing. When we bought the property the following year, the beef went away. I realize now that the dilapidated fencing on this farm would have cost more than the grazing on worn-out hill pasture was worth.

At some point a couple of horses came to us, kept there as a favor to a friend. A white mare, and a chestnut stallion (later a gelding). I rode on occasion with the friend, but it's not my thing. I'm too narrow in the hips, unpadded and hernia-prone to sit a horse comfortably. The horses were there only a year or so. The same friend also brought a pony, her childhood pony, now more than 20 years old. Trigger was there still when I left and presumably died alone. Another twinge of remorse.

And a goat. Annie the goat, source of my career-long aversion to any species of critter that is more agile than I, more single-minded, and smarter too. Annie was occasionally discouraged with a 2x4 when she became obstreperous, especially in the yard when my long-suffering wife was trying to get from the house to her car. Finally Annie ran away, seeking her fortune. A few months later when we had pretty much figured she was long gone or long dead, a sheriff's deputy drove up to the gate. He had in his hand the brass collar tag that identified Annie and gave our location.

"Seems like this goat of yours," he told me, "is romping through people's gardens in Versailles (the county seat). "She's not by herself...she's got other goats with her. Somebody got close enough to her to grab her collar and pulled this tag off...but she gave 'em the slip." I told the deputy to shoot to kill if he had to.

Much more memorable and manageable were the bantams, my game hens. One nice Saturday morning this fellow showed up at our gate—something of an event there at the end of the road—and showed me in the back of his pickup a mighty fighting rooster, a gamecock of high color and a higher attitude. This guy (the rooster) stood tall and strutted boldly considering he was a captive. Once my visitor was assured of my interest he donned a pair of heavy gloves and took the cock into his arms, holding tightly to his feet and the spurs on his shanks. He spoke to the bird, who looked half again as large out in the open and lifted him up. A cry resounded, a rich, far reaching *COCKADOODLE—DOOOOOO*, as piercing as it was loud, a lofty and majestic sound that thrilled me to the heart.

Here was the deal. I'm not sure I ever knew this man's name, for what he was doing—raising and fighting game cocks—was plainly illegal and he was not forthcoming about his identity. In order to keep the lowest possible profile with his neighbors, this fellow, Rooster Man I'll call him, needed to spread out his collection of promising cocks over as broad an area as possible. Rooster Man sought out isolated homesteads like mine in this and surrounding counties to board out his cocks, scattering them over quite a stretch of country. No particular care was required of the landowner holding the role of foster chickenkeeper, for these game cocks were hardy and tough in the extreme, able to live without artificial shelter or feeding. They were smart and tough enough to survive predators (hawks, bobcats, coyotes, men with guns)—or else they weren't. And if they weren't, good riddance. The out-placement of these fighting birds was also a process of natural selection.

In return for my agreement to participate in this dubious scheme Rooster Man offered a couple of dozen game hens, full grown and laying eggs. He must have had a mighty flock of them at home, selecting the best of the best roosters and breeding them back to the home flock, because he had no qualms about handing off 25 of them to me. These were Banties, prolific layers of small and well-hidden eggs, prone to roost in trees and to feed off the land, though they appreciated a little cracked corn scattered on the barn floor at night and this would bring them in for a bit of protection. My own little flock, Rooster Man told me, would tend to keep the lone cock ranging in my woods and pastures reasonably close, for these guys are as lustful as they are wild and

I could be certain of baby chicks before long. Which was true. In fact, everything he told me proved to be true.

Every few months Rooster Man would show up with another game cock in the back of his truck. He would encourage that one to crow and when he did, the farmed-out rooster in my woods would answer. That was how Rooster Man brought them in to have a look at them. Sometimes he'd be satisfied just to hear the distant cockadoodle, know that his unnamed contender was out there and more or less intact; sometimes he'd bring him right in to the truck to assess his aggressiveness, admire his plumage, offer some fond comment. On a couple of occasions Rooster Man took "my" cock away and left another. He never told me where or when he fought these birds and I frankly didn't care. For me it was enough to know that a semi-tamed, highly-trained, and highly-evolved creature was out there, ranging free.

The hens were fun. In spring, when they were setting clutches of eggs and caring for batches of chicks I confined them as best I could to the stripping room in the barn where they and the little ones were protected somewhat. The rest of the year they and their little ones had the run of the place, though they stayed pretty close to the barn and corn crib and the surrounding brush and woods. Dozens were lost to predators, but there was always a new generations coming and these birds were a feature of the place as long as I was there. At one point in the spring chick rearing season I visited them in the stripping room and found there a rather large bull snake, with several suspicious bulges in his tummy. This guy was 4 or 5 feet long and considerably broader than he should have been. In fact he was so bulgy that he couldn't really move, even when I bent down to see. He waited for me to walk to the house and come back with my shotgun. After I blew off his head I opened him up there they were lined up inside, a half a dozen or more week-old baby chicks. The dust from the shotgun blast was still settling when I carried the snake outside and flung his carcass and those of the babies into the woods.

At the tenant house at the top of the farm there was a dug well with a concrete apron at ground level and a hinged metal hatch covering the opening. Except for a few yard trees and spring flowers coming up from bulbs under the broken windows of the house, this was a barren place and I didn't spend a lot of time there. But occasionally I would lift that well cover and peer down inside. Maybe 20 feet below, if the sun was right, I could see the surface of the water and though I don't remember ever dipping any out with a string and a cup, I'm sure it's good water, even now.

During one of these desultory inspections I caught sight of a black widow spider, just under the hatch, as surprised, I suppose, as I was. She wasn't "lurking" there; she wasn't "in ambush" under the well head. She was just living there. Given the same situation now I would thank her for the privilege of meeting her and leave her alone. Then, in youth, I hatched a plan. Going into the abandoned house, I went to a closet where I knew there were some more or less intact canning jars. I found one with a lid and screw ring, went back out to the well head and captured ma spider in the jar, with some strands of web.

I took her home to the garage and set her up in an aquarium with a screen top, little sticks in there for her webwork and a steady diet of flies and moths and such. Ma spider stayed, making herself at home and mighty aloof, I thought, when I would come to say hello. In early summer she quite rapidly built egg cases, all of tan colored silk and the size and shape of my little finger tip. Presumably she filled these cases, three of them, with eggs, for in a couple of weeks spiderlings by the dozens, by the hundreds, emerged. They were barely visible at first. Ma didn't seem to have much truck with them, having done her part. I was curious how she was going to feed them, but that apparently wasn't on the agenda. As I watched over a period of days, no more than a couple of weeks, the little guys and gals got bigger and bigger, and fewer and fewer. Natural selection in action, they were eating each other and may the best few survive out of the hundreds hatched. Presumably by the end of the process the last one or two of them would figure out there is other food on the planet besides siblings, and maybe at that point Ma spider begins to take an interest and teach her adolescent offspring about webs, and prey…wrapping it up and sucking it dry.

* * *

There's not been a lot about gardening in this first chapter because I wasn't into it then. I do remember one season of a marginally productive salad patch, and some flowers in the front yard, but the passion for growing things didn't hit me until later. Now the restlessness was upon me and the need to escape.

What did I take away from this unnamed farm in Kentucky? What lessons penetrated?

If I had been a different sort of person, schooled more in tradition and love of land, I might today be contemplating my own burial in the plot just across the driveway from the house. Up against the Osage orange hedge there was a setting of unreadable gravestones, not quite regularly spaced, and tilted somewhat, as if the ground had shifted. If I had invented myself differently, had I rooted myself on the farm and learned the lessons there for me, I might be scoping out a plot in that tiny graveyard for myself. I could have made a living on that farm and stayed, but I didn't and I am who I am for all that.

I did come to understand that stewardship is not the same as ownership. In fact, ownership is not necessary to stewardship and can even interfere. I learned much later that I could be a good steward...

And I learned that well-founded intentions, enthusiastically pursued, will be blessed, and will redeem a lot of blunders. I'm thinking of those Saturday mornings on the riverbank dragging behind me a damp burlap-wrapped bundle of black walnut seedlings, learning to find the soft, open spots away from competitor trees. Those couple of hundred trees I set in there 30 years ago allowed me to exit with some grace and ease. However many remain, they will outlast me.

The Claymont Mansion many years ago.

Chapter 2 – Claymont School,
Charles Town, West Virginia 1975, 1979-80
Basic Training

Now I have to diverge a bit to the story of Claymont School for Continuous Education and how the inner training I received there—during a summer course in 1975, and during the September 1979 to June 1980 Fifth Basic Course—set me up for further training in Biodynamics and in gardening. All together I spent a year on that red dirt hill and, twice, it changed my life. The summer course made a hermit out of me (you won't hear in this book about my seven months in the Nevada desert—no gardening going on there) and set me on a quixotic course toward mastership in gardening.

It was a different era then. Today, when the Dalhi Llama and Pema Chodron are featured in the front of the bookstore and commuters listen to audio tapes of *The Power of NOW*, it's hard to remember when teachings from the East were something outlandish, half fascinating and half freak show. The Beatles had their photos taken with the Maharishi and Ram Dass was at Lama Foundation in New Mexico writing *Be Here Now*. It was all beards and robes and smiling gurus, exotic as in not-to-be-taken-too-seriously. When Ram Dass was Richard Alpert and along with Timothy Leary was fired from the faculty of Harvard for experimenting with LSD, just 10 years earlier, I was in graduate school, in psychology too, and I thought he was crazy to give up bigwig status in his profession for a knuckleheaded notoriety. But by 1975, having been chastened and broadened some by life, I was ready for Be Here Now, for something…

I was introduced, through friends, to what is called the Gurdjieff Work, or The Fourth Way, which, without going into too much detail, aims to wake people up. *(From Wikipedia: Georges Ivanovich Gurdjieff (January 13, 1866? – October 29, 1949), was a Greek-Armenian mystic, a teacher of sacred dances, and a spiritual teacher, most notable for introducing the Fourth Way.)* Because I was more of a psychologist

13

than anything else, the frankly psychological nature of the teachings was appealing. True, it was psychology over a mighty wide orbit, but I'd been looking for that. The Gurdjieff teachings, as transmitted to the next generation by J G Bennett (among others), involved intellectual work, but the emphasis was on laying siege indirectly to the strongholds of ego: through the emotions and the through the body. Attention to the now, the present moment, was key. Most of the techniques employed by our Claymont teacher, Pierre Elliot, originated in the East, most of those in Islam. But Gurdjieff's teachings were unique to him and eclectic, taken from many sources and fine-tuned over decades. The Fourth Way, it is said, goes beyond the First Way of the Fakir, the way of the body and its subjugation; it goes beyond the Second Way of the Monk, the way of the emotions, of obedience and liturgical devotion; it goes beyond the Third Way of the Yogi, the way of the mind and its control. The Fourth Way is the Way of the Sly Man…the man in a hurry whose teachers, if he is lucky enough to find them, borrow techniques from each of the other three ways and synthesize an accelerated course of development, assuming that the hurried man is teachable.

The great and glowing promise of the Gurdjieff work is that it's quick, made to order for the 20th Century American who just doesn't have 40 years to spare, looking over his shoulder at the sun like a fakir, or to be obedient to an abbot, like a monk.

Mr. Bennett toward the end of his life ran courses at Sherbourne House in England to bring the teachings to a sampling of the younger generation, a few dozen at a time, mostly Americans as it turned out. In a 1974 document "Call for a New Society" he wrote:

> *Progress in self-perfecting is not automatic; it requires use of the right methods and the determination to persevere against all discouragement. Very few people can achieve it alone; and, for this reason, 'Schools of Wisdom' have existed from time immemorial to provide instruction and to create environments in which all can contribute to the common aim. Although such schools have always been present they are little in evidence except in times of crisis and change, when they extend their activities to enable more people to prepare themselves for the task ahead.*
>
> *We are now in such a period….*

Mr. Bennett founded Claymont as a such a school to provide a series of nine-month Basic Courses, a kind of basic training in the manipulation of human energies. Claymont was also seen by Mr. Bennett and his colleagues as a venue for an experiment in intentional community that he pictured in Call for a New Society. After basic training, we were told, we could go from there, taking away what we could of experience and technique toward gathering for ourselves what Gurdjieff called a "kestjan body," a soul. This is not as outlandish as it seems, baldly presented on the printed page. We knew these promises were at least plausible, because of the very guilelessness of the presenters. Fourth Way people are not hard-sell artists, nor are they trained teachers. But they did carry a certain presence...

Pierre came to visit our group in Reno in the winter of 1975, looked us over, gave a little talk on what is called The Work, guided us in the Gurdjieff Movements (more about these sacred dances later), but engaged in recruitment talk not at all. I don't believe it was even mentioned that a summer course was going to happen at Claymont in a few months. I have wondered over the years what Pierre thought of us, a ragtag group of unreconstructed hippies; Pierre, cultured and disciplined, graciously European, well-spoken and courteous—he must have shuddered at the prospect of having us for students. But he had assisted Mr. Bennett at Sherbourne House and knew that young Americans, some of them, were teachable.

WHO WE ARE

We are three-brained beings whose natural harmony of mind/body/emotions has gotten severely distorted by culture and so-called civilization. We were better off before cities and religions were invented and we are all victims of the long, twisted reach of culture. But however damaged and deranged we are by civilization, our role is to transform lower energies into higher ones. That's what is required of all sentient beings. We can do it as an awakened human, embracing the conscious labor and intentional suffering in our lives; or we can do it asleep, enslaved by cultural conditioning and education, programmed like an automaton and dying like a dog, having missed our chance to grow up, to acquire a soul and move on past the cultural illusion. Either way we serve the moon, Gurdjieff teaches. That is to say our personal energies, sent out to the universe, help maintain Luna in her orbit. We can choose to live as a human and have the possibility of becoming more fully so if we are clever enough. This is not an article of faith. It is demonstrable, and exemplars came in droves that first summer at Claymont, presumably marveling over the audacity of the experiment. We had lamas and sheiks, Buddhist and Christian monks, dervishes and bishops and more sheiks. They arrived singly or in groups and once when a veritable symposium of them was meeting with Pierre Elliot in his modest home on the Claymont farm a thunderstorm raged for hours and we students wondered whether it was the landscape angels rejoicing or the powers of darkness unleashing themselves. Each of these exemplars taught a class or two, or led a meditation. Sometimes there were feasts and celebrations, often involving considerable drinking of vodka. However we met with these men—as I remember, it was all men—their holiness and wisdom shone through. Almost none were Americans.

WHO WE ARE NOT

We are emphatically not the "I" of the moment. Within us is a horde of small i personalities, clamoring for attention: "i'm the BIG I—look at me!"

That one, the one of the moment, the one that is cold, or horny or indignant, doesn't even deserve to be capitalized. Temporary, changeable, fleeting small i … who cares? We live with a teeming huddle of small i mini-monsters feeding off the emaciated, un-cared-for core inside us, the only part of us deserving to be called an "upper case I," our essence.

A RUMI POEM

come and see me
today i am away
out of this world

hidden away
from me and i

……….

i have no idea
how my inner fire
is burning today
my tongue
is on a different flame

i see myself
with a hundred faces
and to each one
i swear it is me

surely i must have
a hundred faces
i confess none is mine
i have no face

16

— Ghazal 1519
Translation by Nader Khalili
Rumi, Fountain of Fire
Burning Gate Press, 1984

* * *

All this is pretty abstract, and sketchy, but I can summarize some of what I took away from Claymont, especially as it relates to my education as a self-aware gardener. Remembering all the while that words are slippery and the Claymont experience was much of the time beyond words, ineffable.

In order not to preach any further here, and to return to my main theme, gardening, I shall sprinkle snippets throughout the rest of this book. If these snippets seem impossibly jejune to you as a 21st Century reader, forgive me for bringing them up, for the things I learned decades ago at Claymont—terrifying as they were—prepared the ground in me to be a gardener.

ATTACHMENTS

"Human beings are the only animal that can get addicted to *anything*," Terence McKenna said. "Drugs, each other, the way we look…doesn't matter, we can get attached to it…"

And as any good Buddhist will tell us, the number and scope of our attachments are a measure of our misery. The more we have to lose, the more vulnerable we are. Ego attachments, emotional bindings, intellectual delusions, self image, self justification, self protection—it's all got to go, says our teacher.

We were immersed at Claymont in a community life of household work, farm and forest stewardship, class activities and projects, Gurdjieff's sacred gymnastics—a life calculated to wear away our personality armor, expose our self-centeredness and greed, our many-facades-all-of-them-false. Live in a dorm, cook for 100, and meditate your butt off. Be told by a fellow student, whose role today is House Supervisor, to re-clean a toilet, because your role today is Upstairs Maid.

In the midst of all the self-doubt, personality abrasion, and sheer loathing of your peers that such a life gives rise to, if you're doing it with some diligence, there is the chance to wake up for a moment here and there and be stunned by the glimpse of reality that is visible when the attachments are dropped…when we remember for an instant who we really are.

It was just such glimpses that kept us there at Claymont.

There were times when great efforts could be made, when limitations fell away and we were in touch with an inexhaustible source—always in the present moment when past and future were truly irrelevant.

One of the classes that first summer was run by two garden ladies, one of whom had been a student of Alan Chadwick at the University of California at Santa Cruz. Though he later let go of his teaching of the Biodynamic method, in the early 1970s he did teach the use of the Rudolf Steiner preparations, for garden and compost. At Claymont, the gardeners were applying the Biodynamic methodology, and they gathered some of us students on a July day in an area of the garden recently designated as the compost yard.

At the Claymont farm there were open-fronted stalls that had formerly housed prize beef calves. The manure was old and dry, but we transported it by wheelbarrow to build a long, wide pile maybe five feet high and twenty feet long, and watered it down as we went. Twenty tons, more or less. So the garden lady, I'll call her Linda, had 12 or 15 students there and she said, "Well, we're going to apply these preparations here, put them in the pile." She was vague (or I was slow on the uptake) about just why we were doing this…something about cosmic forces, harmony of energies, whatever. I was OK with that. The packets she had of these preparations, five of them, just filled the palm of her hand. Under her instruction we inserted the tiny parcels of herbs into holes we poked in the pile with little ceremony, tamping the damp stall material around—an ounce or two of them were supposed to have a beneficial effect on 20 tons of compost.

Then it got weirder. Witchier. Linda produced a vial of foul-smelling brown liquid, twenty drops or so in there. She says it's juice from valerian flowers and that we're going to stir it for 20 minutes, and then spray it on the pile as a kind of protective skin. She upends the vial into a bucket of water and demonstrates. With a whisk broom she stirs the liquid vigorously, first counter-clockwise, creating a vortex, then reversing direction, destroying the vortex and creating another, clockwise one. After a couple of minutes' demonstration, each of us in the group took a turn, When it came to be my turn with the stirring I was less skeptical than I might have been. Something was happening here, I knew.

We were taught at Claymont to focus on the present moment and our inner experience within the NOW. I stirred with some enthusiasm. The fragrance of those few drops of valerian wrapped me as I bent to the task and I got the knack of it quickly. The whisk goes faster and faster as more of the water takes up the momentum and finally the vortex is complete. You can see the bottom of the bucket and the outer edge of the whirlpool threatens to spill out. Then reverse, quickly, and chaos ensues. Then a slow rotation in the new direction and gradually the water takes up the motion and the opposite vortex develops. I was enthralled by the energy thus created and lapsed into a profound meditation, drawn in by the valerian solution. I could feel the power of it, the potency.

Years later Barbara, my beloved, would say, "You're the only person I know that can have an orgasm stirring the preps."

Others took their turns stirring and then it was done. We poured half of the solution into a hole in the compost pile and used the whisk broom to flick the rest of it onto the pile, scattering the droplets evenly over the surface. As I participated and watched I came to an understanding, complete and whole as it arose: "*This* is what I've been missing in gardening…the element of spirit, the enlivening dynamic of human intent."

Well, all right…that last bit is bogus. Those are the words I write decades later to describe the unutterable experience I was having. Intuition was aroused…a dim remembrance was evoked, not of the childhood farms, but of lifetimes further back, my peasant days. I knew deep in my being how to do my part to bring forth fertility. It rang in me like a chime—in the vortex was an understanding, in the flower essence was a force that my own intention could ride into the future, into the crops this compost would feed, and the people…in the garden next year, when I was gone. Then, the intention would still be active and potent. We're working in non-material realms where there is no entropy, no deterioration. An effort, once launched, is forever.

In an instant I understood compost. Years later I would teach, "There is no garden problem that isn't solved with compost…righteous, cow manure-based Biodynamic compost." Insect problems? Grow strong, resistant plants in well-composted soil. Disease? Ditto. Soil won't drain? Compost will loosen it. No organic matter…sandy …infertile? Compost…compost…compost.

Two themes recur in my gardens over the decades. Compost stories and greenhouse stories. Whatever else I may have done to feed folks, I always left behind a greenhouse and a compost pile, and garden ground more fertile than when I came.

The Claymont Court property, 300-some acres, well watered and in many places heavily forested, was developed by a nephew of George Washington in the 1820s. The mansion at the top of the hill was dilapidated when we arrived in 1975, but still elegant. Separate small buildings, slave quarters, flanked the main house with its formal dining room and ballroom and verandas front and rear. I know nothing of the human history of the place beyond that it was said to be owned for several decades in the early 20th Century by people who built up a famous herd of Hereford cattle. This was evidenced by the fact of The Great Barn, a two-storey, 400-foot long concrete block structure with a huge octagonal show arena at one end. It was this building, I'm convinced, that sold Mr. Bennett on the place, for, renovated, it would make (and indeed did make) a wonderful school building.

This conversion—from a huge structure designed to house large animals and their hay, into space for human habitation (commercial kitchen, dining and meditation rooms, offices, bathrooms, sleeping rooms for 100, windows, heating plant, raising the roof to provide headroom on the second floor)—was in process during the summer of 1975, with a crew of expert architects and tradesmen, all students of Mr. Bennett's, us, their student helpers, and a very large pot of money—from where I do not know. Between mansion and barn was a shaded two rut road a half-mile long passing by several of the farm staff houses. The oak trees at Claymont were astonishing: monumental trunks supporting many low branches extending horizontally to the ground for 25 or 30 feet, as big around as the trunk of an ordinary tree. One of these would shade a mighty convocation of elves, and perhaps they did. The night before we arrived in June, 1975, there was a terrific thunderstorm and everywhere there were fallen limbs and even toppled trees. A couple of weeks into the course, my roommate Slow Bob and I skipped lunch to do a bit of unasked-for work, sawing up some limbs for firewood. We were feeling good about ourselves, cutting away with light bow saws, working up some righteous virtue when Pierre, also skipping lunch it seems, walked by on the driveway and, a few minutes later, back toward the mansion. He didn't acknowledge us at all, but I knew he'd seen us and my self-congratulations were running high when the saw blade jumped out of its kerf and a single sharp tooth sliced through my left thumbnail, right from bottom to top and blood welled from the wound. I saw this happen in superbly choreographed slow motion, in vivid detail, flabbergasted and delighted before the pain hit, for I knew that Pierre had gifted me with a taste of real consciousness, of grace, *baraka*.

Claymont was set up as a School of Life, an education and a tour in the landscape of soul. It was an experiment in community living with opportunities a hundred times a day to face up to your shortcomings, reflected back to you from the people you lived with, and to rise above yourself to serve the land, animals, and fellow travelers on the path. If I failed to profit from many such opportunities there were still others of them to meet, all day long every day. Pierre Elliot and his helpers, with Mr. Bennett's blessing from the grave, set up the conditions for people to rub against each other and glow in the friction of it all. In the nine-month Basic Course 100 of us students lived, with quite a few other people, in a single long, low building with dorms and private rooms, communal bathrooms, meditation room, theater for sacred gymnastics, dining room for 120, and a commercial-scale kitchen. Everybody was expected to do everything:

cooking for the whole group, baking 24 loaves of bread at a time, stoking the boiler, gardening, animal tending, child care. Learning new things was part of the deal. We were jolted out of the comforting routine of existence, of doing our best, but only at the things we do best (which is the way we would choose to operate), and subjected to trials by fire, with lots of self-doubt, performance anxiety, and failures.

We may never be more awake, I came to realize, than when we're learning to do new things and Gurdjieffian schools have always set up conditions to compel people to live in unaccustomed ways, eating new and sometimes ill-prepared food, working in woods and field and cleaning bathrooms, sleeping in a room with half a dozen others, none of whom love you. All these conditions rouse us from our normal state of comfortable slumber and egoistic self-regard.

My specialty during much of the nine months was not gardening but rather caring for the pigs. Here's how that came about. We often had quick morning meetings on "House Day." Our group of 80 students was divided roughly in thirds and the Claymont schedule provided for one-third of the group each day to do the housework, which included child care. In the first week I'd involved myself with that, only to discover that however adept I thought I was at taking care of two-year-old Sky, my son by default as I'd not yet adopted him, and another 6 or 8 toddlers and preschoolers…this was all beyond my ability to cope, even though I did have partners in the job. They were a mighty force for chaos, those little ones—quite beyond me. So in this morning meeting on the second house day I was intrigued when one of the farmers showed up recruiting for pig duty. This was a different kind of assignment Patrick told us, as it involved a commitment for the entire nine months; the pigs are sensitive critters, he averred, and could not tolerate different keepers every day—they needed continuity of care by the same dedicated bunch of swineherds. This meant that I would not rotate around to child care duty on house days, ever again. I stayed after the meeting with a few others to learn more. The other 20-some students left quickly to their bathroom and kitchen and kiddo duties, slipping out the door away from Patrick's noticeable effluvium.

He took us outdoors, where the pigpens were conveniently located close to the kitchen and the tofu factory. We toured the extensive swineland with Patrick, who introduced us to the brood sows, more than a dozen of them separately housed within plank pens, each with her own shelter, mud patio, feed and water containers. Some were awaiting a birthing (Patrick knew all their due dates by heart), others were accompanied by a litter of piglets. A couple of boars had their own quarters as well, sturdier by far. Other pens held weanling pigs and their elder brothers and sisters. Altogether, this was an impressive facility to a farmboy wannabe like myself—dilapidated to be sure, like much of the rest of the Claymont grounds. Mansion, houses, and the Great Barn where we lived had not been inhabited for forty years before the school took it over five years before. Much had been done toward renovation, but the swine complex had not topped the priority list.

Did I want to sign on as a swineherd? You bet! Did I care that I would be asked to hang my overalls outside the dining room on pig days? Nope!

For the rest of the fall, winter and spring I tended the sows and their numerous offspring. I helped to dig a two-hundred yard trench for a waterline to an outlying pig pasture, went to the livestock auction, either with pigs to sell or to find pigs to buy. I carried the tofu dregs and kitchen wastes to my pig friends in dozens of 5-gallon buckets, slopping through the mud, righting feed troughs that had been played with by 500-pound sows. I fixed fence endlessly as piglets found the holes. I helped to butcher, and I loved it all.

I took on the laying hens as well, a couple of hundred of them, and the moments of animal tending were the anchors in my day. While very many things at Claymont evoked confusion and bewilderment and frustration aplenty, my times with the chickens and pigs made sense; fill the waterer, fill the feeder, shovel shit, observe the scene, observe the self.

ASK THE TASK

I never heard anyone at Claymont put it quite like this, but Ask The Task was my personal code when I was upset or confused and not knowing what to do. Very simple: ask the task in front of you what's needed. Maybe a sink full of dirty pots and pans. It's house day, every third day for your group, and your role is Kitchen Boy. "Why… but I've got a PhD! Shouldn't I be giving a seminar?" Forget it…you're kitchen boy. So you're upset (that is, ego deflated) and confused ("What have I got myself into with this stupid Claymont place?") and Ask The Task pops up.

"Oh. Dishes. Here they are and here I am." And you do the dishes. Ask 'em. How do they want to be done? Done well, of course. And so you apply yourself to the sink and the suds and have some peace for a while from the silly churnings in your head and heart.

I also took on the tools. Anyone who has lived and worked with others can picture the scene in the Claymont tool shed. In my experience people who have not been specifically trained to do so almost never clean tools, sharpen them, or put them back where they belong. Here in the tool room was a jumble of landscape and gardening tools, all the shovels and hoses, piles of axes and saws for forest work, bill hooks, scythes and other old-time tools. Broken tools—dozens of them. Dull tools—all of them. Lost tools—many of them. Misplaced tools—most of them.

One at a time I dealt with the tools, sharpening them, reattaching handles, smearing linseed oil on wooden parts, organizing them in their shed, cleaning out the junk. This was a wholly satisfying job and gave me a place to hang out other than my dormitory room which held a dozen other jerks like me, each more addled than the next.

Often in the winter I did my work with the tools in the boiler house, just a few steps away from the tool shed, where the person on boiler duty fed the fire box from the pile of firewood just outside. If I was sharpening and setting the teeth on a bucksaw or felling saw s/he would obligingly test my work. I was always touched that they were so amazed to experience the difference between a dull saw and a sharp one.

With the animals and the tools I managed to create my own core curriculum at Claymont. I attended all of the scheduled meditations, most of the meetings, almost all of the classes and lectures, all the readings, all of the work sessions. What I skipped, and I'm abashed to say this, was the one offering of the Claymont teachers that they considered most important: what are called Gurdjieff's Movements. G. I. Gurdjieff often preferred to be called, simply, "a teacher of Temple Dances," and judging by the emphasis placed on them at Claymont and in the many memoirs of students, the dances were a crucial part of his teachings. Maybe the most crucial. From the beginning of my involvement with this Gurdjieff stuff, months before Claymont, I was bewildered and baffled by the Movements. Our teachers in Reno did their best to teach our small group the First Obligatory, a series of puppet-like arm, leg and full body positions assumed to a dirge-like piano accompaniment, positions to be taken with no waste motion and with complete precision, not really like a puppet or a robot but like a conscious human being. That means between the time the arm is extended, say, directly in front of the shoulder and the time it is again at your side, just so…no time elapses, there is no lag, there is no delay in the synapses, there is no transmission time from brain to muscles. Movements training involves exquisite harmonization among the head-brain (presumably in charge of intention and attention), the heart-brain (of devotion and motive), and the body-brain (all the workings of the nerves between the spinal cord and the muscles.). This balanced state results in Movement demonstrations (there's one at the end of the film Meetings with Remarkable Men) that show uncanny performances by experts. Of 100 people who try the Movements, probably 20 or so get fairly good at it, good enough to perform in demonstrations; another 5 or so might become good enough to teach. I was at the other end of that curve. I was so bad at this body-heart-brain co-ordination that Movements classes were an agony of self-reproach, nay, self-loathing, and the more I indulged in this negativity of course, the worse I got. Finally, in the winter of the Fifth Basic Course I quit altogether. If anyone noticed, no-one said anything, and certainly there were no consequences. When everyone assembled on the hardwood dance floor in the Octagon, I absented myself, not to goof off, but quite conscientiously to my tool work, or to the garden.

At nearly 40, and never having been the sort of guy who thrives under rules, I felt I could admit failure with the Movements, quit beating myself up about it, and at least in this one thing write my own program. Possibly Pierre noted that I'd done this and possibly someone told him, but there was never a comment. Maybe nobody ever noticed.

* * *

Every afternoon during the course, in the hour before supper, Pierre read to us from Gurdjieff's massive work *All and Everything: Beelzebub's Tales to his Grandson, An Objectively Impartial Criticism of the Life of Man.* The book is full of neologisms, awkward expressions, prolixity, twisted myth and conjured allegory, purporting to be the history of mankind on our planet as told by the exiled devil, now on his way home to the center of the Universe after having been pardoned by our Endlessness, God. Gurdjieff went to great lengths to make it difficult to read and understand the book, and for us students, at the end of a day of hard work and study, the readings were alternately bewildering and soporific, creating a hypnogogic state that may have helped us to absorb some of Gurdjieff's meaning. In his study of *Beelzebub*, J. G. Bennett grapples with the contradiction of trying to explain a "book that defies verbal analysis" and concludes that Beelzebub's Tales is an epoch-making work that represents the first new mythology in 4000 years. He finds in Gurdjieff's ideas regarding time, God's purpose in creating the universe, conscience, and the suffering of God, a synthesis transcending Eastern and Western doctrines about humanity's place in the cosmos.

One afternoon Pierre didn't show up. The thick book rested there on the rug where he usually sat crosslegged to read to us and there we were, ranged along the three other walls, waiting. Five minutes…ten. No Pierre.

I usually sat in the corner of the room at Pierre's left and on this occasion I sidled over to his place, found his bookmark and began to read. I stumbled over some of Gurdjieff's singular renderings of the language from time to time and repeatedly mispronounced the word elucidate as ee-LOOD-i-cate, as one of the students pointed out afterwards, but made it through the rest of the session to the supper bell. Pierre never did come and, again, I never knew if he absented himself on purpose, just to see what would happen.

This sort of thing was one of the features of life at Claymont. We were often faced with challenges quite beyond the ordinary craziness of community in such a setting. Another example:

Every month or so there was announced a "feast," often, as I have mentioned, on the occasion of a visits from sheiks and other highly evolved persons, or on Gurdjieff's or Mr. Bennett's birthdays or death days. The dining room had the picnic-type tables removed and the benches lined up end to end to form low tables. Tapestries, Turkish rugs and cushions were hung and scattered on the floor for guests.

The food prepared for feasts was always a cut above the daily fare. For one such feast during the summer course my old friend Lynda was head cook and I was sous-cook and in the mid-afternoon one of those spectacular thunderboomer storms came through the landscape, rattling our nerves even more. Then the electricity went out, common enough during these events, but crucial for us since the mansion kitchen featured just two decrepit electric ranges and we were cooking for 100 people. (The Great Barn kitchen was not yet ready; the workers were just then raising the roof of the hay mow to provide head space up there for dorm rooms.) We waited a bit, hoping the lights would come back on, while chopping vegetables in the darkened basement kitchen. Nothing.

Finally, determined not to be rendered helpless in front of a 20th Century difficulty, we checked the draft of the mansion ballroom fireplace with a wad of burning newspaper, found that it was OK, and I went to find firewood. Before long we had a nice fire going and big pots of water in the coals to boil. They were just getting going when...the lights came back on.

Now, the question: Did someone flip the switch on us? Was this a cunning plan of Pierre's to push the cooks to the brink? We'll never know. We do know, however, that the conditions of life at Claymont were designed to awaken us from our habitual sleepwalking state, to push us into what Gurdjieff called "self remembering."

BEING AND DOING

We are doers, we Americans. We pride ourselves in getting things done. Like Thoreau's farmer we carry our accomplishments on our backs (the farmer carries his barn and livestock). What we present to the world, masquerading as our Self, is our accumulated deeds and possessions (all bought with our doing), the personality that exults in our performance and seeks recognition for our activities. We mistake activity for progress while hiding from everyone the tender essence that's been larded over by our attitudes, interests, desires, behavior patterns, emotions, roles and all the traits we identify as self. The real kernel of selfhood inside all that blubber, we were taught at Claymont, is our spark of divinity; it's what stays the same, our inner child. It's still a child, when we are in our middle years, because we have let the culture around us reward our doing, while trampling on our being. This has been going on since childhood. If being were to be nurtured, if the inner child had been allowed to grow robustly, we would not be the deluded, smug specimens we are. If we dare to seek the good of our essence we will welcome any assault on personality, anything that peels away some of the suffocating layers of culture and ego and lets the sun shine on that child in there, give it the attention it deserves. We might dare to put some real effort into project of being.

Being still. Being real. Being wholly human. How to do this? Well, I'm thinking that's why I went to Claymont, to find out.

Baby Sky among the marigolds.

Chapter 3 – Fallon, Nevada 1974-5-6-7 More Basic Training

Fallon, Nevada, lies 50 miles or so east of Reno. The Truckee River sluices down from Lake Tahoe, in the mountains west of Reno, flows through town (running right through the campus of the Nevada State Hospital where I worked) and north to Pyramid Lake, which is surrounded by Pyramid Lake Indian Reservation. This vast desert lake evaporates every cubic foot of water that the Truckee delivers, and then some. Some decades ago, by dubious agreements with the Paiute, water was legally diverted from the Truckee into the flat land surrounding the town of Fallon, a landscape that lacked only water to make it fertile. Churchill County is the only market farming area in the state as far as I know.

My friend and co-worker Elwood Koenig lived in Fallon, and somehow took a notion in 1974 to raise cantaloupe...the famous Fallon Heart o' Gold melon. We were living at the time, Elwood and I and another half-dozen friends in a big house just outside Reno, all working for the same state agency. Koenig recruited a number of us to plant five acres of melons, and this we did on a Sunday in May, in a kind of community effort. The field had been furrowed up and we scooped out a depression every few feet in the side of each furrow, sprinkled in a few seeds, covered them and patted the soil firmly down over them. Then we placed a cone of reinforced waxed paper called a HotKap over the seeds and firmed soil around the base.

Melons love heat and the waxed paper cones were little greenhouses that would last through the unsettled May weather, intensifying whatever warmth was there. A "hill" of melon seeds went in every six or eight feet and the furrows were four or five feet apart. It was a big job on five acres, maybe 6,000 plants, but there were quite a few of us there, and the feeling of doing something extraordinary carried us through in good spirits. This stoop labor was new to us all and it was a festive kind of afternoon, with all the city folks in the field.

In June I came back to the field, riding my bike from Reno to Carson City to Fallon, in training for a 2,000-mile journey I had planned for later in the summer. I helped Woody tear the tops off of all those HotKaps, to ventilate the plants that had emerged inside. Row on row of hand-sized melon plants, stretching off into the distance.

The following year, and the year after I helped Woody with the melon crop and in 1976 I was there for the harvest, the final weeding and the marketing of those wonderful melons, and the sweet corn crop that he had added.

By the spring of 1977, I had a job at the community counseling center where Koenig was director and I was living in Fallon, on Cemetery Road. My partner and I had a house in a little compound we called Hoogieville, three or four downscale rental houses and a couple of duplexes with a large graveled parking area and beyond, a garden area. Events conspired for me to engage in the first garden project over which I would have full control for I was now, in effect, a father, or at least I willingly took on the responsibility. The little guy, Sky, had come (out of the blue, so to speak), on April 12. As my job paid only $5 per hour, it was time to get serious about good food, cutting expenses, and doing some productive gardening.

I talked to the landlord and received permission to take over that garden area at the back of the property, a plot maybe 50 by 150 feet; just over the fence was a huge alfalfa field where the roots, we knew, went down 50 or 60 feet in search of moisture. The landlord offered us access to all the water we needed to garden, not a small matter in arid Nevada. Meanwhile two friends joined Sky's mom and me and rented another of the little houses at Hoogieville. None of us knew a lot about gardening, but we had heard of "double digging" and took it to mean digging and then digging again the same plot. We'd started on that when another friend, Lynda, arrived from Claymont on Easter break from the Second Basic Course. She taught us the Chadwickian style of double digging beds about four feet wide. Putting aside all the soil from a trench a foot or so wide and deep in the bed, loosening the subsoil underneath, putting down a layer of grass stems or leaves or other organic matter, then replacing the top layer; the result was a bed four or six inches above the grade level, since everything's all fluffed up. The paths between beds we scalped and left alone. As we built the beds we added quite a lot of old, crumbly pig manure we managed to acquire down the road.

We shaped two or three furrows in each bed and planted seeds in the sides of them, in imitation of the melon plantings we'd done with Woody Koenig. For this garden was to be furrow irrigated, exactly like his fields, but on a small scale. I spent many glorious hours in early morning and evening moving hoses around, gently applying water to furrows, each in its turn, watching as it crept and flowed down the beds, soaking in around the plant roots. Again, as in the compost making at Claymont, I was accessing ancestral memories, this time of irrigation practices, perhaps in Mesopotamia and Egypt. The water flowed and I built little dams to hold it back a bit when needed, destroyed them when the upstream plantings had taken enough water, created clever diversions in order to move the hose as little as possible. Our dark-skinned forbears (I'm thinking of Egyptians or Sumerians) had no hoses, but may have had even more fun coaxing water to run where it was needed.

We planted onions, cabbage, Brussels sprouts, corn, tomatoes, peppers, melons, squash…many flowers. All along the front, on the parking lot edge, and along the sides, we planted dwarf French marigolds

At the far corner of the garden, as far away from human traffic as I could locate them, I placed a beehive, on an old pallet.

I was quite young, maybe 12 years old, when I read the Sherlock Holmes books and discovered that Holmes, in retirement, became a beekeeper. I held that thought for many years. If my hero Holmes was interested, so was I. To be a beekeeper, in my mind, was to understand mysteries of Nature few people know about; it was to work with these mysteries as manifested in a tiny insect governed by instincts and sense endowments we infer but cannot experience. Wisdom was there to be found in the pursuit of beekeeping, I was convinced.

Two years earlier, we had arrived to attend the summer course of the Claymont School the day after a horrendous early summer thunderstorm that caused extensive damage to many of the very old oak trees on the property. The evening of my first day I spied Eric among the chaos of fallen and broken limbs, trying to manipulate a wooden bee box into a buzzing mass of live bees, a swarm dispossessed of its hive in a hollow trunk by the storm's fury. Eric had a cast on his arm (he'd fallen from a high rafter working on the Great Barn) and needed some help. Fascinated by the prospect of trying to hive a swarm, I approached cautiously. As I knelt down before the swarm and entered its aura, its fragrant and portentous buzz, I felt a peace and animated awareness that's rarely been granted to me. I knew little about it all, except that there was probably a queen in that seething throng of bees. I knew little but somehow I understood much.

Our attempt to entice the bees into our dilapidated bee box failed and the next morning they had gone, no doubt to a much more suitable home. Other events at Claymont kept me from any further investigation into the world of bees that summer.

In Fallon, in 1977, the spring of the birth of my son, I finally became a beekeeper. One of my counseling clients was a bewildered boy of 12, doing poorly in school, uncooperative at home. When I interviewed his mother she told me she was a beekeeper, working several hundred hives, on shares. In one of those happy and easeful mergers of life (my gardening life) and work (my job) I agreed to this lady's offer to spend a Saturday with her and the boy, visiting hives. The idea was to see what needed to be done with each after the winter, assess their strength, combine weak colonies, and open up the entrances to the spring. It was a learning day for me, and my young client was much happier to show me his expertise in the bee yard, than he had been to sit in my counselor's office trying to talk about feelings. He was competent and deft as he showed me how to manage the hives, and in a delightful role reversal, I got a of useful information and even more important, technique. Everyone has seen the standard beehive, made of several stacked drawer-like boxes, the stacks often arranged with three others on a pallet—several groups of these in a corner of a field, often placed up against a grove of trees. This is a bee yard, and my bee mentor and his mother and I worked a couple of these that Saturday morning, a hundred or more hives to inspect.

I learned facts, but more important that morning were the feelings and intuitions that were drawn forth. To hold a frame of honeycomb (there are ten of these, hanging parallel like picture frames, one "bee space" apart in each box) with hundreds of bees clinging to it, going about their business in the full light of the day; to be bathed in the exquisite blended scent of honey and pollen and beeswax; to give yourself to the *Hmmmmmmmmmm* of the workers, to realize that vibration in the depth of you; to observe the beginnings of new life—the eggs, affixed by the Queen ever so precisely to the exact bottom center of a six-sided cell; to discover other cells next door covered with tan wax and containing—you're told this, but you don't disturb it to see for yourself—a pupa that in a few days will emerge as a worker bee; other cells packed with honey and pollen to feed the larva; later in the year, full frames and supers weighty with surplus honey. Sometimes the boy and I were able to see the Queen herself, ringed by attendant worker bees. To participate in these events, I knew, was a privilege granted only rarely, and I was grateful.

The boy's mother, grateful herself for my attention to her son, and generous, gave me a hive of my own.

By the time we were done and I'd hauled my new hive home to the garden corner at Hoogieville, I figured I'd gotten a good introduction to the perils – yes I got stung, plenty – and promise of beekeeping. And so it was. I would continue to keep a hive or two or four at most places I gardened.

Always I could find peace with the bees, most often situated a little way from the garden where I could be alone to meditate or think about garden problems without interruption, for few apprentices or customers would venture near the hives. Again that immersion in the sound and fragrance, the vibration of the hot, blossom-y day vectored by the thousands of bees into that place.

I watched carefully the bees' arrivals and departures as they homed in on and leapt from the launching board at the hive entrance, seeing the color and quantity of the pollen the bees carried, and viewed the drunken weaving of over-laden nectar carriers; all this led me to conclusions and understandings about how the bees fared. The more activity, the better. It was when the incoming bees were empty and hungry, when the guard bees just inside the entrance attacked them, then there was trouble in the bee yard and robbing going on. Perhaps the subject hive was weakened by some mishap, or the honey flow had been interrupted by weather or changing seasons.

These troubles were rare, however, and mostly I hung out with the bees because it uplifted me to be with them, just as I knew it would when I was turned on to them by Sherlock Holmes.

On another edge of the garden we erected a teepee. The little guy, three and four months old this summer and the only infant I've ever seen with a serious tan, often slept in a cradle basket suspended by the center tie-down rope where he could swing for hours and dream of marigolds and honeybees and have visions of the gyring, tapering pine poles above.

In the hottest days the voracious larvae of cabbage moths attacked our cole crops: broccoli, cabbage, cauliflower. As a novice gardener this took me by surprise and I watched dumfounded as those green caterpillars grew fat on our produce, eating holes in the leaves, laying down beads of green shit and doubling in size every day. The cabbage, growing strong, wrapped new leaves around the worms as they ate non-stop and they didn't care, just kept munching, growing and finally pupating in the nourishing dark greenness.

Our garden partners consulted with the pig-manure lady and concocted a plan to use "Sevin" a broad-spectrum insecticide developed by Union Carbide, notorious a few years later for an industrial accident in Bhopal, India, which killed 20,000 people. Sevin is known too as a honeybee killer, though I didn't know that for a fact at the time. What I did know and communicated at full volume to our partners, was that there was NO WAY we were going to use poisons in MY garden, where MY son and MY bees spent their days. I shocked myself with that blast and them too, I'm sure.

That vehemence anticipated an as-yet-unformed set of convictions that later guided my thinking about being an organic gardener.

· It would never occur to me to use poisons of any kind to eradicate problems or for weed control; better to lose a crop than to resort to these practices;

- Nor would I bolster plant growth with chemical amendments to the soil; no muriate of potash (the chemical sacks stacked in piles in the hay barn at my farm in Kentucky), no anhydrous ammonia, no Weed n' Feed, no "fertilizers" other than composted manure;
- No quick fixes allowed; I would always take it as a given that Nature would provide the bounty if I took care of the soil;
- Furthermore, why should I ever have to prove any of this to an organic certification agency for marketing purposes? Or to argue with garden partners about what to me was a matter of plain common sense and moral behavior?
- If I needed my buyers to know about the way I gardened—that I did not use poisons and so forth—then I would *tell them face to face,* rather than rely on third-party certification and marketing at a distance.

With little experience in marketing at all I intuitively committed myself to direct marketing: farmer's markets and Community Supported Agriculture projects and, better yet, captive markets for the next 30 years and I never looked back. I still believe this is the only reasonable way for a gardener/farmer to make a living and as the current trend toward *local* food gathers momentum and as the true costs of shipping produce become known and unacceptable, it's all the more reasonable.

Chapter 4 – Fossil, Oregon 1977-9 More Basic Training

Fossil, Oregon, lies in the north central part of the state, a very sparsely settled region between the wooded hills to the south and wheat farming country to the north. With fewer than 500 people, Fossil is nevertheless the largest town in Wheeler county and is the county seat. We moved there, Sky's mother and the little guy, just under a year old, and I because that was where I found work as a counselor, through the good graces, once again, of Elwood Koenig, who had moved to Oregon the year previous.

We first landed in Enterprise, a larger town near the Wallowa mountains in the northeast corner of the state, arguably the most beautiful place I'd seen on a 2,000 mile bike journey through the Northwest a few years earlier. But there was no job for me there.

At Fossil I was the sole mental health counselor in a two-county area but had plenty of time on my hands as clients were scarce. We arrived, bee hive and a wringer washing machine in the back of my pickup, and set up housekeeping in an old dwelling in the middle of town. This place had a big yard for Sky, for the bees just outside the fence and, of course, for a garden.

There were to be two gardens in Fossil at two different houses. I'll be writing only a little about them, for they were very modest and designed only to feed my little family. But they were properly double-dug and productive, adding to my confidence and by the end of my time in Fossil I began to consider myself as a journeyman gardener. In the back of my mind, however, I understood that I had not even begun to fathom the mysteries of Biodynamics.

I did gain ground during those two seasons toward three other important skills. I built my first greenhouse, was able to gather some insights about composting, and found many rewards in my relationship to bees.

Greenhouse Rhapsody

Not long ago I said to Barbara, "If I had a greenhouse to work in, it would add years to my life."

The greenhouse work can begin in January: mixing up potting soil, filling up flats and pots, working ground beds, sorting and ordering seeds. When the sun is shining it doesn't much matter what the outside temperature is, you're working inside in your T-shirt, basking and breathing an atmosphere alive with negative ions, oxygenated and enlivened with the growth-vibes of the plants and the soil underneath. There is joy in abundance in the greenhouse as the late winter advances toward spring and the sun rises higher. Seeds are sprouting, seedlings ready to be transplanted, either into their permanent place or given more root room in larger pots and wider spacing. Shifting rainbows glisten as I water with a misting nozzle. Watering happens sometimes two or three times a day as the intensity of the sun warms everything, the floors, the benches, the flats, the soil. From March until June these early plants thrive and bloom and produce, and right behind them are regiments of summer greenhouse plants, set to go outside.

A well-planned garden greenhouse (as opposed to a commercial greenhouse) can generate plants that are worth tens of thousands of dollars once their produce is marketed. A single square foot of greenhouse space, warmed artificially from February until April, then sun-warmed the remainder of the year, can yield $40 or $50 in a season, having supported a spring crop of seedlings for transplanting outdoors, say 20-30 cabbage plants, then a late-spring harvest of lettuce, then a cucumber or tomato plant to bear in mid-summer. The timing of all this is an exquisite exercise, half intellectual and half intuitive, and the opportunities for gratitude and humility in the face of nature's abundance are there to be taken and remembered.

How would seasons in the greenhouse lengthen my life or anybody else's life?

- Breathing that enlivened atmosphere is like a trip to the spa, all day every day;
- The repetitive and occasionally physically demanding (loading wheelbarrow loads of compost, mixing it with soil, filling a hundred, a thousand, pots and flats) is life-enhancing hard work with a purpose;
- The manifest cheerfulness of the whole thing…seeds germinating, plants growing, music playing, sun-warmth, worms working, playing with water… how could anyone be glum?
- And finally, the many occasions there are in the greenhouse to express what is best in me: humility, gratitude, a sense of proportion and balance, an

appreciation of my place in the harmony and inevitability of a living system designed to feed people.

The second home we had in Fossil was much more suitable than the first, which had been huge and hard to heat. It also had a south-facing front porch eminently suitable for a sun porch/greenhouse. In February I managed to strike a deal for salvaged glass, a lot of it, with a fellow who had demolished an old-style glass greenhouse, and studs, grooved along the edges, to hold the glass in place, enough of both to glass-in the whole thing. It took a few days to do the job, which the landlord approved as it obviously created a winter time heat source.

Soon I had seedlings started and as the winter cycled into spring these grew mightily in the green porch atmosphere. On fine days I began double-digging beds in the vacant lot next door, with help from Tom Smart, who lived with his wife Minnie and little boy, a little older than Sky, in the house on the other side of the lot. The boys, Sky was just two that April, spent hours chasing each other around a big tree in Tom's yard on their 3-wheelers while their dads dug in the garden.

Tom and Minnie held a Bible study in their home every Wednesday evening and there I met Edwin Derrick, a rancher and lay preacher whose place was on the edge of town. Edwin ran a few cows and their calves on leased land during the grazing season, kept a bull or two, and cut hay on an irrigated field at his home place. On my country walks—you're never more than a few blocks from the country in Fossil—I eyeballed that hayfield and noticed an unused triangular corner where the irrigation reached but the hay equipment couldn't turn around. I'd had a notion about growing sunflowers on a more-than-garden scale and a scheme to press oil from them with a home-made hydraulic device, but if that didn't work out I would be satisfied to let the wild birds eat the seeds. This field corner seemed a likely spot and I asked for Edwin's permission.

He was one of the kindest, gentlest, most modest men I have ever known and something about my idea struck his fancy I suppose. He was all for it. In his kindness he downsized my proposal of three acres of sunflowers to much less than that, not because he was being stingy with his land but because he didn't want me to fail. He knew that three acres of hand weeding would be beyond my capacity.

In the end it was a wonderful sight, that sunflower patch, with the bright yellow flower head bobbing and turning with the sun, and in the end the blackbirds got all the seeds and the cows got the stalks.

The two years in Fossil were marked by two triumphs in my career as a beekeeper, my first honey harvests and successful increase, which is what beekeepers call the process of making two colonies from one very strong one.

I was not prepared to invest in all of the equipment needed to harvest extracted honey which has to be spun from the honeycomb with a centrifugal device–even one holding only two or three frames and spun with a hand crank–is bulky and expensive, unsuited to a nomadic lifestyle like mine (though, come to think of it, so are beehives themselves). This summer of 1979 I opted for a system of comb honey production called Ross Rounds in which the bees build their comb in round plastic cassettes, 28 of them in each shallow box sitting atop the main colony. When filled with honey— they weigh about a pound—these round combs are very attractive and require only to have clear plastic covers and labels put on. One of these little honeycombs sitting in a saucer on the breakfast table is a gourmet delight and, with beginner's luck I harvested more than a hundred of them. Many we gave away as gifts.

The honeybee queen is less a monarch than an egg-laying phenomenon. Under good spring conditions, when weather favors nectar and pollen production, lots of flowers and good foraging for the field bees, queens can lay a thousand or more eggs a day. Colony population increases rapidly and swarming, the bees' natural tendency to increase, becomes a distinct possibility. At this point the alert beekeeper, reluctant to allow a significant number of his charges to fly off yonder, will order a new queen bee or two and "split" the overpopulated colony into two or three portions, each with its complement of worker bees, feed (honey and pollen) and brood, that is, developing bee babies of all stages of growth: eggs, larvae and pupae. The queen stays with what is left of the original hive and new queens are installed in the other one or two new colonies. With luck and continued good conditions in the field the result is two or three surplus-producing hives by the end of the season where before there was one.

Beginner's luck again favored me those two seasons in Fossil and the increase went well, with the one colony I'd brought from Nevada expanded to three. I was not so egocentric as to consider this a personal accomplishment but rather as a privilege, being allowed to participate in Nature's plan for the continued welfare of the bees. The increased honey production was gravy.

* * *

Meanwhile, as I carried on my counseling work that summer and saved some money, two thoughts nagged.

One was that I was no closer than I had been three years ago to finding a way to learn about Biodynamics. We did hear that Alan Chadwick was teaching at a community in Virginia, having left California and the various gardens he created there: the University of California at Santa Cruz program he founded, the garden at Green Gulch, the Zen Center, and the Round Valley Garden Project at Covelo. We inquired at Virginia's Carmel in the Valley only to be told that this startup community had no housing for a family, nor any provision for communal child care. We had no way to know, of course, that Chadwick would die at Green Gulch in May, 1980, the following year.

"We need to create the beauty and the quality first. The quantity will follow"

"It is, you see — though many people seem to find the idea amusing — the garden that makes the gardener."

— *Alan Chadwick*

The other nagging thought, was this: I had come out half-baked from the Summer Course at Claymont four years earlier. Those three months of Gurdjieff teachings with Pierre and the Sherbourne House graduates had had a huge impact and sent me spinning off into the Nevada desert to find answers and since had informed many life decisions, but I remained soggy inside. We heard from Sky's biological father, who sometimes taught at Claymont, that if we wanted to go to a Basic Course—the nine-month one, of which there now had been four—we had best figure on going to the fifth one which would begin in late September, for there might not be a sixth.

And so the late summer at Fossil, which might have been a quiet time of garden and honey harvest, became a frenetic period of selling stuff, including all the bees and bee equipment, of closing out therapy sessions with clients, of phone calls and application forms to Claymont. Pierre, I think, recognizing my half-baked condition, made it easy to re-enter the situation there. By mid-September I left Fossil with less impedimenta than I had come with, to join the boy and his mother in Reno for a few days before leaving on a cross-country train ride for West Virginia. It was not the most impulsive thing I've done in my life, but it certainly ranks among the top few.

Chapter 5 – West Virginia, Florida, Eden, New York, Blacksburg, Virginia, Kimberton, Pennsylvania 1980-1

In this single year, my fortieth, a major flurry of opportunities arose for learning certain aspects of community, family, and farming, each of them giving way in due course to the next. From June of 1980 to June of 1981 I moved from Claymont in West Virginia to Lake Jem Florida to Eden New York to Blacksburg Virginia to Kimberton Pennsylvania.

The year-long Claymont course finished up on schedule in June, 1980, and, more or less penniless, I chose to believe an ad at the back of *Mother Earth News* announcing a new community arising in Lake Jem, Florida, on the Gurdjieffian principles. I'd gone there to scope it out on Easter break from Claymont and realized that this outfit, a 5-acre smallholding in the midst of orange groves wasn't going to become a viable community any time soon, but rather was a non-self-sufficient homestead run by this fellow, I'll call him Murphy, and his wife and consisting of a double-wide trailer home, a poly greenhouse, a couple of shade houses, an acre or so of garden, and a couple of acres of oranges. Both worked away from the place as well as tending it. But it looked to me at Easter like a cheap place to live while I took a few months to try to digest whatever had happened to me at Claymont.

So I arrived at Lake Jem in early June with a couple of packs and a box of books, eager, actually to take care of the plants, meditate during the heat of the day, and learn whatever it was that the situation had to teach me.

If I had any illusions about Florida as a balmy, paradisiacal place, I lost them quickly as the 100°F days and extreme humidity took their toll. True, Lake Jem was in the center of the state and blissfully distant from the traffic and overcrowding of the coastal communities and from the Disneyesque and SeaWorldish claptrap around Orlando. Not a lot of mega-hotels or freeways out among the groves.

However, industrial agriculture, complete with monocultures, pesticides and peonage was dismally present there in Lake County. One day watering in the shade house I heard what might have been a jet airplane landing next door. When I went to investigate, walking through a neighbor's grove and approaching the sound, I came upon the sight of mature trees whipping in a machine-made hurricane and realized that what I was hearing was a tractor-pulled spray rig with huge fans dispersing a pesticide, making sure that every leaf, every fruit and every nook and cranny of bark was dosed with poison. I quickly pulled back from there. Murphy was raising his oranges organically, but his place was surrounded by conventionally managed places.

Murphy fancied that he was a Gurdjieff-style teacher, creating conditions for spiritual growth by demolishing the egos of others. Now Murphy was not a Claymont person. In fact he seemed to be slightly contemptuous of the Bennett stream of Gurdjieff teachings. His own training in The Work seemed to have come from what is called the Foundation lineage with 50-60 affiliated groups in 30 states and many foreign countries, all flowing from the teachings of Madame Jeanne de Salzmann, an early and very highly regarded student of the master.

I was a more-or-less willing, if slightly bemused, victim/student of Murphy's manipulations. On one occasion his wife was away for the weekend and he and I were to cook the Sunday meal, which included a lovely beef roast. (Whatever else the Lake Jem experience may have lacked, including any wages, I was always very well fed.) I was to make the gravy. This I did and soon a deep frying pan, half full of bubbling, savory gravy was simmering on the stove top, the last component to the meal. Just at that point Murphy called me away from the kitchen on some pretext and stretched out the distraction until the gravy was ruined. Had I been ego-involved in that gravy scene, I would have been furious, but I wasn't and I wasn't. Another time, Murphy asked me to mow the grove, using his sweet little Farmall Cub tractor and a sickle bar mower. It had been many years, since the farm in Kentucky, that I had driven a tractor, but I was confident. When we went to the outbuilding so he could explain the controls to me we found that the left side big tire was flat. Now I knew there had to be an electric air pump somewhere on the place but Murphy brought out a hand pump and began the job. He set a fast pace, challenging me, but at 39 I was strong and I kept up, sweating in the 95°F heat. Eventually the tire was inflated and as I mowed in the grove I reflected on Murphy's clumsy, but harmless machinations. At Claymont I had been subject to subtler, far more expert schemes designed to deflate ego.

I never did any real gardening there as it was high summer and, as I was to appreciate years later in Arizona, in these sub-tropical conditions spring and fall gardens were the norm. High summer was a resting time for the garden. After about six weeks I'd had about enough, of Murphy and of Florida. I wrote a reasonably gracious note to Murphy and his wife, thanking them for their hospitality and promising to send money and an address to ship my pitiful couple of boxes of possessions. I left everything except a backpack of essentials and began to hitchhike north.

Before I left Claymont I'd had a phone call from Dan Winter in New York state, inviting me to come to his Crystal Hill Farm in Eden, near Buffalo. I knew Dan from the 1975 summer course at Claymont. In fact I was at least partially responsible for his staying on the course after his ego got severely whacked in the first few days. While sitting in a cold bath (there was very limited hot water in the Claymont mansion where we were roommates in a 5-man bedroom) I talked to him like the proverbial Dutch uncle about just why we were there. Dan was an intellectual of the first rank, a computer geek even in 1980 when I arrived at his place, but psychologically a little immature, I thought. He had many talents and held down a very nice position as researcher, technical trouble shooter and customer support guy at his family's electrical services and equipment firm. There wasn't much that Dan didn't know about electric cars, wind generators and electrical applications of all kinds. He even had an electric tractor on the farm, with a little front end loader on it.

Crystal Hill was a smallholding that must have been a much bigger farm at one time than the five acres he had purchased, for it came with a huge seven-bedroom house complete with conservatory-greenhouse and a beautiful old barn with hayloft big enough to play basketball in. That gable roofed barn with cupola on top would cost at least half a million dollars to duplicate today.

Dan had three goats, two milking nannies and a kid, a few chickens and a neglected garden. What he wanted was a Biodynamic farm and he needed me to initiate it. I don't think I ever told Dan that I could do that, but it was what we both wanted. I didn't have whatever it took but I did have a clue.

In Florida, at Lake Jem, Murphy had a calendar on the wall of the dining room, "*Stella*Natura*," published by the Camphill community at Kimberton, Pennsylvania. No eye candy here or 4-color photos of mountain lakes or wildlife. Rather, it was a plain Jane black-and-white publication with informative articles on Biodynamic gardening, charts on planting in harmony with cosmic events. I didn't understand the astronomical basis for the calendar's suggestions, but overall it seemed to be a sophisticated rendering of lore surrounding planting by the moon. I was only mildly interested in that part, but on the back cover there was a brief mention of an apprenticeship program. That really piqued my attention—the notice that Kimberton Hills accepts a few interns each year as part of a several-year training in Biodynamic agriculture. Here it was, the opportunity I'd wanted. I wrote to the place while I was still at Murphy's, but with all my subsequent moving around, the first reply might have been lost.

At Dan's place I made myself useful, cutting firewood for the cook stove, cleaning up the workshop, milking the goats and caring for them, working in the garden, driving his Ford 8-N tractor and bush hog mower to keep unused land clear. Dan shopped; I cooked supper. We were a couple of eccentric bachelors, rattling around in that huge house. In the attic Dan had stashed enough grain and beans in 50-pound sacks to feed us for years, if it came to that. He didn't pay me and I was OK with working short days in exchange for room and board.

Then my family showed up. The boy was three and a half years old now and what I saw as a cozy state of affairs his mom saw as serfdom. We made the best of it through much of the winter, but the chemistry of the situation just wasn't right. Nobody's fault. By the first of February we left Eden for Blacksburg, VA, where I had the vague possibility of a job, which, in the event, fizzled.

Blacksburg, home of Virginia Tech, was an OK place, but it wasn't getting me any closer to the Biodynamic training I craved. Shortly after we arrived I got work at a big nursery, at first balling and wrapping trees for landscape plantings—some of the hardest work I've ever done—then working at the nursery itself and finally as foreman for small crews, going out homes to install landscaping designs sketched out by our salesmen-horticulturalists. Lots of hole digging, tree toting, lifting and carrying of plant material and heavy sacks of this and that.

I was going on 40 years old and I've never been physically powerful. I certainly couldn't keep up with the 18-year-olds on my crews. The pay was $4.50 an hour and it was all very depressing. After a few months of this a note came from Kimberton, inviting me to come and present myself as an candidate for internship. I wanted to go and with the family's agreement I did.

The next five years, devoted to Biodynamics and two Camphill villages was one of the most productive and happiest times of my life.

Chapter 6 – Camphill Village Kimberton Hills, Pennsylvania 1981-5 A Community that Works

I arrived at Kimberton on Whitsunday, the seventh Sunday after Easter, in early June… strawberry time. I met Joel Morrow, the head gardener, that first evening and the next morning when I showed up for work at Morningstar Garden my first assignment was to learn the names of all the houses in the community—Springfield, Oberlin, Hyacinth, Kepler, Garden Cottage, Farmhouse, Sancanac, and several others—and to make signs to mark the strawberry rows for picking by the folks in each house. Our garden crews would pick every other fruit and vegetable we grew, but we could count on a U-Pick scheme for strawberries—the house mothers would somehow find the time to come, or send someone, to get those! My second assignment was digging up thistles, Canada thistles, vicious invaders with no business in a garden. The root goes down straight for more than a spade's depth, but it's not enough to pull up this tap root and call things good; for between vertical roots runs a horizontal one eager to send up through a foot and a half of soil a brand new plant if necessary. Thistle removal is a chore to test the patience of a would-be gardener and a means to test his resolve.

Camphill Village Kimberton Hills was founded in 1972, nine years before I arrived, and is part of the world wide Camphill movement begun in Scotland in the early years of World War II by Dr. Karl Koenig and other refugees from Nazi oppression, all followers of the teachings of Rudolf Steiner. Steiner (1861-1925) is often called simply "an Austrian philosopher," but he had a devoted following of people dedicated to carrying on the practical applications of his work in education, medicine, agriculture, architecture, religion and other areas of human endeavor. His work was immense in depth and extent, preserved in many books and more than 6,000 lectures during his lifetime. Immerse.

Steiner died less than a year after he gave the "Agriculture Course," the week-long series of lectures that became, in farmers' hands, the art of Biodynamics. This was what I'd come for, to learn the techniques and lore of Steiner's agriculture. I'd had a taste of this at Claymont and now it was time to plunge into it thoroughly. What I didn't realize until much later was that much of the learning I was going to absorb would come from retarded people.

Rudolf Steiner's teachings in education and what came to be called "Social Therapy" coupled with Koenig's vast compassion and considerable expertise as a seasoned pediatrician, inspired the life at the first Camphill which was set up as a school and community for mentally handicapped people. The premise was simple: work with people's strengths, and immerse them in a community culture that values every individual's contribution as a vital piece of the whole. Know that if you program for success and let the whole community adapt itself to the best elements of all its people, wondrous things can happen.

Other such schools were developed in Great Britain during the 1940s and 1950s and when it became clear that no place existed for the students after they became adults, Camphill would carry on the compassionate and life-affirming work with them. "Villages" were established as places where they could live as adults and work in healthy environments designed to encourage their fullest potential. There are more than 100 Camphill communities in over 20 countries in Europe, North America, southern Africa and India where those with special needs are offered the support they need to develop their potential. The first of these Villages in North America was Camphill Village USA at Copake, New York, founded in 1961. Kimberton was the second.

The premise was simple but in its execution complex as only a community of human beings can be, even elegant. Camphill Villages are not institutions. There is none of the architectural or administrative inflexibility that characterize, say, schools or mental institutions. They are truly Villages in their structure and their culture, self-contained and managed by the Co-workers themselves... housemothers, gardeners, grounds keepers, bakers, store keepers, farm workers, maintenance people. There is little or no hierarchy, excepting that in all reason and justice, the judgment of a core member who has been there since the beginning is likely to hold sway over that of a summer intern.

The housemothers are the heart of the place and the household you live in—probably no less than five inhabitants, nor more than 10 or 12—is her domain. She is chief nurturer and the special ambiance of the home she creates is carried like a bouquet by the people she sends out into the Village in the morning—well nourished, scrubbed, cared for and cheerful.

The so-called handicapped adults we worked with, the reason-for-being of the place, would have been lost in the society at large, either sheltered at home by aging and anxious parents (for what would become of their autistic or Down's Syndrome son or daughter when they passed on?), or in a group home and "sheltered workshop" kind of existence, medicated into docility and forever infantilized. Here in Camphill however, they led lives of dignity and their sense of self-worth was fostered at every turn. There were about fifty of these folks at Camphill Kimberton, ranging in age from 20 to 60+. For the most part their stay at the Village was open-ended, a lifetime place for almost all, for it would be hard to conceive of a more sustaining life for them. I wrote "so-called" handicapped people, because it became clear to me after a while that they taught as much as they learned, and they cared for us Co-workers as much as we cared for them, though not so self-consciously. For instance, if you were paying attention to what was going on in your relationship with these folks, especially to what it was that most irritated you about someone's behavior, you found invariably that they were reflecting unappealing traits in your own presentation to the world; their special gift was this all-unaware mirroring.

My garden crew were fine wheelbarrow drivers, and berry pickers, carrot pullers, bean harvesters. At a certain point in the mid-morning (we'd been harvesting all of the first part of the day) we would load produce into white plastic buckets, each with the name of a Village house on it, load the buckets into big two-wheeled garden carts, and send teams off to the various houses, in time for the cooks to use in the main meal of the day, around one o'clock. In a summer, for a Village of 120 souls, uncounted tons of tomatoes, beans, squash, peas, broccoli, cabbage, salad of all kinds, plus potatoes and sweet corn from the farm fields. We all ate like kings, even if we were poverty-stricken from the standpoint of the wider culture. For in Camphill, Co-workers receive only a stipend.

It was during that first summer, walking on a path from Springfield house over the hill to the garden in the middle of the night—going to move irrigation sprinklers from one section to another—that I had an epiphany: My life and my work had merged and I really couldn't tell the difference. Here I was, just having been awakened from a sound sleep by the alarm, trekking halfway across the Village to drag hundreds of feet of garden hoses around on the soft ground and make sure things got evenly watered. Work, yes…and interrupted sleep, but the balmy farm-scented air and bright stars exalted me too and I was intensely alive and aware and thankful as I've never been in a job that paid money. In a "real" job you work so you can have a life on the weekends and on vacation. In Camphill you love your work or you leave; there's nothing to blur the tight connection between work and life, money doesn't matter and neither does social status. It's not who you know that matters, but rather who you are and what you can do in support of the people, the land, and the life of the community.

My garden mentor Joel Morrow had been the master of Morningstar garden for a year or two. Joel was a high-energy type, not only a superb gardener but also a fine writer and later the editor of the bi-monthly journal of the Biodynamic Farming and Gardening Association. His articles for that publication were brilliant and provocative. His understanding of how to work with mentally handicapped people was compassionate and practical. During that first summer Joel challenged me, inspired me and energized me. I had come to here to learn Biodynamic gardening, to immerse myself in it, and Joel was my guide. I lived in Springfield house with him and his wife Julie, their two small children, and two young Villagers.

Mealtimes in Springfield house were a pure delight. Julie was a fine cook and the quality of the Camphill fare—the garden and farm vegetables, the milk and cheese and butter, fresh bread, the farm-butchered meat—was superb. We worked hard and were fed wonderfully, but not before Joel led us in the grace before meals, a Camphill custom from way back. Grace was often sung and there were dozens of them. An example:

> *Earth who gives to us this food*
> *Sun who makes it ripe and good*
> *Dear Earth, dear Sun*
> *By you we live*
> *Our loving thanks*
> *To you we give*

Then we all held hands and sang out: "Blessings on the Meal!" We ate better, I'm convinced, than the richest of the rich.

My mentors in community life were Helen and Hubert Zipperlin, who were among the founding members of Camphill Kimberton. Helen was a prime mover in the Village, a bright and vivacious Scotswoman, the closest thing we had to an executive director. Within an hour of my arrival Helen was there on the scene welcoming me but also with gentle probing seeking to discern my motivations and intentions in coming. Was I going to be an asset to the Village or was I here to escape something? Was I thoroughly unmarried…did I have obligations in that realm? I apparently passed muster. Hubert was maybe 20 years older than Helen, a native of Germany who found himself interned as an enemy alien on the Isle of Man during WWII. Semi-retired, he was a figure of great respect at Kimberton. For many months early on in my stay there I came to their home, Garden Cottage, on Tuesday evenings for supper and conversation.

The 430-acre property at Kimberton, was one-half of an estate which had been the home of Alaric and Mabel Pew Myrin. Thirty years before, they had given one half of the property to help found the Kimberton Waldorf School across French Creek. In 1972 Camphill took on the rest, including the hilltop mansion, Kepler House, which was the Myrin's summer home, and a dozen other residences which had housed staff. The land rises from Pughtown Road uphill to the mansion and down the other side to French Creek. It includes the homes, farm fields and farm buildings, woods and gardens, wonderful perennial plantings and ornamental trees. The houses were soon inhabited by Co-workers and Villagers and the work of social therapy began.

When I came to Camphill Kimberton nine years later the Village held about 120 people, roughly 50 "Co-workers," 20 of their children, and 50 "Villagers," so-called handicapped folks, adults aged from early 20s to their 60s. The terms are in quotes because in Village life the distinctions got thoroughly blurred. True, there are things I as the head gardener could do that members of my crew couldn't do—plan the timing of the season's crops, wrestle the rototiller, read and interpret the indications on the *Stella*Natura* garden calendar—but then there were plenty of things other Co-workers could do that I couldn't—bake the fabulous bread, make cheese, keep a home spotless and inviting. In fact there were things Villagers could do that I couldn't, including being at peace with their lot in life. Certain autistic savants in the Village would ask your birth date and tell you the day of the week you were born, or Roger Maras' batting average in 1976. Other Villagers had the patience to weed almost endless rows of tiny carrot seedlings and a sense of humility that would make a saint blush.

So, in effect, we were all Villagers and we were all Co-workers.

Joel Morrow was a little younger than I, but vastly more experienced as a Biodynamic gardener and as a community member. He almost single handedly ran Morningstar garden, two and a half acres of a south facing slope just on the left as you entered the driveway and began to climb the hill toward Kepler House. Lines had always been drawn between garden and farm at Kimberton, with the farm producing many of the space-hogging vegetables like potatoes and sweet corn, which lend themselves to mechanized cultivation, and the gardens growing the crops that required less space and more hand work—salad, tomatoes, onions and such.

I worked with Joel and his crew that first summer in Morningstar garden, gradually taking on more and more responsibility. It took a while to be taken seriously by him and by the community and what counted was just that, responsibility-taking. Kimberton attracted all sorts of visitors: idealists of all kinds, young tourists from many states and all over Europe, newly-minted Biodynamic farmers from training programs in Europe, parents of so-called mentally handicapped folks, and potential community members. Some of these people stayed only for a few hours, some for several days or weeks. Anyone who stayed for more than a day or two was expected to help out with the work, either in the gardens or the houses, perhaps, in high summer, with food processing.

At the center of the Village, near the Kepler House mansion, was a building that housed the bakery, walk-in coolers and freezers and a large commercial style kitchen in which housemothers and helpers preserved food for later use, canning or freezing. In July, August and September we sent thousands of pounds of tomatoes, green beans, peas, cucumbers and other produce up the hill from the garden to this processing kitchen. Often enough the slicing, dicing, blanching, water bath boiling, canning and such went on from mid-afternoon until late at night, for we all took Village food security very seriously. With the dairy cows, cheese making, bakery, farm and gardens, very little of the Kimberton budget was spent in grocery stores.

A short walk from Morningstar garden was the greenhouse, a 50-year-old glass house 100 feet long and 30 feet wide, divided into three roughly square rooms by glass partitions. This structure was connected to a large potting and storage shed by a smaller glasshouse, maybe 20' x 20', a tropical house presided over by an older Co-worker. The former owners of the estate had raised flowers to supply the homes and to compete in shows and exhibitions… chrysanthemums, I think.

This elegant structure, almost a relic, was designed and built by Lord & Burnham, a 150-year-old company known for high quality and high prices. It had a very practical function under Joel's management as a place to grow seedlings for the garden, but I puzzled over the fact that it went unused for three-quarters of the year. It was pretty much empty when I arrived in June and wouldn't be utilized again until February. This struck me at the time as a shame, for a mighty asset was lying idle much of the year.

Glass has many advantages as a greenhouse covering. It's permanent and does not deteriorate like fiberglass or plastics. My experience is that it transmits a wider range of sunlight to the sheltered plants. It's clear and beautiful. But, of course, it breaks. Once a hapless (and here nameless) farm intern at Kimberton broke 25 or 30 panes on the greenhouse when he neglected to turn the output chute of his tractor-mounted snow blower away from the greenhouse as he cleared snow from the driveway alongside it, sending a cascade of gravel and ice chunks onto and through the glass roof. Glass shards and debris showered down on the plants inside and the mess, including replacing those panes, took a couple of days to clean up.

By late winter I had acquired enough credibility with Joel to be given the entire responsibility for the seedling preparation for the coming season's garden. The greenhouse growing began in early February when we sowed onions and leeks into freshly composted soil beds up against the south side of the greenhouse where there was the most light. Joel taught me the technique to handle the tiny black seeds—"You have to watch every seed drop…"—taking a pinch of seeds between the tips of thumb and forefinger and releasing the seeds by sliding the fingertips, while slowly moving your hand along the soil furrow. With practice you can pick up a consistent number of seeds from the pile in your left palm, maybe 25, and drop them evenly along the row so you get a reasonably consistent stand of plants a quarter-inch or so apart. Working with dark, moist, rich soil and black seeds, "watching every seed drop" is a real exercise. I'm grateful to Joel for holding me to the standard on this and proving that it's possible. The beautifully even stand of allium plants that resulted from his insistence on method proved his point. In a few weeks we had a 20-foot bed of onion (three kinds) and leek seedlings in eight rows three or four inches apart, slender and gloriously green. Since these alliums are slow to grow to transplant size, they were the first to go in. By mid-April, when the maritime climate in eastern Pennsylvania had settled and the soil had warmed a bit we had thousands of onion seedlings ready to go outside.

I took to that first greenhouse work as if I'd done it all my life, or in a former life. The atmosphere of it was wonderfully familiar. So was the rhythm of it. I felt I had the best job in the Village, working in a T-shirt in spring like, sun-captured warmth when it was below freezing outdoors, sowing seeds, mixing potting soil, filling flats, working out the schedule. For nighttime and cloudy days supplemental heat from the oil furnace was necessary, the warmth rising from the floor where hot water pipes run through in trenches under the beds, a far better system than the propane hot air furnaces blasting away in most commercial greenhouse.

First onions, then brassicas—cabbage, broccoli, cauliflower, Chinese cabbage, bok choi—which can go in the garden or farm field about the same time as the alliums but grow to transplant size much more quickly. Parsley, another slow grower like the onions, also needed to be seeded very early in the greenhouse for summertime eating. Happily, parsley is perfectly content in a low light situation that would frustrate other crops and cause them to become "leggy," reaching and reaching for the light. Parsley could be started early when daylight hours were still on late winter schedule and be transplanted into an bed on the north side of the greenhouse where light was minimal.

Meanwhile, thousands of salad seedlings—lettuce and spinach mainly—went into the waist-high soil-filled benches in the first two sections of the greenhouse. These we packed in closely, perhaps four inches apart, for it's not until the outer leaves of adjacent plants touch each other that we are taking full advantage of the sunlight which is, after all, the object of the game. When this happened, we could cut every other plant—the remaining plants, now growing vigorously, would soon fill in the spaces—for distribution to the Village houses for first salad of the year in early April. From the greenhouse, then from the main garden, and from the greenhouse again in October and November, the aim was to provide fresh, crisp, healthy greens for the folks in the Village for almost nine months. During my second winter in the greenhouse I kept a dozen 5-gallon buckets going with alfalfa sprouts and delivered a quantity of these to each house every few days. That year there were fresh greens at lunchtime every month.

By far the biggest challenge in my first greenhouse spring was starting the tomato seedlings. In Morningstar garden we grew more than 500 tomato plants of many different varieties and at transplant time, the last week of May, we wanted sturdy six- to eight-week old plants with robust root systems. The ideal is a stocky plant at least as wide as it is tall and this requires quick growth and lots of root room; if one plant's roots touch those of its neighbor, or the walls of its container, growth is checked. Fortunately tomato seedlings love to be transplanted and always show a growth spurt as they settle into fresh soil. When the tomato seeds were sown in flats around the first of April, the plants came up close together in the rows, a half-inch or so apart, so one flat held a hundred or more babies. At about two weeks it was time to transplant them into flats, now about two inches apart, say 35 to the flat. Another week and each plant needed to go into its own four-inch pot, and 10 days later each went into a 6-inch pot, to stay until transplanting time outdoors.

Not only did we have to find room for all these plants in the greenhouse, rapidly filling that time of year, we also had to create potting soil. Joel's formula for this, which I never found any reason to alter, was one-third Biodynamic compost, one-third garden soil, and one-third sharp sand, to loosen the mix and help it to drain. The mixing of potting soil and filling of flats and pots was a mighty job in April and May, but thoroughly satisfying work. To have this done just in advance of the need for the new, filled containers was tricky, but doable.

Tomatoes were not the only garden plants we were working with in the greenhouse at this time; we also had hundreds of pepper plants to deal with (much slower growing than tomatoes, but every bit as demanding), eggplants, cucumbers—all those warm weather transplants. Meanwhile, outdoors in the garden, I was tilling up beds for peas, early, and, once the soil was warming well, green beans—both staples in the Village food scheme and candidates for blanching and freezing efforts. Also for direct seeded spinach and lots of lettuce transplants. The onion plants started in the greenhouse in February are also ready to go outside in April.

By tomato transplant time in late May the greenhouse season under Joel's management would have been coming to a close but this year I had another idea: in the end house, four thirty-foot ground beds, I planted double rows of cucumber plants, the old-fashioned "Straight 8" variety. Later, when the plants began to run, I installed fence wire hanging from the roof frame for them to climb on. Within weeks there was a jungle of cucumber curtains, growing up, rather than sprawling on the ground. This was a clever way, by no means original with me, to maximize the limited floor space in the greenhouse. There were about 250 plants bearing fruit instead of perhaps 50 in the traditional sprawling mode. Another couple of weeks, about mid-July, I began to harvest 60 or 80 pounds of cukes twice a week and this went on for six weeks or so. A half a ton of cucumbers, more or less, for salads, pickles and the Philadelphia market.

A year earlier when I first met Joel on that Whitsunday evening he had asked, "You're not one of those marketing guys are you?" It seems that a couple of visitors were in the Village promoting the notion of selling Kimberton Hills produce in the wider market. Already the Village sold raw milk, bread, cookies and cheese in a few stores in Philadelphia, which was less than an hour's drive to the East. Since we already had a refrigerated truck making the trip, the theory went, why not grow surplus for sale? Jim Baurausky's wife Andrea was overseeing the marketing logistics and by the time I planted all those cucumbers, the greenhouse was already contributing parsley and a bit of salad to the effort. But on that first night with Joel this was still a relatively new idea and he was against it, feeling perhaps that we gardeners had enough to do feeding the Village and sending once-a-week buckets of produce to housemothers at Beaver Run, the Camphill School not far away.

This was in the days before CSAs and farmers markets were not nearly so popular as today.

The middle greenhouse section, with four waist-high beds, I filled with eggplants, two or three hundred of them. These were well grown plants with six or eight leaves and a blossom or two and in the congenial greenhouse atmosphere they grew very well indeed.

My rationale for these two plantings, the cukes and the eggplants, was this: Outdoors, cucumbers were sorely beset by the Cucumber Beetle, striped horizontally or lengthwise, or spotted, these guys eat a lot and carry disease. My hope was that cucumbers under glass would escape the problem and in the event that's just the way it happened. And even in the benign maritime Pennsylvania climate eggplant didn't seem to thrive outdoors. In the greenhouse that year my little monocrop of eggplant bushes was a true sight to behold, each with a couple of glossy black shmoo-shaped fruits dangling, flourishing in the summertime heat and humidity, extreme in the greenhouse.

I determined early on in my stay at Kimberton that I would not enroll in the apprentice program. I had heard murmurings among the long-term Co-workers and especially housemothers to the effect that the apprentices were **in** the community all right, and they made a true contribution with their work, but they were not **of** the Village, that is they had little feeling for the true heart of the Village, the work with the so-called handicapped people. I was sure there were some apprentices for whom this criticism was more or less justified, others less so, but out of a longstanding interest in community living and now finding myself in the midst of one that actually seemed to work I wanted to be accepted as a fully fledged participant, not merely a bystander.

I came to discover that there were several routes to being perceived in that way, always with the assumption that you are reasonably competent in your job. I have said that there is very little bureaucracy in Camphill, no entrenched managerial class. Rather, the management of the Village is taken on by committees; the Admissions Group, to which I belonged by my second year there is a good example. The question was put to me whether I would join this group to help decide who could come to the Village among all those who applied. Helen Zipperlin was the point person for the group *ex officio* literally as she, of all the Co-workers, was in the office the most and naturally fielded incoming phone calls from people interested 1) in "placing" a more or less handicapped person in the Village, or 2) in coming to visit/work/stay for a while. From others, letters came. The Village was pretty much always full, but there was a lot of churn…people coming, people leaving, especially among the young Europeans on an American tour of intentional communities, Camphill Villages and Schools, Anthrophosophical initiatives of other sorts like Waldorf Schools, Biodynamic farms and the retirement community in the Hudson Valley. These youngsters came mostly during the summer, stayed a few days or a few weeks, and if they were good workers, as almost all were, and cheerful, as they were, they were sorely missed. Some stayed a year or so, took on real responsibility, and were treasured.

Also coming for usually short visits were Camphill old-timers, equally cherished for having been in on the beginning, or nearly so, of the now worldwide Camphill movement.

We paid special attention to inquiries from mature couples contemplating an extended stay at Kimberton, as these folks might be candidates to be houseparents, There were a dozen houses in the Village, from the mansion at the top of the hill, Kepler House, where two houseparents, a couple of assistants and six or eight handicapped adults; down to Springfield House where I lived at first with Joel and his wife, their two children and two young men, Villagers. (Though we were all actually "Villagers," in practice the so-called handicapped ones were called Villagers, while the so-called normal adults were "Co-workers," though I suppose in these more politically correct times the labels might have changed a bit.) The houseparent roles were well-filled by experienced folks, Camphill veterans, in all but two of the dozen Kimberton houses when I arrived. The houseparent situation in these two was seen to be dicey. In one case the role was filled by two sterling Co-workers from abroad, both female, who would be leaving in a matter of months, but who because of their demonstrated maturity and empathy with the Villagers were recruited for the job. The other slot was filled by a new couple whose marriage was faltering. Like the wider culture around it Camphill had the requisite instances of divorces, wandering spouses, mismatched pairs, odd couples and eccentrics among those who came to serve. The core Co-workers—the ones with long experience and who had been at Kimberton since its beginning 10 years before—kept a close eye on such situations, not by inspecting the households directly as that would have been intrusive, but rather by assessing in the course of daily life the well-being of the Villagers from those houses. Our handicapped friends do not cover up their miseries well and if the home life is lacking in love, or nutrition, or comfort, the Villagers show that.

So I found that committee work was one avenue of acceptance and my work with the Admissions Group was certainly eye-opening, a window on the need for Camphills in the world.

I was able, halfway through my first year at Kimberton, to gain credibility and acceptance in two other areas: festival work and house parenting.

Almost unique to Camphill life is the lively and cheerful celebration of the Christian holidays, both the traditional Christmas and Easter, the more obscure ones like Whitsun and Saint Lucy's Day, and the peasant celebrations like the plowing festival and harvest celebration. The activities surrounding these festivals are a rich source of cultural life in Camphill, with plays, musical events, special meals, land walks, readings and, most touching of all to me, Christmas eve midnight caroling in the cow barn, where the cows stood in their festively decorated stalls and listened attentively and appreciatively. In peasant lore this is the one moment of the year when the animals are given the gift of speech.

That first Christmas at Kimberton I played Joseph in the Christmas play, an artless performance marked by sincerity, at least, if not by my singing voice, for the Camphill Christmas play is a musical. Happily, my partner Beth, as Mary, was a highly talented musician and her patience and clarity of voice carried the show. This was a presentation in front of the whole Village on Christmas eve.

By my first fall at Kimberton, that houseparent marriage at Hyacinth House had imploded and the cobbled-together team that replaced those folks the past few months was coming apart. Two of the three members had to return to England as their visa had run out. I was asked to become a houseparent with a more experienced Camphiller, a fellow gardener who'd been in the house with the English couple, and I accepted. I was to remain house father in Hyacinth during the remainder of my time at Kimberton, three years and more.

One credibility-strengthener I failed to comprehend or, comprehending, failed to appreciate, were the ongoing study groups in Rudolf Steiner's teachings, usually around one or the other of the dozens of books he wrote, or collections of some of his 6,000 lectures. I attended one such study group where participants were expected to read chapters by the week and one designee was supposed to explicate the text for the others at the next session. With little or no experience with Steiner I found his writings dense and impenetrable and the attempts of my fellow sufferers to explain I found an exercise in bewilderment. I soon dropped out of the group.

At one point Helen encouraged me to begin another one of these study groups and I replied that however wonderfully Steiner's ideas worked out in practice, in Camphill life, in Waldorf schools and in agriculture, I had great resistance to his philosophy, the basis of Anthroposophy. As a recovering Roman Catholic and a student of Gurdjieff, I was suspicious beyond all reason (I admitted) of any dogma or ideology. I had great faith in my hands, I was becoming conversant with my emotions, but I didn't expect to enter heaven on the strength of intellect, particularly as expressed in words…slippery words from another language and a century past.

I know I was a disappointment to Helen and Hubert. If I'd humbled myself to ask about Anthroposophy and explored with them how I could gain access to these teachings, starting from where I was and from the gifts I had…if I had been able to squelch ego and my burgeoning self-confidence as a journeyman gardener and animal tender…I might have learned from them, I might have accepted the grace they offered as my mentors. But even at the age of 40 a certain self-satisfied callowness marked the face I put to the world. They forgave me, those good people, out of their deep wisdom and compassion, and they accepted me for the energy and competence I brought to my work, but they never again invited me into their world and I apparently blew my chance to become a full member of the Camphill Community.

Meanwhile I was traveling back and forth between Hyacinth House and the greenhouse and Morningstar Garden six or eight or ten times a day. From time to time I had a vehicle, a battered pickup or van, and for one long summer, a moped, but I often walked, over the hill and through the woods and fields, and relished the life I had, demanding as it was. I was in my prime, I felt, productive and creative, and fully appreciative of how the Village, especially for me the farm/garden/household alignment worked, in all its details. Every couple of days one of our Hyacinth people came home from the milk room with a gallon or two of fresh, whole, raw milk; another would return from the bakery daily with fresh bread; I would send garden produce by the basket full to all the houses and the farm would send field crops, including some that I had started for the farmers in the greenhouse. If there was extra produce it went off to market in Philadelphia and brought needed cash into the Village economy. The Village was every farmer's dream, a captive market where everything is dealt with on the retail level (wholesale for the small proportion that went to market), and value is added on the spot, from wheat field to cleaned grain to flour to baked goods; from garden truck to processing to vegetables for the winter; from milk to cheese, from cream to butter. For all its quirks and personalities this system worked, and worked efficiently.

From Joel I learned to garden on a scale I'd not done before. Morningstar was a two-and-a-half acre plot, with only a few perennial plantings of herbs and berries. All the rest was laid out in rototilled beds and planted to annuals, either direct seeded, as for beans (200-foot rows) and carrots (400-foot double rows) and beets; or transplanted, as for tomatoes (500 plants), brassicas (say, 200 broccoli plants or 500 cabbages). All weeding and thinning was done by hand and many beds were completely renewed with compost and tilled again in mid-season for a fall crop; beans could be followed by lettuce or spinach, an early spring salad crop could be followed by mid-summer brassicas, cauliflower, say. There was a certain seasonal plan followed, but opportunity for "catch crops" appeared serendipitously. Often enough, by late spring, the garden had gotten away from us with weeds rampant, but this was all fodder for weed-and-soil-based compost piles in the garden. As part of the partnership with the farm we gardeners received all the Biodynamic, cow-manure-based compost we could use, and, for one dubious experiment (Joel was enamored with the idea, I wasn't) a slurry pit of fresh cow manure mixed with a thousand gallons of water in a disused septic tank on the edge of the garden. This, the only time I used it, we spread on half-grown onions, but it was a mess and it stunk. I know now that such a manure tea requires aeration we weren't providing then.

From Joel I learned to try to see the whole garden at once, then sections of it at a time, then beds in a section, then to see every plant in a row...really look at them, one at a time. There are times in the season, different times for different vegetable varieties, when it pays to look at every plant, even a mile of potato plants (not much to an Idaho potato farmer, but a lot in a garden with dozens of other vegetables to tend), say when the potato beetle is due. The first sign of leaf damage, the first beginnings of the second generation (eggs on the underside of leaves—you might have to turn over 500 leaves to find an egg cluster), and what's needed is not just walking by and having a look, but real scrutiny, coupled with action, smearing the eggs and clusters of just-hatched larvae. Early attention in the first week of a potato bug infestation and you can ward the whole thing off. Miss the timing and you're in big trouble.

With the Mexican Bean Beetle, however such "spot 'em and squish 'em" techniques will be speedily overcome by the bugs' reproductive exuberance. I did discover, however, a solution to that one in my second Morningstar season. There's a parasitic Pedio wasp that can be introduced to the garden and will extend the harvest from three harvest pickings, say, to five or six.

From Joel I learned that in Biodynamics we cultivate the atmosphere with the horn-crystal spray, enhancing light and air, cosmic forces drawn on by the plant leaves fully as enthusiastically as roots seek out nutrients. No other organic practice ever mentions the atmosphere. We tend to think of "atmosphere" in terms of schoolbook diagrams of "the vast envelope of gases surrounding the earth or another planet" as my dictionary puts it, but there is also the close-in Earth-aura we and the animals walk around within, in service to the plants. Composting, good tillage and mulch for the soil, to be sure, but no thought of the atmosphere until Steiner taught about it and later when the man who brought Agnihotra to the West, Shree Vasant, began to tell about Homa farming. (See the chapter on my work at the B-Bar Ranch.) For the past 15 years all of my gardens have utilized Steiner's Horn Crystal spray in conjunction with daily practice of Agnihotra fire ceremonies at exactly sunrise and sunset, when the etheric wave of sun energy sweeps through.

From Joel I never did learn to prioritize as we did a walk through the garden, sometimes at speed for that was the way he was. I would note that the beans needed picking in this bed here, but not yet in the bed over there; I heard him when he said we'd better pull those thistles on the edge over there before the seed blew across the garden; there are hundreds of things like this to notice in a garden in high season. Joel was adept at noticing them and I was becoming so, but neither of us was good at making the daily and weekly plan that would address them in a prioritized fashion. The work went on in a catch-as-catch-can manner from day to day, most often with the priorities set by outside forces, the need to harvest for the processing kitchen or the households, or by a clear need to rescue a crop that would be otherwise lost to weeds.

I learned from Joel how to attend to the job at hand in the garden—the hours-long tomato harvest every other day, or the endless rows of beans or peas to pick—while also keeping an eye on my crew in their corners of the garden, or being well aware of them out in the Village with their delivery carts. This is the great, learned skill of a Camphill workmaster, who is under some pressure at least to produce, and even larger demands to be responsible for people who are naturally distractible. Joel once shouted across the garden, "Joshua! Use your senses!" and our best wheelbarrow driver, autistically stuck in a repetitive full-body nodding gesture, going nowhere, came out of that trapped place and carried on with his task.

We're all like that, aren't we? Our mind wrecks the program at hand, our bodies go slack. When you live day in and day out with autistic or "retarded" people you become clear that it's all a matter of degree and their symptoms and quirks mirror our own, and the advice, "Use your senses!" can be the quickest way back into our bodies where the action is, back into the present moment. The mind, where Joshua was, is full of associations, memories, conjectures and frights, but the body is the place for direct experience.

Oddly, I learned little of Biodynamics from Joel directly. The garden had been under Biodynamic cultivation for nine years when I arrived and had had dressings of Biodynamic compost each of those years. It was thoroughly imbued, I came to understand, with those cosmic energies. On a few occasions Joel had me walk the garden sprinkling BD#500, the Horn Manure preparation, or spraying #501, the Horn Crystal preparation, but never with much instruction and never a word of the theory behind the practice. With Joel, it was all practical and ad hoc.

There was a clear division between the farmers and the gardeners at Kimberton. There were the two gardens, Morningstar, the larger, and Owlring, run by Sherry Swartz (later Wildfeuer), who edited the *Stella*Natura* calendar and was housemother of Sycamore House, one of the larger households, hard by Morningstar garde. The gardens were staffed by a head gardener, often a second-in-command gardener, casual help from visitors, and a crew. The farm was organized differently, with two main departments, the dairy (including hay and other feed crops) and all row crops not grown in the gardens—potatoes, sweet corn, storage beets—including row crops specifically for market like broccoli and leeks.

Farmers and their apprentices were machinery-minded. As a gardener I had a Troy-Bilt rototiller and a lawnmower for the edges, that was all. It was the farmers who ran the big stuff, tractors, manure spreaders, combines, hay balers. And I couldn't help noticing that the best and brightest of apprentice candidates wound up in the dairy barn. It takes an exceptional human being—patient, empathic, quiet, unexcitable—to work with dairy cows. More than once I was disappointed when a young garden apprentice-to-be would spend a day or two in Morningstar garden and then find that the dairy barn was where she (it was usually a *she*) wanted to work during her Kimberton stay.

Approaching the end of my own Kimberton experience, always having been pretty much isolated in the garden/greenhouse, I came to realize that I was wholly cut off from the source of fertility of the place, the cows, and that the next step in my Biodynamic training was to connect with them.

As before at Claymont I took care of the chickens, a laying flock of 50 or so hens and, on one occasion, worked with one of the farm apprentices to castrate a couple of dozen piglets. This was all familiar territory, but the cows were a mystery to me.

By the end of my fourth season in Morningstar garden, where I had been in full charge for two years after Joel and his family left the community, the opportunity arose for me and my little family, who had joined me at Kimberton (so much for being "thoroughly unmarried"), to go to the newly-established Camphill Village in Minnesota where a gardener was needed and I would have the chance to work in the cow barn.

Chapter 7 – Camphill Village Minnesota 1985-6 Another Community that Works

Camphill Minnesota had been founded three or four years before by Hartmut and Gerda von Jeetze in response to requests from parents of mentally handicapped adults in Minneapolis. The von Jeetzes had been at the Camphill Village at Copake, NY, for many years when they set out to pioneer Camphill in the prairie. Several Kimberton Co-workers had already spent time in Minnesota helping out as two new houses were built, a dairy herd assembled and a number of Villagers and Co-workers were gathered. Now the Village was ready to call on the work of a full-time gardener.

Beyond the prospect of working with cows, I was attracted to Minnesota because of an article written by Hartmut in 1977 called "*In Defense of 'Old-Fashioned' Training: A few words of wisdom for all trainees, apprentices and master growers alike.*" In this piece Hartmut points out the un-looked-for lessons that a learner might encounter in a training to truly prepare her or him for life as a master gardener or farmer, lessons such as *the necessity for order* (picture an Amish farmyard), *the need to submit oneself completely to doing what one is asked to do* (Ask the Task), *submission to repetitive tasks* (which leads to an inner stability and sense of rhythm), *perseverance* (which lends certainty and tranquility to all our work), and *non-preference* (no task on a farm is to be preferred over any other, Hartmut says; again the task is what counts, not the self.) Noting how similar these italicized points may seem to those involved in spiritual training, he concludes, "Is there any true outer training which is not at the same time an inner one?"

As strange and unaccustomed as these instructions may seem to the apprentice, in his examples and encouragements Hartmut made them seem at least attainable. He gives little help in his article, however, to the master farmer who must try to instill these virtues in the trainee. In the years since my Minnesota experience I worked with many apprentices and found that most, not all, were tetchy about obedience and that the trainer needs to be oh-so careful about not hurting feelings. Self is in ascendance, social correctness is all, and we are spoiled, spoiled, spoiled. Only in military basic training, monastic formation of novices, or another spiritual training will people stifle self and ego. Note the repetition of the word "submit," above and ask yourself, in your recent experience of life, if you have actually seen *anyone* surrender self to anything except under compulsion. Mothers, maybe. In any case Hartmut reflected great and hard-won wisdom in this article I read and I was ready to meet up with him. On my visit to scope out the village and in turn be scoped out myself, I rang him up from the café in town at 4:00 AM, figuring he would be up to go milking, but rousted him out of a deep sleep. Not his day to milk, it seemed. He was kind enough about my imposition and came to get me in his own time.

The farm consisted of a couple of hundred acres north of Sauk Center and south of Long Prairie, hay fields, pastures and woods, with the Sauk River running through. There were two new houses with handicapped folks and Co-workers, the original farmhouse, and a trailer home where we were invited to live. The trailer also became the Village bakery one afternoon a week.

I began immediately to work in the barn, appropriately at the low end of the organizational chart, washing udders. We were milking 25-30 Guernseys, beginning at 4:30 AM and 4:30 PM. Earlier for the person designated to bring the cows in from pasture, which might take 30-45 minutes since they would not be rushed. It is not in a dairy cow's, nor the dairyman's, nature to hurry. There were four of us on the milking crew: the farmer, Don Wilson, who was raised at Camphill Village USA, Copake, NY, and had his Biodynamic training in Germany; two experienced Villagers, who detached the milking machine cups and carried the milk to the bulk tank, and me, the lowly udder washer. We each milked 13 times a week, with one morning milking time off, when we got to sleep in.

We arrived in Minnesota in early November, so the daylight hours were already quite short and I walked to the barn each morning under a dark sky with brilliant stars. Dawn would not break until we were almost finished milking at 7:00 AM or so. When we arrived at the barn each had his job to do, bringing the cows in, distributing hay in front of the stanchions, measuring out the grain ration each cow received, based on her production that week, getting the machines and the wash buckets ready. All this was facilitated because the barn had been made clean and tidy after the previous milking. There was not a lot of chatter among us as we got ready to milk.

I squatted alongside each cow with warm wash water and rinse buckets and gently and scrupulously washed teats and udders, the first line of defense against contamination of the milk. This was not too difficult unless the cow had lain down in a manure pie, which happened often enough in the small fenced lot just outside the barn, not so often when they were on pasture. This washing, rinsing and drying process, the massaging, scrubbing, and kneading, stimulated the cow to let down her milk from the reservoirs in the udder into the teats. If our timing was working well, Don would be ready right behind the cow with a milking machine in hand as I finished. These were relatively ancient machines that hung on a belt around the cow's middle and attached by a hose to a vacuum line running at the back of each milking stall. Meanwhile our Villager partners would be weighing the milk from the last cow and carrying it to the next room—steam cleaned that morning—and pouring it through a filter into the bulk tank.

It was all an elaborate rhythm, a clunky dance featuring guys in muck boots and barn overalls, performed twice a day. The little talk we engaged in was mostly low murmurs of encouragement or caution to the cows, "Whoa, Miranda…easy there… move that foot," "Whoop, Buttercup…now then…be still," "Step forward there, Girl, let me in there…" The cows were rarely fractious; they knew the routine as well as we did and they had their food in front of them. Their calves were near at hand in their own pen in the barn waiting, not all that quietly, to be bottle fed. The calves—perhaps it seems cruel and unnatural, but there's no other way—are taken from their moms the first few hours after the birthing, after they've had their first drink of colostrum. Thereafter for a few days they continue to get their mom's first milk. After that, any cow's milk will do.

After morning milking, turning the cows out into their lot and cleaning up the milking machines we would gather at the Farmhouse for breakfast, then have a bit of a break before returning to the barn. One of us would walk the cows to their pasture, during the months when the grass was available, roughly from April into November, and the rest would clean the barn, forking manure and straw bedding from the stalls where the cows stood during milking into the gutters behind, then into the manure spreader which I learned to back into the barn. Then a good sweeping and dusting of lime to provide sure footing for the cows the next time they entered. In all, with preparation time, milking, feeding the calves and cleanup the whole process took three to four hours. Typically we'd done almost half a day's work before 9:00 AM. There are modern dairies where many more cows are milked in such a time span, but none where it is done more humanely than at Camphill Minnesota. Nor where so-called mentally impaired people were valued, much appreciated members of the team.

Three weeks after we arrived at Camphill Minnesota my father died. I talked with Hartmut after my sister called with the news and he assured me that the Village would pay for my flight to Kentucky from its social fund, reserved for just such emergencies.

It was a Saturday and, since I couldn't fly out until the following day, he invited me to Bible Evening at his and Gerda's house to tell a bit about my dad.

Bible Evening is a feature of Camphill life I haven't mentioned. Every Saturday evening Villagers and Co-workers in each house got spruced up, lit candles, and sat around the dining table to talk of happenings in the house, the Village and perhaps the wider world during the previous week. My contribution that week was to speak of my dad, his boyhood in a St. Louis orphanage, his 55-year marriage to my mother, the long walks we took together when I was a lad, and his exemplary, upright life. Hartmut's kind invitation helped to focus my grieving and perhaps helped the folks at Coleman house to know me better.

After conversation, the Bible Evening program included a reading of the Bible passage specified for the coming week, a little explanation of it, then a snack. This simple agenda, along with the Sunday service, anchored the week for all of us, closing and opening it in a graceful way.

Camphill is not a religious movement. These activities were definitely optional (except perhaps for house parents, who were more or less obliged to make them available for their Villagers). There is no liturgy (the Sunday Service is austere in the extreme), no priesthood, no chapel. Humility replaces hierarchy and the goal is not to convert mankind but rather to spiritualize the landscape, uplift the ordinary and raise everybody's vibration in so doing.

Laurens van der Post writes, "…Camphill, to put it the Christian way, is doing New Testament work in a modern idiom, through its care of the despised and rejected, the physically handicapped and the unloved. In doing so, it is characterized by a rediscovery of what are the first and highest values in the natural life of man."

Another fixed point in the week was the Village meeting on Tuesday evenings. In a Village the size of Copake or Kimberton this would have been difficult or impossible, but at Minnesota the group of 20-some Villagers and Co-workers fit nicely in the living room of St. Christopher house. All attended except mothers or dads of small children who had other responsibilities that time of day.

Hartmut suggested for me the role of facilitator of the meeting, and I accepted. There was no honor in this but only the responsibility to run the meeting smoothly, encourage everyone's participation and hear them all out without letting the gathering run on too long. Since the milkers had to be up at four the next morning and others were well aware of this, cooperation on that last point was not too hard to come by. In the Village meeting announcements were made—guests and others coming and going, new regulations by the State of Minnesota, building projects initiated or completed, a calving—festivals planned, individual achievements acknowledged.

One such announcement came in January: a Mid-Winter Festival, toboggans and snow fun, warm snacks and drinks out in the hillside pasture! One morning in January the thermometer was just touching minus 40 as I headed for the barn—happily, the cows were in the barn these nights, content in their stanchions with thick straw bedding and each other for warmth and company—and the barn was comparatively toasty, in the mid-40s. The udder washer guy was happy to snuggle next to the cows with his hot water buckets and the metabolic furnaces rumbling at his shoulder. They went outside to their holding pen during the morning while we cleaned the barn.

I was in charge of the mid-Winter festival and loaded a pile of firewood and a wood stove onto a hay wagon with the food and drinks and straw bales for people to sit on, the toboggans and snow saucers and skis. There was maybe a foot of new snow, not too much to prevent pulling a wagon with a tractor to the hillside site I'd chosen. The Villagers and Co-workers were in high spirits, well-acclimated to the cold and set to have fun. We enjoyed each other's company, tobogganed gleefully down the slopes, made snowmen and snow angels. We gathered around the wood stove in between times for hot chocolate, cookies and toasted cheese sandwiches until the afternoon light began to diminish and the milkers needed to get back to tend to the evening milking.

The farmers were aware that the time from mid-January to mid-February is known in Biodynamic idiom as the Crystallization Period, when the water and earth elements beneath our feet are most open to cosmic influences, when "...the strongest formative forces, the strongest crystallizing forces, can develop within the Earth..." as Steiner says in his agriculture lectures. This sets the stage for the growth of the plants in the next season, just at the time, incidentally, when the gardener's imagination is trending in that direction as well and uplifted by the seed catalogs coming with every mail.

At one point in late winter, discerning a tendency of mine toward independent action, Hartmut encouraged me to share my intentions for a new project with the Village. I had gone with him to check that a set of old storm windows stored in a shed and that I wanted to use to construct an improvised greenhouse were truly available for my purposes, and he let me know that it would be most appropriate for me to tell in the Village meeting about my plans. Otherwise, he said, people would see what I was doing in building the greenhouse and wonder why they'd been left out, not told what was happening. This was a lesson in community for which I was grateful once I thought about it, but in the moment I may have had a flash of irritation at such an unwonted curb on my usual much-cherished autonomy.

This little greenhouse was designed with two unique features that, in the end, actually seemed to work. First, I built it against the south wall of the chicken house a visitor had built for the community just before I arrived. This effectively determined the length of the greenhouse, about 14 feet, and its design as a lean to house rather than a free-standing one, but more importantly gave it a warm north wall instead of one exposed to the winds out of Manitoba with just a few barbed wire fences in between. The other feature presaged a much larger greenhouse I built many years later in Arizona: this little house was built pit-style, that is, one went three steps down into it, the theory being that warmth of the earth would moderate the temperature in there. A window into the chicken house allowed some of the chicken-warmth in there as well.

The glazing for this greenhouse was old wooden frame storm windows left over from the renovation of the Farmhouse, and all the other materials were salvaged as well, wood for the foundation plate and kneewall, the end walls and a used door.

I was able to build this little house after a thaw in late winter, in time to use it for garden starts that summer season and for tomatoes and peppers grown all summer, since the Minnesota summers are (can be, at least) uncongenial for such warmth-loving critters.

Don Wilson, using the big farm tractor, plowed and disked and spread Biodynamic compost on a nice, flat acre-and-a-half parcel with a creek on two sides, situated below the farm buildings. I was able to pull irrigation water from the creek later in the season. For that first Minnesota garden I concentrated on staples, nothing too exotic. Potatoes (which were planted in the middle of May), sweet corn (early June), onions (mostly from sets, and a lot of them), some salad and brassicas (cabbage and broccoli). We prepared a separate field, a little under an acre in a different location for space-hogging winter squash grown in place from seed, again considered a staple crop for winter.

I would have been happy to have had a large rototiller for between-row cultivation in a garden this size, but Hartmut and Don opted for a small utility tractor, a 25-year-old Massey-Ferguson, with a cultivator. This choice made sense for such extra-gardening tasks as pulling hay wagons and the manure spreader, but it was kind of clumsy, I felt, in the garden. In the end I did a lot of the cultivation with a push-from-behind high wheel cultivator bought from a yard sale in Sauk Center for $25 and fitted with a bicycle wheel to replace the old, heavy iron wheel. This item worked beautifully for me and I'm sure similar cultivators worked ten thousand gardens grown by these sensible Minnesotans over many decades.

Overall, there was nothing beautiful about this garden, but it was a highly productive one and, I'm sure, fed the folks at Camphill Minnesota right on through the winter. I wasn't there to experience that for, after a little less than a year, I left to join my little family in Quincy, Illinois. After five years in Camphill it was time to strike out on my own.

Lynda the cow in Illinois; behind, Woody with the bees.

Chapter 8 – Quincy, Illinois 1986-89 Smallholding/CSA

We found ourselves, my little family and I, in Quincy, Illinois, a city of 50,000 or so on the Mississippi River. I took a job as a counselor at the local counseling center, my fallback position over the first decades of my long career. When there seemed to be no immediate way to make a living farming or gardening, my degree in psychology often opened another avenue.

Exigencies of family life caused us to choose Quincy and we were resigned to apartment living in town without a garden. Very soon, however, we began to realize that we were *starving*, quite literally. Though we had ample funds to buy mostly organic stuff at the health food store, such as it was in a Midwestern city at that time, it was not locally grown and certainly not Biodynamically grown. We began to appreciate fully that the food we'd been eating for years in the two Camphill Villages had been sustaining in a way far more satisfying than what we were now eating, stuff that lacked that Biodynamic pizzazz. We were feeling undernourished, seriously so.

Less than a year after my dad died so did my mother, as so often happens with couples who spend 50 years and more together. Again my sister called with the news and again I traveled to Kentucky, now as an adult orphan. A couple of months after the funeral came a letter from my sister, who was the executrix, with details about our parents' estate. They were never wealthy, my folks, and were modest in their lifestyle, so the news from my sister set me back more than a little. Dad had made solid, conservative investments and over the decades they had paid off. My share in the estate was going to be enough to buy and outfit a smallholding of some sort, free and clear.

Having lived in penury in Camphill—though eating very, very well as I have said—we were now situated nicely, with real (that is, paying) jobs and a bank account sufficient to enter the housing market. In a month we contracted to buy a 5-acre place in Fowler within quick commuting distance of Quincy. A habitable home, outbuildings, good well, pasture and garden sites.

The place would be designated a "hobby farm" by realtors in a landscape dominated by farms with many hundreds of acres of, this being Illinois, corn and soybeans, varied by soybeans and corn, intermixed with corn and soybeans. Then the occasional "hog farm," not a farm at all but, even then, a confinement operation with the animals imprisoned inside buildings with scarcely room to stand and stretch. Sows and young ones never saw the sun, never rooted in the earth, never wallowed. They ate scientifically formulated feed; the brood sows were artificially inseminated, and the piglets had nothing to do but put on weight until reaching the predetermined marketable size when they were butchered. This insane industrialization—cash grain farming, animal confinement and outdoor feedlots for cattle—had become the norm in just a generation here in the Midwest and it was all around us. Our little Biodynamic farm would be both an anachronism and a harbinger of the future.

We moved in at Christmastime, fully decorated tree and all. Looking back 23 years I have trouble wrapping my mind around all the effort we put out (and all the money we spent) those first few months to secure our hold on the land and build a rural and domestic life we could live with.

Some projects we contracted out: a new, large garage; a weaving room off the dining room; a screened-in porch; greenhouse foundation.

Others we did ourselves:
·   Building a redwood and glass greenhouse, a solarium against the south side of the house;
·   Barn renovation to accommodate a cow—box stall and stanchion;
·   Interior painting to cover cigar smoke odor;
·   Conversion of shed to chicken house;
·   Fencing for cow and chickens and pigs.

All of these projects ran over budget, of course.

Then there was the equipment we required to do our work. Very early on I had spotted an old Ford 8N tractor for sale down the road, complete with disk harrow, plow, small wagon, and another odd implement or two—the whole works for $2,000. These tractors were produced from 1947-52 and are among the most solidly made machines ever conceived. Almost 35 years old at the time I bought it, this little tractor worked perfectly for me until I sold it three years later for the same price. No planned obsolescence here, just great functionality. I'd used one of these at Eden, NY, and the small tractor at Minnesota was of similar vintage and usefulness.

We also purchased a Troy-Bilt rototiller, same as the one at Morningstar garden at Kimberton, a chipper-shredder for mulch and compost material, a half-mile of soaker hose for garden row irrigation, and a riding mower.

By March the gardens were laid out, seedlings were started in the greenhouse and we were well on the way to growing much of our own food and some to sell.

Even before all this equipment buying, Lynda the cow came to us. I'd inquired of several large animal veterinarians for local dairymen who milked Guernseys and Jerseys—few enough, as the usual milking cows in that area, and indeed all over the country, were and are Holsteins, those massively-uddered, 1,500 pound, black and white beasts pictured on milk cartons and in children's books. But some dairies kept a few Guernseys or Jerseys in their herds to boost the butterfat content of the product in their bulk tanks, the Holsteins being valued more for the quantity of their milk than the quality. I was able to locate one farmer with a Guernsey he was willing to sell, a big cow, already bred and with an udder suitable for hand milking, that is, teats large enough and set forward at a reasonable angle. She was a gentle and responsive animal, I could tell. For $1,000 the farmer was willing to guarantee that she had "settled," that is, she had a live calf in there, and would deliver her to our place.

Lynda, named for the old friend who taught us double digging, proved to be a true gem and within a few weeks of moving onto our little homestead I was back in the swing of morning and evening milking, six AM and six PM, before and after work. Lynda gave a nice two-gallon bucket full of milk every time; the weighty 20-pound tug of it as I walked from the barn to the house balanced by the equal pull of the wash water in my left hand, its bucket kept full just for the sake of balance until I dumped it alongside the driveway. Lots of milk, yogurt, soft cheese and butter for us, and milk to sell to colleagues at work, at $3 a gallon, I recall. I mention the price because here we are as I write, 21 years later, paying $11 in a marginally legal herd-share arrangement providing raw milk. Now, as then in Illinois and 40 years earlier when I was a child refusing commercially denatured milk, the demand is there for healthful, tasty raw milk—never mind the dairy lobby, the doctors and the health departments.

That first spring, with Lynda happily grazing in the pasture behind new fencing, we raised 50 baby chicks, began to feed two piglets looking toward fall butchering and added two beehives to our smallholding. Lynda thought all this activity was just fine and seemed content to be with us; she was the whole herd in our one-cow dairy.

We cared for Lynda only secondarily as a milk provider, important as that role was for us. Primarily she was a manure donor. We blessed and honored her as the bringer of fertility to our gardens. She came indoors to her stall at the evening milking time and remained there all night, even in the summertime when it would have been perfectly OK for her to be outside, so that I could gather her manure and urine-soaked bedding for the compost pile, 25 pounds of it at least in a day. This I forked onto a wooden sled located conveniently just behind her milking stand and every week or so pulled the sled around behind the barn with the tractor to the compost pile. It took a few months to build up a pile twenty feet long, by eight feet at the base and four or five feet high. This was a nice size for the Biodynamic preparations to be applied and in another few months the compost was ready to apply to the garden and another pile ready to be prepped. Once in a while we would clear out the chicken house and the pig palace and all this additional manure and bedding we would add to the pile. All of the kitchen waste and garden trimmings went to the pigs.

This process created the living heart of the farm and insured the cycle of fertility and tilth in the soil. Our dear Lynda stood at the center of that cycle—grazing, eating hay, giving milk, shitting, fully connected to the great cow oversoul, to the farm and to us, her family.

Years later I would write about another cow:

> *I don't consider the labor expended for Bessie's care as anything but a service. It's a service to the farm, to Biodynamics, to the planet. As a service it's my choice to render it and no cost accounting can touch it. The exercise keeps me healthy; the morning and evening rhythm is grounding; the attention to detail sharpens my perceptions; the nurturing character of the work allows me to express my feminine side. I am a better person for taking care of animals...and who will account for that? Who will tell me what that is worth?*

> *Leaving aside finances, we come to the intangibles, the interesting stuff. In a way, Bessie represents, calls forth, the spirit of the place, the farm individuality. In her singleminded metabolic nature she is the biosystem around here. Her energy, her presence, her connection to the oversoul, knits the place together. As she grazes or chews her cud, she's aware of everything going on, seldom reacting with more than a looking up in the direction of the disturbance. But she knows. When the dogs got into the poison a clueless neighbor set out for coyotes, Bessie knew. When the bull was slaughtered, Bessie knew.*

> *Bessie's calm being, her knowing, permeates every corner of the farm, and, through her compost, enlivens especially the seed garden beds. When we contemplate more than the material details of our daily lives, when we take time to consider the layers and webs of existence in which we're enmeshed, when we*

remember what it's like to be a peasant and to be possessed of the instinctive wisdom Rudolf Steiner spoke of so wistfully—we are grateful to know Bessie and to have our lives enriched by her.

The gardens that first year, growing on rototilled sod, were just fine. Compost was ready by mid-summer, so fall plantings of quick growing salad crops and herbs were made in newly enlivened ground, the ceremony of composting repeated each fall and spring for the whole time we were there.

We did not name our smallholding, too diminutive perhaps to name, but for the sake of a credible presence at the farmer's market on the square in Quincy on Saturday mornings we had painted on the old van we purchased, "Homegrown Naturally," which I thought had a nice ring to it. A blue van with that yellow legend painted on each side with a stylized image of a sunflower. The first year and the second on the land we tested the possibilities at the farmer's market. These are the impressions I took away from that experiment, the first and last time I attempted to market that way. Understand that all this was happening in the mid-1980s when "organic" was still a miniscule sector in the food marketplace, not the $20 billion commerce it is today as I write. 1) Buyers at farmer's markets habitually return week after week to the vendors they are accustomed to trade with and are very likely to pass by unfamiliar ones, regardless of presentation or quality; our lettuce and broccoli might be just as good and equal in price to that featured in the stall next door, but habit wins out and why shouldn't it? Loyalty, after all, is a virtue. 2) The agony of watching stuff wilt in the intense summer heat, no matter what you do to try to prevent that. 3) The hidden costs of going to the farmer's market with your stuff: the per-mile cost of getting there and back, the impedimenta (tables, signage, canopy) to deal with, the payments to the market organizers, the sheer amount of time involved—never mind getting up at 4:00 AM to harvest—all this puts whatever profit is gained into a realistic perspective. The conclusion was, it ain't worth it. This, remember, from a grower who had been spoiled by a captive market; the Camphill households were happy with what the gardeners produced. End of story.

Another cautionary tale about the perils of growing for a farmer's market: At one point early in the season the second year I planned to grow some 300 broccoli plants to take to the Saturday market. In early March, then, I sowed the seeds in flats and carefully grew the plants to be sturdy transplant-sized broccolis in mid-April, by which time the soil was warm, and well composted and beautifully tilled in the chosen spot between the barn and the shed. I put the irrigation hose in place, weeded those broccolis, fussed over them, grew them up to size by late June. Now in those days I wasn't committed to open pollinated varieties and these were a hybrid, Premium

Crop, a broccoli I'd had wonderful success with at Kimberton. Now one of the features of this hybrid is that *all the broccoli heads mature at the same time.* I had planned for 300 perfect, beautifully-sized heads to sell, maybe $750 worth, but I hadn't planned for them to mature on a Tuesday, which is exactly what happened. By Thursday they had to be picked, all of them, or they'd have become over mature, tough and bitter. This I did and put them on ice in the basement, hoping they would hold until Saturday, market day, but they did not. The crop was a total loss and came to nothing financially speaking, though we did freeze some of it.

This was another reality check for me about farmer's market sales, and it also spelled the end to my dependence on hybrid varieties. An open-pollinated broccoli type would have been a better choice, as the heads would have come to maturity over a period of many days. If I'd been paying attention here I might have noticed a pattern, going like this: whenever I focus on the numbers at the end of a project before I consider the *gist* of the project—the living beings involved: plants, animals, people, the life and energy flow of the thing, I'm headed for trouble. It would happen again with the meat chickens, and yet again with bees, before this chapter is finished.

I was on the lookout for a different marketing method, but that didn't come to me for another little while. I had no way of knowing in that 1986 season that growers in Massachusetts and New Hampshire had independently come up with an alternative that would change the face of the farmer/eater relationship.

In late summer Lynda presented us with a calf. We had ceased milking her, as is customary, two months before her due date, to allow all her internal energies to go toward growing the calf in her belly. We watched her closely and she got bigger and bigger and bigger that summer. As the due date approached I let my boss know that I might have to leave work suddenly to attend to the birthing. She was slightly bemused by that, but when the call came during a Wednesday afternoon staff meeting, and I told people I had to leave, and why, I got a jolly sendoff.

I found Lynda in her stall, in labor but no particular distress and stayed with her through the delivery a few hours later of a huge calf, a bull calf of such size I named him Jupiter.

The big guy stayed with his mom for a day, then I shifted him into the small stall I'd built adjacent to hers. As I rested from that—no trivial thing to "shift" a 100-pound gawky long-legged calf out of sight of his mother—I watched open-mouthed as this day-old critter half jumped, half climbed over the side of his stall, which was common with his mom's stall (not smart of me, eh?). That top board was a 2"x12" armpit high on me and that baby bull scrambled over the top of it in a flash, and was right back at mom's side. There he stayed until I lag-bolted yet another 2"x12" up there at head height. And another, on the other side; and another over top of his stall gate. Once again, later that day, I manhandled Jupiter into his own stall and there he stayed to be bottle fed until he was weaned. He did go out on pasture during the day in a grassy pen out of sight of his mother.

By the middle of my second summer the gardens were flourishing but my frustrations with marketing remained. Then came the Summer, 1987 issue of *Biodynamics*, the journal of the Biodynamic Farming and Gardening Association, with an article by Jan VanderTuin about a concept, new to the U.S., called "Community Supported Agriculture."

VanderTuin told briefly about the relationship between the growers at Indian Line Farm in the Berkshires of western Massachusetts and their customers who paid up front for twice-weekly boxes of produce during the season. In this system the farmers are paid early in the season when they most need the money for seeds, equipment, and so on, and the eaters have a stake in the farm, sharing the risks of unfavorable weather or a poor harvest. They also share in larger-than-anticipated harvests. Instead of buying one head of lettuce or a couple of tomatoes at a time at the farmer's market or the grocery store, they "subscribe" to their share of the entire season's bounty. I was to discover later that another initiative, the Temple-Wilton Community Farm in New Hampshire, independently started the same sort of scheme in the same year, 1986.

It's more than a marketing innovation. There is for the eaters the sense of belonging to an economic initiative that makes sense for all concerned, of being stakeholders in a farm that's doing things right.

The light strobed in my mind, dazzling me: here was a melding of Steiner's agricultural insights and his Threefold Social Order, a cooperative venture between growers and their customers that resulted in a sacred compact—"support my efforts and I will feed you to the best of my ability." It removes from the equation the deadening competition between growers for the buyers' dollars, the dreadful uncertainties of marketing, and opens the possibilities for the families who eat the food to see how it is grown, to help a little if they wish, to have a more comprehensive relationship with it. Go to the farm, kick the soil, taste it, inspect the chickens, sniff the compost pile; bring the children and pet the pig, sample the green beans—this is the reality folks, it's got dirt on it, bugs over there, but it's all of a piece, food without the packaging, the hype, the coupons and the adverts.

I was seriously fired up about the concept of such a captive market situation with shared risks and real involvement between farmer and eaters, but couldn't wrap my mind around how to manifest it in a bastion of conservatism like Quincy—where "farming" meant cash grain crops from here to the horizon—until New Year's Eve.

We were invited to a party unlike any we'd ever experienced—lots of camaraderie, good food and conversation, but *no booze*. This was specified on the invitation. Just after midnight and a somewhat subdued observance of the turning of the year, the 12 or 15 couples were invited by our hosts to gather in a circle. The ground rules for our New Year discussion were these: we were to tell the others of our dreams for the new year, what we would do if all limitations were removed, if all was possible, if we could accomplish our heart felt aspirations. We were encouraged to truly listen to each other and to respond in the same "as if" mode, that is, in the spirit of the evening, that anything is possible, and yes we would help each other realize the dream. What a contrast to the drunken, content-free commotion at most New Year's Eve parties! Here was an opportunity to share our heart's desire with friends, no matter how outlandish, and accept pledges of support.

I spoke of the CSA concept and the little bit of history I knew and was heartened by the response from the group, which boiled down to "What a great idea!" I told the folks about our little smallholding, that we had sufficient garden space and compost on hand and that given a bit of encouragement I would quit my job in early spring and undertake to become a CSA grower. Our CSA would be the first in the Midwest and among the first 20 in the USA. Within minutes several people expressed serious interest in becoming core group members; the response was far more than I could have hoped. Alise and her husband Todd offered to head up the effort to recruit members; Otto, who had done much of the renovation of our farm house, was willing to help with special projects; Al, an accountant, would keep the project honest in that realm. These folks would lend credibility to the venture, for they were long-time Quincy residents, and I was a comparative newcomer.

In a week or so I called the first meeting of the core group. It's the rare farmer who possesses the people skills, the organizational skills and the communication skills to run an efficient and effective organization, or, for that matter, who has the head for business. To get the CSA off the ground I needed help and credibility. This group of would organize itself over the coming weeks to set flexible policies around pricing and collecting shares, gatherings of shareholders at the farm for festivals at spring and autumn equinoxes and the summer solstice and to do some of the bookkeeping and other record-keeping chores. This group of loyal folks was a major Godsend, helping out on the farm with special projects, recruiting members, and cheerfully boosting the energy surrounding the project. At that first meeting we determined that if we could enroll 25 members at $350 that would be an encouraging beginning and I would commit my time and resources to make the project work.

I prepared a news release for the local paper and TV stations and came to realize that CSA was a newsworthy concept. Early in the season there were a couple of front page news stories with photos of greenhouse activity in the Quincy *Herald Whig* and also TV interviews. This media attention drew some 25 folks to our home for an early February recruitment meeting. By then I had my rap down pretty well:

Quincy Community Supported Agriculture Project was to be part of a growing movement in this country connecting real farmers with real people who eat; fresh food is good, fresh and local food is better, fresh, local and Biodynamically-grown food is better yet; in the past, before industrial agriculture, food growing, food gathering, food preparation and preservation were social occasions or family affairs; here is a chance to bring human values back into our relationship with food: festivals, bringing children to the farm on distribution days, trusting the process.

Dennis Hurley had arrived that same day. Dennis had called a few days before this from his home in northern Illinois to inquire if I needed an assistant, an intern, for the CSA garden. On the day of the meeting we'd had time to discuss this and Dennis signed on. As events unfolded, he was an able helper and indispensable right-hand man for most of the season. A lawyer and CPA by training, but one who wanted to connect to the earth. In the evening meeting Dennis gave a good account of himself and his status as an educated professional person interested enough in this project to devote a few months of his life to it, unpaid, lent serious credibility. So did the enthusiasm of the core group members.

By the time Dennis arrived to spend the summer, though we didn't realize it, the drought was already underway. This was the year Yellowstone burned.

From the NOAA website:

The three-year drought of the late 1980s (1987-1989) covered 36% of the United States at its peak. Compared to the Dust Bowl drought, which covered 70% during its worst year, this does not seem significant. However, the 1980s drought was not only the costliest in U.S. history, but also the most expensive natural disaster of any kind to affect the U.S. Combining the losses in energy, water, ecosystems and agriculture, the total cost of the three-year drought was estimated at $39 billion. Drought-related losses in western Canada exceeded $1.8 billion dollars in 1988 alone.

By 1988, the drought intensified over the northern Great Plains and spread across much of the eastern half of the United States. This drought affected much of the nation's primary corn and soybean growing areas, where total precipitation for April through June of 1988 was even lower than during the Dust Bowl.. The summer of 1988 is well known for the extensive forest fires that burned across western North America, including the catastrophic Yellowstone fire.

In addition to dry conditions, heat waves during the summer of 1988 broke long-standing temperature records in many Midwestern states.

This was the year I chose to risk starting a CSA, taking people's money and committing to grow food for them! Yes, June was hot and dry, but nothing too much out of the ordinary. We spent a lot of time moving hoses and sprinklers, burned a lot of electricity drawing water from the well, and prayed for the well to hold out. I went to bed every night grateful for that well.

About this time, out of the blue, a gentleman arrived from out of town—his name was Andrew, but I don't remember where exactly in Illinois he came from—and told us he had heard what we were doing, supported the idea, and wanted to help us the best way he could, which was to teach us to dowse. He spent an afternoon with us showing us how, making it clear that there was nothing magical about the tools (we used L-rods, pendulums, and Y-shaped willow sticks). We dowsed for the water lines running to the barn and to the pasture from there and reliably found them. We dowsed for produce quality, asking the pendulum how a particular specimen rated on a scale from one to nine, and the results confirmed our (admittedly subjective) judgment. We thanked him profusely and off he went, leaving me scratching my head, wondering what that was all about. We'd been taught that dowsing is a dependable adjunct to intuition and since I've used the technique literally thousands of times to good effect, even in the grocery produce department to evaluate the quality difference, say, between bagged spinach from one source and loose spinach from another.

Jupiter grew apace. An adolescent calf, well fed on grass and hay, can put on three pounds a day, close to 100 pounds a month, growing from gangly, long-legged gawkiness to sturdy young bull-hood from spring to fall. Two things needed doing while he was still young, then he cold be left alone to grow. First, halter breaking. Within a few days of his birth Jupiter, thriving on his mother's milk, outweighed me and was stubborn as could be. I purchased a small halter (and would buy three more in ever larger sizes over the next several months) and after only a brief tussle got it on him, then snubbed the halter rope, thick and soft and easy on the hands, to a post in the barn, talking to the little guy all the while. He had to get the idea that he wasn't going to get loose on his own, but only by cooperating, that is, calming down. When he was ready—the first time he nearly exhausted himself fighting the restraint—I loosened the rope from the post and walked him in a tight circle and quickly snubbed the rope again to the post. He mustn't get any notion of freedom as long as the rope was latched onto that halter ring. Nor could he ever get the idea that he was stronger than I and could pull me right off my feet, thus the tight circle, which kept him a little off balance. Soon he was walking out the barn door to the pasture where a handful of grain waited for him, happily walking at my side on his rope; any rambunctious behavior and it was the tight circle again. We practiced daily for quite a while until I was satisfied he was controllable, even when he got to be seven or eight hundred pounds, a formidable nine-month old animal. Second, he needed to be castrated. I bought an "Elastrator," a device that stretches a small elastic band to fit over the neck of the scrotum; the band then compresses the blood vessels and a while later the tissue just sloughs off. It was only a 10-minute job and caused the little guy only a little discomfort until the parts went numb. (Notice how offhandedly I assure the reader that my surmise of "only little discomfort" is factual; if someone were coming at my privates with an Elastrator I reckon I would rethink that supposition a bit.)

Meanwhile Hubert and Helen, the piglets, grew even faster on garden wastes, kitchen wastes, excess skim milk. Whatever we brought them, they ate.

Hubert and Helen came to us in springtime and by late fall they were about the right size for butchering, which was their destiny all along of course. There was a dilapidated chute attached to the pigpen which I renovated the last week before the pigs' appointment with the butcher and on the day I put the sides on the pickup truck and backed it up to the chute. With the truck tailgate lowered it was a straight shot from pen, up the cleated wooden ramp and into the truck. The trick was getting the pigs to see that. The oddly-angled unfamiliar surface under their trotters baffled the pigs and made them uncooperative; tempt them as we would with luscious garbage and other goodies, they were immovable. Finally I recalled a trick I'd read in an old farming book. A pig who cannot be pushed or pulled, compelled or coerced, to move forward will move backwards on his or her own, *away* from a basket placed over the head. I got the first pig, it was Helen, situated with her butt at the bottom of the ramp and jammed a peach basket over her foreparts. In utter confusion at this insult to her dignity, she rapidly backed up the incline and found herself in the truck bed; Hubert, who loved his sibling dearly, joined her with no need for persuasion at all and the loading was done.

I had participated in butchering pigs at Claymont and knew the routine, but chose to take these guys to a professional because we did not possess the requisite band saw, sausage grinder or work tables that could be properly sanitized and we were selling half a pig, cut and wrapped, to pay the costs, so the meat needed to look professionally done.

At the butcher's shop in town we reversed the process and the pigs happily entered the place. They weighed out fairly close to the 225 pounds I'd hoped for.

The year of the CSA we discerned a ready market for frying chickens among our shareholders and raised two batches of 100 meat birds each, three weeks apart. These chickens, unlike the pigs, we butchered ourselves and after the fact I said, "Never again," and meant it. Meat birds, Cornish cross hybrids, are amazingly quick to grow to full size, six weeks or so. As it was summer and the cow was dry, we left her and her calf out in the pasture while we turned the central part of the barn over to the chicks. Chicken wire barricades kept them out of the odd corners of the barn and from exiting through the big barn doors, which we left open for ventilation and sunlight. With plenty of feed and water and fresh air, they grew…and grew some more. With a wide stance to support a husky body and especially the over-developed chests, a result of decades of cross-breeding, these birds were a marvel, and by the time six weeks had passed they weighed, on average, six to seven pounds, which translated to four or five pounds dressed weight—a large fryer or small roaster.

Meanwhile I recruited folks who would pluck and dress the chickens in exchange for taking a few home for free. I was the designated beheader. Years ago, from studying farm supply catalogs I copied the idea of a killing cone from the commercially produced ones on sale there. My cone was a sheet metal affair, ten inches across the top and tapering to a three-inch opening at the bottom, maybe 30 inches high, fastened to a fence post. In use, the chicken is slid inside and thus immobilized with the head emerging at the bottom, to be cut off with a sharp pruning shears. No hatchet, no chopping block; no flapping wings and headless birds running around. It's as humane a killing method as can be, quick, and no fuss. After giving the birds a couple of minutes to bleed out into a bucket, I dipped each of them into a washtub of scalding water with a small fire underneath to keep the water up to temperature, to loosen the feathers, and delivered them in small batches to the people on the plucking and gutting assembly line in the garage. I had the easier job, out in the sun and moving back and forth from the barn to catch the birds, to killing cone, to garage. The folks at the tables were stuck inside with gut and feather stinks and heaps of offal. But as each cleaned bird was slipped into a plastic bag and put on ice we were closer to the goal, fifty of them one day, fifty the next, and three weeks later, the same deal all over again.

The meat sold readily at a dollar a pound and certainly improved the cash flow of the farm that month, but, as I said, "Never again…" This was too much like industrialized agriculture. We had no real relationship with birds who were genetically destined for death at an early age, who were never really part of the farm organism, rather, just a blip on the balance sheet representing a hell of a lot of work, blood, feathers and death. Here's that pattern again. The profit is foremost and then all the "how to" details—

never mind that we're dealing with living creatures and depriving them of perhaps 95 per cent of their lives—for financial gain—(well, yes, for food too, and that takes some of the curse off of it, or does it?) Jupiter, however, was a different story. We'd lived with this guy for a year or so and he was a gentle, sweet bullock. We'd met a couple, Ted and Marcie, down the road who raised a few beeves every year and had all the equipment for butchering. They agreed that I would bring Jupiter to their place for slaughtering then the cutting up of the meat, the latter being an all-day job after the carcass, in halves, had hung in the barn for a few days.

To lead Jupiter on his halter rope down the two lane blacktop for two miles I chose to take the tractor and fasten the rope behind the seat. The animal did not know about cars and I knew that if we were walking and he heard one coming behind and bolted I could not hold him. As it was, we had no problem, putt-putting along at a slow walk speed on the country road and Jupiter followed along happily, taking in all the houses and fields and vehicles he'd never seen before. Shortly, we arrived at Ted's place and I drove the tractor around the barn to the corral and Ted closed the gate behind us. It was chilly day in a chilly October.

Jupiter nuzzled happily at a flake of hay Ted had brought for him. Ted had his rifle at his side. I was admiring Jupiter, thanking him for his being and letting him know he was appreciated as Ted edged to one side a bit to get a square shot at the bullock's forehead. Quicker than I expected he fired and the animal went down, kicking once, then again. Ted handed the gun to me and climbed the steel fence panel in front of us, whipping his sticking knife out of its sheath as he hit the ground. I was a little slow on the uptake here—we hadn't rehearsed this after all—but I found a safe place for the rifle, leaning it against the building, and I was on the ground inside the corral shortly after to lift a foreleg while Ted plunged the knife in alongside the breastbone and worked it back and forth until there was a gush of blood from the incision. He'd cut the main chest arteries. I pumped the leg a few times and we waited while Jupiter bled out.

It took another two or three hours to hang, behead and gut the animal, skin him, and cut the carcass in two. During that time, in my mind, he went from being "Jupiter," the character, the stall jumper, the image of bovine contentment out there in the pasture…to two sides of beef hanging from a rafter in the barn, 450 pounds, more or less, of fine meat. Thank you, Jupiter.

Meanwhile, Tuesdays and Saturdays were CSA distribution days. Half of our group of 27 families came on each of those days to pick up the produce Dennis and I harvested for them in the morning—salad crops in spring and early summer, then the summer stuff: tomatoes, peppers, okra, summer squash, green beans and the crop that saved us that drought year, sweet potatoes. I had ordered 500 sweet potato slips from a grower in Georgia, knowing that many people like them and that they can grow well in dicey conditions such as poor, dry soil. We put them in three feet apart in the row and the rows three feet apart, each slip with a shovel full of compost to give it encouragement; this was on a dry slope in the pasture, a north-facing eighth of an acre that I'd not used for gardening. Each slip got a good gulp of water and we strung a temporary electric fence around the plot and left it alone. Either they would grow or they wouldn't. In the event, they did very well indeed and by late summer we had more than 700 pounds of sweet potatoes to distribute to shareholders, despite the lack of rain.

In late summer, digging sweet potatoes in drought-hardened ground, Dennis blew out his knee, the right knee he'd injured as a high school quarterback, and that was pretty much it for the season for Dennis. He returned home and not long afterwards had that knee operated on once again. I missed his help and his cheerful good nature for weeks.

For our customers during the season the visit to the farm to pick up their share was often just another chore on the list of things to do and they were in and out again with their vegetables pretty quickly. But some moms with little ones were able to take time to go visit the chickens or greet the cow and we were happy to spend time with them. For real getting-to-know-you socialization we invited families to the farm for festivals at the spring equinox, summer solstice, and Michaelmas, the autumnal equinox. Our wonderful core group folks organized these events—kite flying, balloons, pot luck meals, farm tours and all the rest. At Michaelmas honey tasting was a highlight.

* * *

This same season I had the opportunity to move a hive from nearby Quincy to our place, add it to my little bee yard, and enjoy what promised to be a fine crop of honey, for I'd seen the hive—two brood chambers and three honey supers—and knew that it was very heavy. In my greed to possess this treasure and my recklessness, I failed to take several things into consideration:

It was August and very hot;
- The hive had been neglected for at least two years;
- As I said, it was very heavy;
- And, very much to the point, I'd never done this before, never tried to move a colony this populous, one that did not know me as the *beemeister*, nor one that hadn't been frequently inspected.

Nevertheless, in the early evening I set off in my pickup with all the tools and contrivances I figured I'd need. I knew this was a risky adventure I was on but I'd failed to hive a swarm the month before—someone had called me about this beautifully accessible swarm hanging from a tree limb in a public park in Quincy and somehow I'd blown the job. I was therefore anxious to prove myself (to whom—myself?)as an intrepid beekeeper. I parked some distance away from the hive, which was in the backyard of a rambling old house, inhabited until now by friends from the CSA, who were moving away. I suited up, already a little uneasy, because I could see from 100 feet away that masses of bees were hanging off the landing board of the hive, a sure sign of overcrowding inside. These guys clustering outside were making room for cooling air movement between the frames. If they didn't do this, bringing into play their fine discernment of heat and humidity in there, the beeswax, with precious honey, pollen and baby bees would begin to melt, resulting in a huge, disastrous mess. Overheated bees are not happy bees, and here I was, about to disturb their peace. Discretion would have been in order here…never my strong point.

I fired up the smoker, put on my hat and veil and gloves and immediately got overheated myself. By the time I'd approached within arm's reach of the hive I was sweating profusely…not an auspicious sign. Already the fabric of the arms and shoulders of my bee suit was sodden and plastered to my body. Already as I began to smoke the outside clusters angry workers were emerging from the entrance and zeroing in on me; I began to collect a few stings.

I should have backed off and reconsidered the situation but instead I endured the stings and pried the lid off. The mess I found in the top super should have deterred me as well: the frames there were welded tightly together with propolis and burr comb. I knew there was plenty of honey in there because of the weight, 80 pounds or so, about as much as I could pick up and carry. I pried the top box from the next lower one; again, the solid adhesion of one box to the other.

And the bees are getting very pissed off. And me stinking with the sweat of exertion, 100°F temperature, and, yes, fear. You see, the bee suit is not entirely impervious to the thrust of a stinger, especially where the fabric is tightly stretched and wet across the shoulders and the back. I was getting stung at a rate I'd never before experienced.

I began to work hurriedly and none too gently to separate the five boxes, knowing I could carry just one at a time to the truck, and then restack them and try to plug the gaps for the journey home. There I would have to reverse the process and set the colony in place next to the other hives.

It took half an hour to restack the colony in the truck bed, to tape the gaps (the boxes set none too squarely, each on the other), to screen the entrance, and to tie the whole works down securely. Thousands of bees were in the air, searching for the hive and their sisters. They were left behind as I drove a few blocks, with my helmet and veil in place since I'd brought plenty of bees into the truck cab with me. I stopped and opened the doors, got out and took off the veil and helmet—sweet relief!—and surveyed the situation. I was running on adrenalin and had blocked the pain, but I knew I'd taken several dozen stings. In the back of the truck, things were about as secure as they could be.

Back home, staggering and exhausted, I installed the new hive in its place as best I could and went to the house. When I stripped off the bee suit I found dozens of stingers embedded in the fabric and the smell of venom was even stronger than my own. I needed a bath, a cold bath to lower my core temperature and to help with the itching hives I was beginning to experience.

The next few hours are blurry, for I was either delirious or unconscious most of the time. I was floating in a cold tub with a scum of puke, trying to explain to my partner what had happened. I was in a bathrobe, lying on the back seat of our mini-van going somewhere. I was hearing my partner and the doctor in the hospital ER, her explaining, him harrumphing and examining and injecting.

Then I was back home, somehow in bed and beginning to realize I'd narrowly skirted death from anaphylactic shock.

Beginning to realize how stupid I'd been, not to have realized early on that I had bitten off more than I could chew, not to have stopped what I was doing, not to have sought help, and to have let greed override common sense.

* * *

My 27 CSA customers were very kind and uncomplaining about the relatively small amount of produce they were getting, which was less than they might have liked. It was certainly less than I would have liked. The drought concentrated the life force in the vegetables, however, and the flavor was superb even if the quantities were not there. We could not water all the beds as much as we wanted to, out of concerns for the well. Day after day, week after week of brutal heat assailed us and some crops just burned up. But three years of Biodynamic composting and the Biodynamic spray preparations had imparted a certain resilience to the garden and things were not as bad as they might have been. One of the features of Biodynamically-grown produce is its wonderful aroma and flavor. For the most part my customers were down-to-earth folks, most with rural roots, and they knew what good garden truck tasted like; they also understood what drought was and gave me credit for doing all I could to assure abundance. Each week I published a newsletter that people picked up with their share of vegetables, outlining developments in the garden, prospects for the following week's distribution, news and commentary. I strove to keep things light and place disappointment regarding individual harvests in perspective, but the fact remains that some people must have been disenchanted with the CSA concept and felt they were paying a fairly high price for involvement with a new social initiative. Probably most would not have signed up for a second year.

This realization led me to understand that I was not going to sign up again either. The first year of the Quincy project would also be the last. I reconciled myself to that and was able to come up with a self-absolving case to prove that the shareholders had gotten their money's worth: #1 – they'd been introduced to associative economics and the experience might have opened them to other possibilities than the producer/middleman/ consumer scheme; between the grower and the eater there's a direct transaction a life-affirming exchange of energies, not just money and goods. #2 – They had the chance to experience Biodynamic produce, and some of them to experience the making and using of the preparations; I heard week in and week out phrases like, "I don't even like (spinach, green beans, whatever) but yours tastes like candy to me!" or "The kids won't eat any vegetables but yours…" #3 – They got the chance to belong to something new, just starting out, and I'll bet even now 20 years later, they remember Quincy CSA as having been something worthwhile; some may even belong to this year's version of the same kind of thing.

We would not have been so eager to leave after the demise of the CSA had we not had occasion to sell out and move to southern New Hampshire, to associate with the Pine Hill Waldorf School and the Temple-Wilton Community Farm. That initiative, by Trauger Groh, Anthony Graham of Lukas Foundation, and Lincoln Geiger began in 1986, the same year as the Indian Line Farm CSA in western Massachusetts.

I would not be gardening for the Temple-Wilton farm, however, and the next short chapter will cover my impression of membership in Temple-Wilton Community Farm. Otherwise, 1989-94 is a five-year hiatus in my hands-on gardening career.

Chapter 9 –
Temple-Wilton Community Farm, New Hampshire, 1989

Again, circumstances of family life determined the timing and destination of a move and southern New Hampshire seemed to be the place. This was a hilly, lightly populated, town-hall-meeting kind of area, a "real New England" place where people from the populous areas to the south and east come to peep at the gorgeous autumn leaves. That's what the locals call the tourists who flock there in October, "Leafpeepers." An area of many played-out farms and a few functioning ones, but always vest-pocket kinds of places compared to the spacious Illinois farmscape. Pine Hill Waldorf School was located at Wilton and so was the Temple-Wilton Community Farm, beginning its fourth year in 1989. While we were able to join T-WCF as members, it was clear than no one was going to pay Woody to farm in New Hampshire, and that the cost of living was roughly double that in Illinois. It was time again for me to take my fall back position, a job in the social service sector working with mental hospital patients who had been returned to the community.

On occasion I was able to make myself useful in Trauger's fields hoeing in the row crops, or rototilling the raspberry rows at Temple Gardens but my connection with the initiative and the other members really took form at the March budget meeting for the farm.

There were about 75 of us sitting there in March, 1989, to pledge our support in dollars to the year's budget for the community farm, sitting in a newly constructed meeting room attached to Trauger Groh's home, where he lived with his wife Alice Bennett Groh and their new baby. We were representing the 60 families who would receive shares of vegetables, fruit, milk and other dairy products every week during the season. During the winter the fresh produce would be minimal, and maybe not worth the trip to the farm to collect, but if you were a raw-milk customer, as we were, you'd pick up your gallon or two for sure and perhaps a bag of beets or carrots. That phrase "the trip to the farm" distinguishes what I consider a crucial difference between CSAs: 1) Most larger CSAs deliver their produce in boxes or bags to one or more distribution points in their geographic area. Subscribers pick up their portion and take it home. Many will never see the farm, although the farmer or core group may sponsor festival activities there; 2) Smaller CSAs often have the shareholders come to the farm to pick up their shares. Self-evidently, the traffic can be a problem, as is the demand on the farmers' time to schmooze with customers, but the public relations aspects are good. Shareholders may take the time to at least look at the cows or feed the chickens, ask a question or stay and gossip a bit with other shareholders. Certainly they will feel more involved.

There is a difference between what the CSA ideal represented 20 years ago and how the business of CSA is run today. Most of the larger, most successful CSAs now simply offer vegetables in exchange for a set number of dollars. One such, serving 950 families from New York City and other towns, offers 25 weeks of vegetables, roughly 20 pounds per week, for $600 or so. It's pretty straightforward, much like buying a magazine subscription, with some flexibility built into the system for lower income folks. Perhaps there are opportunities for shareholders to visit the farm individually or at a festive event.

This is the "vegetable box" scheme discussed and found wanting by Wolfgang Stränz in a 2007 posting to the BDNOW! email discussion list, which I'll quote extensively later. Wolfgang is involved with the Buschberghof Farm in Germany where, I believe, Trauger Groh farmed before romance brought him to New Hampshire.

Many of the most successful CSAs have flourished with an additional twist, based on inspired convictions about the ultimate relationship between land, farmers and eaters, a relationship that faces up to risk and responsibility. The T-WCF blurs the distinctions by calling all members "Farmers" and has remained quite small, just over 100 families. The following is from their current website, in this their 23rd year (2009).

The Temple-Wilton Community Farm is a free association of individuals which aims to make possible a farm that provides life-giving food for the local community and respects the natural environment. The members are economically organized in households. Out of their household income they cover, individually and together, the operational costs of the farm. They are not legally connected and have, therefore, no legal claims on each other. So: -- if a member does not do the farm work that they promised to do; -- if a member does not pay the share of the farm cost they declared they would pay; -- if a member harvests more produce for their household than is socially responsible; -- if a member does not come to meetings to discuss their needs, and the needs of others in the community; -- if a member works on the farm without first coming to an understanding with the other farmers; in short, if any of us goes against their own expressed will and intentions, the others can have no claim against them. The only thing that the others can do in these cases is to jump in, in order to prevent an eventual loss. Everything concerning the farm originates from the constantly renewed free will of the participants.

But I was telling the story of the pledge meeting that cold March evening in Temple, New Hampshire. The farmers passed out copies of the proposed budget and discussed it briefly. I remember that it was in the neighborhood of $68,000 that year. There was general consensus that it was a reasonable budget. Trauger gave a high-minded little talk reminding people of the significance of the occasion—that they were engaging in a very unusual activity here, the application of principles of brotherhood in the sphere of economics, a radical departure from the prevailing economic ideology—cheap goods at the lowest possible price. He offered a peroration to help strengthen resolve and lighten the mood, which was actually a little heavy, I thought.

This was the one mandatory meeting of the year: you came to make your pledge, or sent a proxy, or lost your share. It was a thrill to be part of this, to put the "I" in Idealism and vote with our pocketbooks for food of the highest quality, grown by farmers who were first of all stewards of their land. Everyone, I think, was stoked, but most had been through the process before; this was my first time. For me, to speak aloud before this circle of strangers to tell what I could afford, to undergo such an exposure of private matters…this was exhilarating, humiliating and disconcerting.

It was clear that the average pledge was going to have to be more than $1,000 and it was understood that some could afford to offer more to cover the shortfall caused by others who could only give less, like me. I was prepared to pledge $650 for the year's share, as much expense as we could bear. Most of the others in the room had kids in Waldorf school too and were sorely burdened by that tuition as well as the high cost of living in the region, but many were employed by high tech firms and making three times what I did in my social service work, or they were professionals of one kind or another. Then there were the farmers, total masters of their craft, who were taking only a pittance for themselves.

I have not analyzed budgets of the most robust CSAs in this era, to see what wages the farmers are earning—probably pretty good, considering—but this brings up another point: all CSAs I know about or have been involved with have been subsidized in some fashion, often enough, as with T-WCF, by the capital investment represented by the farmers' land and equipment. I'm sure that by 1989 the budget covered normal operating costs for the tractors, mowers, swathers, balers; the fixing of fences and purchase of supplies. Farmer Groh had all this equipment and more besides, along with a few cows and fields for crops; blueberries and an ancient apple orchard as well. Farmer Graham worked the land belonging to the Lukas Foundation, a Camphill-inspired life sharing community occupying three houses at Temple, and Farmer Geiger, on land next door to Lukas, was continuing the dairy operation he'd run for years. My point is that none of the eaters, in their share price at this time, was paying for the capital assets: land, equipment, animals or housing for farmers. This, too, along with the living wage issue, may well have been addressed in more recent years, and Steven McFadden points out in a New Farm article (http://www.newfarm. org/features/0104/csa-history/part1.shtml) that the town of Wilton assessed itself $40,000 for the farm's support, this, as Steven reports, in "skinflint New Hampshire." Clearly the town cherishes the farm.

And so the protocol went: Each of us around the room, one by one, spoke out our pledge, without too much editorializing or justifying, so the process could keep moving along. As each firm pledge figure escaped a shareholder's lips, a dozen poised fingers homed in on calculator keys, and a running total was kept. First round, $29,000 short; second round, $12,000 short; third round, DONE DEAL! We applauded lightly, many grinning faces and nodding heads. It was late. We congratulated ourselves and headed home.

Now we hear from Wolfgang Stränz, from Germany:

> *At Buschberghof we are an all-year CSA with a full range of food, including bread, meat, cheese. There is no need to go shopping anymore for us. And the other difference is that we (the members) decide personally, how much money we want to give. There are no fixed prices. Trying to let the social threefold thing to come alive.*

> *Talking of sharing risk and responsibility in agriculture CSAwise means for me that it has to happen reciprocally. To run a CSA scheme only during the summer season and let the consumers go to the supermarket during the rest of the year and let them buy the crap from there, is not a mutual commitment. I do guarantee the economical stability for the farm and I do expect from the farmers that they don't let me starve.*

Which is the clearest explanation I know of why one would belong to a CSA and embrace the heart-centered commitment Wolfgang is proposing.

From the Temple-Wilton website, details of the financials:

The following formula has allowed the farm to operate smoothly since its inception: All unprocessed farm produce (vegetables and milk) is available to members free of charge, if they meet the proposed budget through contributions over the course of one year. This enables us to sever the direct link between food and money. Pledges are made, based on the ability to pay, rather than on the amount of food to be taken. Having made a contribution, the member is free to take as much food as is needed, dependent on availability. Processed goods (yogurt, cheese, meat, bread, etc.) and eggs, are sold at a price that will enable the processing costs to be covered.

And the nitty-gritty of co-operation, after the "new" wears off and the ideals have been tested time after time:

The farmers agree on certain principles to make cooperation in the agricultural community possible:

1) All farmers (members) are individually responsible for their actions and the consequences thereof. To enable others to help them in their initiatives, each farmer (member) must let the others know what they intend to do.

2) Each farmer generates expenses to serve their initiative. The expenditure made by each farmer increases the cost for all the others. Therefore, the individual, in cooperation with other individuals, has to declare what costs they project to fulfill their initiative. The projections of those that intend to spend money, combined together, make up the annual budget. This budget has to be approved by the assembly of farmers (all members). Once the budget is approved, the individual farmer is free to spend the amount of money they have in the approved annual budget.

Every farmer who spends money agrees to keep books and records of such expenditures. The farmers agree on a scheme of categories in which the expenses are accounted for. The books have to verify annually how far the economic aims have been achieved.

3) All farm members agree to share the cost of the annual budget. Any farmer (member) can leave the Community Farm at the end of the year, when they have paid their part of the annual cost. If the need arises to leave the farm before the end of the year they can either pay out the rest of their pledge, or find another member to replace them.

4) Every farmer gives all the other farmers the right to substitute for them in their work if they fail to do, or complete, something they have taken on.

5) It is understood that when the cooperation between the farmers is working, fewer goods and services will be brought into the farm organism by individuals at the expense of all others. It is our goal to be as self-sufficient as possible with our labor.

6) The motivation to do things on the farm should always be directed by our spiritual and nutritional aims rather then by our financial needs.

And Wolfgang contrasts this level of brotherhood with the more typical CSA:

What we have here in Germany is many vegetable box schemes, which is less than CSA for my taste. Because it is so easy to stop your subscription. To take over risk & responsibility in agriculture is something different. But possibly these veg box schemes are similar to many CSAs in the U.S. of which I know too little.

I say *All Blessings* on the named and unnamed heroes at Temple-Wilton Farm, and on all those in Germany. They provide elegant models for the almost 100,000 families involved in CSA projects around the country to strive for greater involvement and commitment...for the sake of the land and the children.

I was commuting back and forth to Manchester, a city of 100,000, an hour and a half at least per day to the various places we lived in the Temple-Wilton settlements and their surroundings. We never could find quite the right place to live and garden there. Then, after two and a half years Waldorf school was over and there was no way we could afford to send young Sky to the Waldorf high school at High Mowing, which is a boarding situation. And so there was no real reason not to move to the city and give me back that seven or eight hours a week I was spending behind the wheel. He could go to public high school there.

Another year and a few months went by with me, the gardener...bereft of land to care for, away from the light, the smells, the colors of the garden. My work was with highly medicated schizophrenics or bipolar folks, all of whom had been through hospitalization, most many times. The support available to them in the community was scattered and sparse and ill-advised. I learned a lot about compassion working with my people, and a lot about anger, working with conventional medical bureau-crazy they were enmeshed in. My rope was getting mighty short and I went to a psychic for advice. The question was why I was stuck in this job and lifestyle so far from my natural home on a farm, and was there a way out? The psychic was a drooling old fraud (he'd had a stroke, but his wife was at his side to dab him off with Kleenex and interpret his very impaired speech) who came up with a delicious story for me to chew on, about the relationship I had with my son several lifetimes back for both of us. When I asked "Am I ever going to have the opportunity to garden again…" he answered "Of course. What you have to do is want it badly enough." And that old cliché, which I could have had for free in any number of self-help books, carried me in the next few months.

In this winter of 1993-4, in the meantime, I met up with the Landmark courses and I took the basic one, The Forum, in January, and the Advanced Forum soon after. I very quickly "got it" that I was creating my own misery and that there was a bold and terrifying thing to do about it: I could "really want" something better for myself.

Soon came a phone call from Dennis, my helper from the Quincy CSA times five years before. He'd read a classified ad in *The High Country Times*. The B-Bar Guest Ranch in Montana was advertising for a Biodynamic gardener. Decent salary, housing included, a captive market. Oh my. I took all I had learned from the Landmark courses and went for it. Applied for the position, had lengthy sessions on the phone with the ranch guest manager; she consulted with the owner (my big negotiating point was that I needed a winter job as well, since I would be supporting my son from a distance with half of my salary) and the deal was struck.

And so by grace I was offered a gem of a gardening job at the B Bar Ranch (next chapter) and much sooner than I might have expected I was to be showing up for work there, most of the way across the country, in my beloved West. The obstacles fell away, fell away, until I was on the road in the last week of March, with everything I owned in a small pickup. Along the way, somewhere in South Dakota, the landscape became visibly, spiritually Western and I pulled over into a roadside rest, plucked a sprig of sage for the dashboard; I wept with the beauty of its scent.

Suffolk Punch draft horses.

Woody at the B Bar Ranch

Photo credit:: Maryann Mott

Chapter 10 – B Bar Ranch, Tom Miner Basin, Montana 1994-96

Easter Monday, April 4, 1994, I arrived at the B Bar Ranch in the Tom Miner Basin, just north of Yellowstone National Park, in the midst of a snowstorm heavy enough that my pickup got stuck a couple of miles short of the ranch. I had to slog my way through the wet snow to the B Bar's nearest neighbor and call the ranch manager to come and tow my truck the last two miles. This was the inauspicious beginning to what turned out to be one of the best of my gardening jobs.

The B Bar is a high-end guest ranch and the owners wanted to present the best possible cuisine—fresh, local, and Biodynamic, prepared by a superb chef—to their clients, and I was hired to supply the best and most produce I could, direct from the garden and greenhouse, located just steps away from the kitchen. Early in the morning I was to consult with Linda, the chef, let her know what veggies would be available for the main meal at 1:00 PM, harvest and give it all a good wash in the garden and take it to the kitchen by 11:00 AM for preparation.

In my mind the situation was made to order for these reasons:
- A captive market which required no selling, no storage or transport of produce;
- An appreciative, discerning group of food preparers and eaters;
- Abundant water;
- Unlimited compost on hand;
- Paid and motivated garden help;
- Generous salary and budget for supplies;
- Challenges aplenty, mainly the climate.

The Tom Miner Basin is located above 7,000 feet elevation and surrounded by mountains, the ones to the south belonging to the northern border of Yellowstone.

The April snowstorm I encountered on my first day was by no means uncommon, and frosts could and did occur in any month of the year. In my first year I had young ankle-high potato plants zapped to the ground by a hard frost on June 21, the summer solstice. I quickly learned that half-hardy plants needed frost protection, and tender crops such as tomatoes, basil and peppers would have to stay in the greenhouse for the entire season.

There was already in place a 50 x 28 foot greenhouse, hoop-style, with a double polyfilm cover and a propane hot air furnace. My predecessor gardener had been a young graduate of the Agroecology course at the University of California at Santa Cruz, where he seemed to have learned little or nothing about greenhouse work. When I arrived the interior arrangement of the greenhouse was all higgledy-piggledy and disorganized. With snow on the ground and the soil still hard-frozen, my first priority was to make this plastic building useful and efficient. I chose to build long soil beds out of 2x12s and installed a long waist-high counter for flats, the soil-filled trays I used for germinating seeds and growing seedlings for transplanting. Underneath these flats were rubber heating mats to hold them at the proper temperature.

Before long the south sides of the compost piles were thawing and I could bring loads of finished compost to the greenhouse to mix with a peat soil mix and fill the beds, 24 inches deep. I began to sow seeds in the second week of April for guest meals starting in June—lettuce and spinach, peas and carrots. Quick stuff and prime candidates for the early spring meals. One of the high points of any B Bar meal was salad and we grew 39 different varieties of lettuce and greens that first year. That very week I was asked if I could supply salad for a group of businessmen coming to the ranch for a working retreat, and I could reply with confidence—Yes! Salad for 20 for a week towards the end of June.

Whee-whoo! I could do it, *Inshallah*. I said it and I meant it

I had just escaped from the city and a job—40 hour weeks under fluorescent lights—five years of frustration, a hiatus in my gardening career that almost did me in. Now all was good; I was gardening and getting paid for it, living again in the West, my true home, in a setting half-wilderness and half luxurious. I was 52 years old and as happy as I've ever been in my life to that time. I was grateful to be there and gave good account of myself, I believe. I exuded confidence.

By the end of May when my garden helper Josh arrived from California—he was another Santa Cruz graduate—the greenhouse was in good shape, with salad and peas and the quicker root crops in and growing well, and many flats with tomatoes, peppers and squash to stay in the greenhouse for the summer, and cole crops and flowers for outdoor planting. In the garden, potatoes were in but many beds had yet to be double dug and that was Josh's job. With his energy and occasional help from an interested guest or one of the landscape crew, I had time to create a nice-looking garden, trim and full of flowers, with benches for grandmas, and sandbox for little guests; a bit of rustic/artistic sculpture in the middle, flowforms and separate small beds for each of the biodynamic preparation plants I could grow there: yarrow, chamomile, stinging nettle, dandelion (people were shocked when I planted dandelion on purpose), valerian. Missing only an oak tree for the biodynamic preparation #505, oak bark. There was a bird feeder too, and a pole fence all around. For the first time in my garden career the spring and summer work was not balls-to-the-wall, flat-out, dark to dark grunt work. Yes, I was a gardener, but I was also an administrator, a manager, and certain nice things went with that.

The ranch was run by two managers, Cathy who dealt with the guest side of things—bookings, guest needs and comfort, employees, housekeeping, food (the garden was in her purview)—and Les, the ranch manager, who was responsible for livestock, buildings, equipment, and ranch guys: cowboys, irrigator, maintenance man. I worked closely with Les, for any time I needed use of a tractor or a load of lumber from town, he was the man to see; and in the winter when the guest side of the business was shut down, I worked directly for him. It always surprised me that Les was ready to trust me—over educated, not really at home with machinery in the way someone is who was raised on a farm or ranch—with a tractor that cost $100,000 or more, but I never pretended to be any thing other than who I was, unafraid of learning new things, ridin' and ropin' come to mind, and settled enough in life to be careful. I learned a lot from Les.

Maryanne Mott owned the ranch. A lady about my own age, an inheritor of a large slice of the General Motors fortune. I knew before our first meeting that Maryanne was a supporter of rare livestock breeds, Suffolk Punch draft horses at the B Bar and White Park cattle at the Seed Savers Exchange farm in Iowa. She manifested this and supported other worthy causes through (at least) two family foundations. I met with Maryanne the first week I was at the ranch. We looked out the lodge windows at a snowscape, knowing there was a garden out there behind the jack-fence. She made it clear to me that she understood something of intensive gardening, having done a three-day intensive course with John Jeavons, the gardener/author who popularized Bio-Intensive gardening methods in a series of books and with well-attended workshops at Bountiful Gardens in Willits, CA. If I'm not mistaken, Maryanne's family foundation donated funds to his work.

"Bio-Intensive" is short for "Biodynamic-French Intensive" gardening, which was what the method was called in the early days of Alan Chadwick's work at Santa Cruz.

I don't know if Jeavons ever knew Chadwick, but he made no secret of borrowing the techniques and adapting them to his own unique system.

Chadwick definitely knew Rudolf Steiner's work and taught the use of the Biodynamic preparations as sprays on the land and inserted into compost. Paul Lee, his great supporter at USC, remembers that in the early days of the garden there was a great deal of skepticism about his methods from the university scientists, angry enough at the notion of organic growing and "planting by the moon." What they would have thought of burying cow horns full of manure and spraying ground-up crystals is hard to imagine. This is in the late 1960s. If Chadwick taught the preparations, he did it on the sly. The Claymont garden lady, Linda, certainly learned about them somewhere, and she said it was from Chadwick.

But Maryanne also made it clear that she would leave the gardening to me. She would not interfere, she told me, and I don't think she ever did. It was already clear to me from phone conversations that salad was a big deal for the ranch kitchen. I was instructed in that first meeting to grow as many varied kinds of greens as I could, and it turned out to be 39 different varieties of lettuce and other salad greens. When I neglected to produce cilantro, she asked me, through Cathy, the guest ranch manager, to produce lots of it, and I did. Maryanne and I talked at length that April afternoon and I think I startled her when I stood up to leave and gestured to hug her, which she was graceful enough about, and told her, "You know I've never known a really rich person before, but I see your heart is in the right place." She said, "Well, you know, the biggest difference is that wealth just allows us to make our mistakes on a bigger scale!" I liked that.

By the third week of April glorious Montana sunshine had thawed the piles of horse corral scrapings that were to provide the compost for my greenhouse and garden operation and I turned one of them with a backhoe-equipped John Deere tractor. Under the deep, insulating snows the piles had heated somewhat and there were rich compost makings there, along with head-sized rocks. I invited Cathy and Maryanne to participate in placing the Biodynamic compost preparations in the steaming pile I'd just turned. They met me there in the "Boneyard." Every ranch has one, an area set aside and fenced which holds the obsolete and broken machinery, discarded building materials and such like. This was where the dump trucks had brought the corral scrapings last summer. I had plenty to say about the preps and about Biodynamics, and the ladies seemed to take it all in. When we stirred the valerian they took to it, just as I had many years before. The witchy-ness of the whole scene, which I did little to dispel, impressed them, I know.

Flowers, I was told. Fresh flowers for the guest cabins, the lodge dining room and office every day. And so the first beds Josh and I dug, three great arches at the very front of the garden, nearest the entrance, were reserved for cutting flowers. Those were some of the first seeds to be grown in flats in the greenhouse too, for transplants outside when the time came and some to stay in the greenhouse as they matured.

In early June a shipment of leased horses arrived from a ranch that specialized in providing unassuming, docile horses for guest programs at other ranches, and I was shanghaied, along with Josh and office helpers and landscapers to go for a long ride to test the new mounts. Duke, the wrangler at the B Bar, and I were already good friends. He was a fireplug kind of guy, thick as he was wide, good natured and ready for any job, as long as he could do it from the back of a horse. Now I had almost no experience on horseback, but that was precisely what Duke needed in order to evaluate the new horses—people with little riding expertise and whose maladroitness in the saddle would test the animals' patience and tolerance. Duke could look on with serenity while my mount went in circles or tried to scrape me off on a low pine branch and draw conclusions about the horse's suitability for a housewife from Dubuque.

I'd had a hernia operation the winter before and I'm built too narrow in the hips to wrap conveniently around a saddle, but at the B Bar you didn't get any points unless you were game for new experiences so, uncomfortable as it was for me, I did climb aboard once in a while, on these tryout rides, moving cows and, in winter, long rides on elk patrol, keeping tabs on the hunters, who were allowed only on specified sections of the ranch.

By late June, when the first guests began to arrive (there were six cabins, each sleeping four people, so there were never more than 24 guests at a time, most often fewer than that), tender lettuce, spicy greens, spinach and baby carrots were on hand for their salads. By the time produce had been flowing regularly for a few weeks (and the kitchen wastes coming back to the garden in the same white plastic buckets) I realized that the presentation of the fresh stuff needed to be upgraded. Josh and I installed a washing station in the garden, with wire-mesh surface and a handy hose with sprayer, and we took to washing everything very carefully, so the chef and her helpers could skip that step, and arranging it artistically in plastic trays and wire baskets. I got them to agree that no leafy greens were to be stored in the fridge; we brought absolutely fresh salad for every lunch and many evening light meals. The plastic trays and wire baskets, with their mounds of lettuce, cut spinach, a couple of hands full of peas, cut flowers and spring onions, bright carrots and beets—every color of green and maroon and orange—these were carried by the gardeners ceremoniously into the luminous kitchen and placed like offerings on the work tables. Often enough a guest or one of the managers or Maryanne herself was on hand to see this presentation, and I can attest that the gardeners' stock went up at these moments.

Josh, Eric and Mark—these were my garden assistants during the three seasons at the B Bar Ranch and I acknowledged my debt to them, for they made me look good. As I have mentioned, they were (relatively) well paid, which is a rarity in the world of garden apprentices, and thus more highly motivated than most. I expressed my gratitude to them, every chance I got, referred to them in conversation with Maryanne or the managers as my "garden partners," and introduced them as such to ranch guests. I did have one complaint, in the middle of my second season at the ranch, from a garden partner who chided me for spending so much time "administering this piddling little garden" and, thus, not helping him with the double-digging I was requiring of him. This fellow, half my age and twice my muscles, had no idea of the record keeping I was doing in support of hundreds of different heirloom varieties, the weekly reports I was writing, or how many long beds I'd double-dug in my career, but I was disinclined to defend myself. Claymont had taught me that it's only the ego that's damaged by false, unjust or ignorant criticism from others, and I refused to rise to the defense of ego, or to remind him sharply that'd he'd come to the ranch in May bragging of the 80-foot beds he'd dug, for free, for a CSA in New Mexico.

My appreciation of these guys was not feigned. Very often in the garden I would call out, "Hey, help me look at this a minute…" This was genuine, not just an attempt to draw my garden partner into my sphere of influence to direct or instruct him. What I needed was just what I called for: someone to help me look at something that was puzzling me or had me stymied in some way. It might be a critter, maybe a construction problem (I often require help for building projects from a mind that can visualize better than my own), a peculiarity of plant growth or animal behavior. I have never been so impressed with my own opinion that I couldn't ask for another viewpoint.

As scheduled, these apprentices finished up at the end of September leaving me to put the garden to bed for the winter and to contemplate the prospect of working as a ranch hand during the next months, under Les's direction. Much of one winter we spent upgrading a two-car garage on the driveway into a three-bedroom bunkhouse. Then there was feeding the horses every morning, hitching up a hay sled to a team of Suffolk Punch draft horses, driving it to the hay barn, loading up a dozen or so bales and off loading them, flake by flake, in the snow-covered pasture. I took care of the chickens; participated in re-building the big horse corral and building a chicken house. There was a period of long weeks one winter writing up a MSDS (Material Safety Data Sheet), for every cleaner, chemical, can of paint and lubricant on the ranch—an

Occupational Health and Safety Act requirement. One winter assignment I was not too happy with, and this was patrolling the outer boundaries of the ranch headquarters area on horseback during elk hunting season. For reasons of public relations and simply because it was customary in that wild piece of country, hunters were allowed on certain outlying 640-acre sections of the ranch, but not on the four or five sections in the middle where the buildings, pastures and irrigated fields are. Hunters in hot pursuit of game, or clueless, lost hunters could be forgiven for encroaching on the inner boundaries, but they all needed to know that ranch personnel was watching, so on many mornings during the six-week long elk season I was delegated to take rifle and binoculars and ride, like it or not. I didn't much like it, because of the cold (we're talking January here at 8,000 feet elevation) and because horseback was never my strong seat. But I would never turn down an assignment—I was not raised that way and it was not part of the can-do ranch culture to welsh and expect someone else to do the job you were detailed to do.

Another cold and tricky job was snow removal. We had an 8-foot snow blower on the big Ford articulated tractor and this served to clear all the ranch roads and the long driveway. We often had to do this in the middle of a snow storm (these came pretty regularly every week or two from December through March) because one storm could drop snow fencepost-high, more than the blower could handle. But this work was done from a comfortable tractor seat in a heated cabin, and in radio communication with the ranch office.

A late-winter project I was very happy to take on was building an addition to the hoop-style greenhouse. When I came, the greenhouse was 48 feet long and I proposed a 27-foot addition to bring it to 75 feet. Les and Maryanne approved and I learned certain skills on this job that would stand me in good stead on my next two assignments when I would build similar greenhouses from scratch. The hoops themselves came in kit form, identical to the ones in the 48-foot portion. I needed to cast 14 concrete anchor/piers, partly buried, to secure the bottoms of the hoops, build baseboards on each side, and build the end wall, hanging a door and positioning windows there. I had help on some of this when I needed it, but it was my project until, on a more or less windless March day it was time to re-cover the whole greenhouse with two new layers of Polyethylene, the translucent 6 mil (a mil is one 1/1000th of an inch) covering. For this we needed as little wind and as many hands as we could muster, for we are talking about two pieces of poly 75 feet long and almost that wide (to go over the top of the hoop). I'd talked this procedure over with Les quite a bit in the week leading up to the event and we thought we had it figured.

This is an appropriate place to mention in fond appreciation just how much I learned from Les Urbin. Ranch raised as a child, a journeyman ranch hand when I was still in school, Les was a seasoned practical genius, both with animals and machines, a fixer, a builder and a natural observer of life and people. Ten years younger than I and in his prime, Les had a bit of a reckless streak. He proved this when he overturned a new-to-the-ranch Bombardier 4-seat snow cat, with myself in a front seat, and Duke, the wrangler/cowboy who was my bunkhouse mate that winter, and Scott, the ranch handyman, in the back. We had to wait for a couple of hours for Duke, who was the youngest and built like a tank, to break a trail to ranch headquarters and drive the big tractor back, so we could get the snow cat back on its tracks. I had fun from time to time with these guys and, as I said, learned quite a lot from Les and from the others too.

Now picture this: all the hoops are up, baseboards new and renovated, end wall in place, the thing looks like the keel and ribs of an overturned boat, waiting for its skin. First thing in the morning now for four days I have gone to Les in his office where we checked the forecast and, more importantly cast a wary eye to the anemometer readout over his desk. We shook our heads over it each day. Not right. Both of us were cautious for dealing with a sail-like piece of polyfilm 75 feet by 70 or so in the wind would be no fun at all. On this fourth day, however, I was getting really anxious (I had a schedule of seeding for greenhouse plants, and I was way behind) and the wind was, I thought, manageable. Les agreed and we got on the telephone and radio to bring as many helpers as we could muster. "Meet us at the greenhouse…today's the day!"

I did this same exact routine two more times in the next three years, erecting new greenhouses in Arizona and New York, but it never went more smoothly than at the B Bar. The ranch staff was a well-picked team—practical geniuses all, in their realms—and we went forward with a problematic, awkward job. Long baling strings, prepared earlier with a weight on one end were thrown over the top ridgepole to the other side and one person assigned to each string. We rolled out one of the poly pieces, grabbed and twisted a piece of the near edge at intervals of 6 feet and tied the string to it. I'd practiced this maneuver. Pull on the strings evenly, everyone, and, with glitches to be sure, the poly slides up over the hoops and the first skin was in place, to be fastened at the baseboards temporarily. Same routine for the second skin, which slides quite easily over the inner one. There were some scary bits along the way when an errant breeze caught an edge a few times, but now, with a lot of adjusting and tweaking, the lower edges at ground level could be wrapped around 1"x2"s and screwed to the baseboard, just tacked there with a few drywall screws because further adjusting was going to be needed once the space between the two polyfilm skins was properly inflated.

Other folks could go to their other business now, with the gardener's heartfelt thanks. I could take it from here. The cleverest piece of this classic hoop house configuration is the inflation, by means of a blower not much larger than one on a hair dryer. This is positioned to blow air at low pressure into the space in between the two coverings, so that ultimately the outer skin balloons out and nowhere touches the structure except at bottom and the ends; just as predictably, the inner cover is pooched inwardly along the hoops so it takes on graceful curves. This is what you see from the inside. From outside you see the balloon-like outer covering only. On average the space between the covers is less than a foot. The brilliance of the design is that the wind bears against the outer ballooning surface and spills off without affecting the hoop structure, the framework, much at all.

My second season I was led to introduce an innovation to the greenhouse, the flowforms. These are sculptural forms cast in concrete aggregate, each the size of a small washtub and each having three cavities through which the water flows, from one to the next. There are many styles of flowforms and they are set up in different configurations. The flowform concept grows out of the work of an English sculptor, John Wilkes, and I was privileged to attend an early hands-on workshop demonstration with him of the flowing, fluid world of flowforms at Kimberton in 1982. Now, 12 years later, his student and protégé Jennifer Greene, had developed Waterforms, Inc. in Blue Hill, Maine. I bought her "Bristlecone" cascade, three flowforms, 60 or so pounds each, which I set up in the center of the greenhouse, stair step-fashion, with a little 20-gallon pool sunk into the greenhouse bed. The bottom flowform discharged its water into the pool and a small pump raised it to the inlet at the top flowform. None of this verbiage can capture the magic of the water as it wells up in the topmost cavity and enters the course dictated by the sculptor's intent, falling, swirling in a replication of the movements of water in a natural watercourse—the laminar ebbing, flowing, vortexing, and pulsating that clearly enlivens and energizes. Negative ions dance in the air and exuberant minuscule droplets escape gravity altogether and spin off into the energy field created around the cascade.

In each of the three flowforms—there are three basins that collect the flow from the form a step higher—the water is nudged by the incoming flow into a gentle vortex, then moves in a figure-of-eight pattern to the adjoining basin, where the vortex takes the opposite direction. Some water streams back to the other basin, taking on the turn of the resident vortex there, while some flows off the spout, waterfalling into the next lower form.

The figure-of-eight movement takes on a rhythmic pulsation, an oscillation of high- and low-tides 30-35 times a minute.

Plants placed around the flowforms grew prodigiously: a sunflower grew to the greenhouse ridgepole 14 feet above the planting bed, then bent over and grew another two or three feet. A Kwintus pole bean plant yielded half a bushel of beans. Whenever I had a potted plant I wanted to encourage, I would place it there and watch it flourish. The flowforms create a enlivening atmosphere for plants and people and the greenhouse became a healing spa for everyone.

The flowforms are also a tool for the devoted Biodynamic gardener. With their vortex action repeated and rhythmic they serve to stir the Biodynamic preparations in elegant fashion. In practice, the limiting factor in the use of the Biodynamic preparations is often the time needed for stirring/potentizing. Whatever the grower's good intentions, the press of business in field, garden, and greenhouse sometimes interferes with the preparation applications one hopes to be able to perform, or knows s/he "should" perform. Many growers resort to stirring machines, but this would have been patently ridiculous in our situation here, a highly intensive small scale greenhouse and garden situation. This spring I have been for the first time soaking all seeds in appropriate Biodynamic preparations before sowing. Since here at the ranch biodiversity is encouraged both in garden and salad bowl, I am growing out more than 350 varieties of vegetables, greens, herb, and flowers. On a given day in April I may sow seeds in small amounts for two or three dozen separate varieties and require seed soaks of two or three different preparations, each with its hour-long stirring. This couldn't be done without the flowforms. With them, multiple stirrings are both simple and efficient.

At a pump capacity of between three and four gallons a minute, a given "particle" of preparation solution flows through the system about 80 times, subject to at least 480 vortices and several hundred chaos actions, between forms and in the pump. Sufficient, I asserted, but ran into the official opposition of Anne Mendenhall, the head of Demeter USA, the Biodynamic certifying agency after I published an account of flowform use in the greenhouse in *Biodynamics*, the organ of the Biodynamic Association.

The journal *Biodynamics* has been published more or less bi-monthly since the 1940s by the Bio-Dynamic Farming and Gardening Association in the U.S., a group with the mission to promote the cause of Biodynamics. I began writing for the magazine from the B Bar with this flowform report, then another two articles on the ranch garden and greenhouse, and would continue writing for a decade and more despite the fact that they did not pay. The journal was spotty with articles sometimes brilliant—especially during the several years Joel Morrow and, later, Allan Balliett were editors—and sometimes warmed-over pieces from past issues, decades old. If these happened to be by Heinz Grotzke, who was the original editor and ran

Meadowbrook Herb Gardens for eons, they were wonderful. Heinz also wrote a slim book, *Biodynamic Greenhouse Management* which I took as my bible in my early days as a greenhouse-person. Then there was a period when Alan York, as editor, managed to make cutting edge discussions of life-energy (bio-dynamics) as dry and unappealing as could be done, by recasting the journal graphically on the boring model of scientific periodicals.

In my opinion the BDA has a lot of catching-up to do with the spirit of Biodynamics in this country. The days when Dr. E. E. Pfeiffer had to dissemble about the alchemical aspects of the preparations, in order to get them out there on as much farm acreage as he could—those benighted days are pretty much over. Look at the BDNOW! email discussion group where Biodynamicists from Portugal, Australia and New Zealand, Canada and the UK, and many from the U.S. gather on a high-traffic forum to question the Biodynamic orthodoxy and promote hundreds of innovations and variations, to support in real time newbies to the field and to rail against the established order as represented by the BDA and Demeter International, which holds the trademark on the term "Biodynamics." Never mind.

In the fall one year we had the corral scraped. A road grader, a big front loader and a 5-ton dump truck arrived on the scene, and with much billowing diesel smoke, proceeded to scrape the horse shit, then the trampled-flat top layer of soil, compressed horse shit and melon-sized rocks. This arrived at my garden staging-area near the greenhouse by the dump truck load and during the long day an 80-foot long windrow of compost-making material developed. From time to time the front loader would shape the pile a bit for me. Peculiar, that on a ranch where from 300 to 500 cows and young steers and heifers spent five months, that I couldn't scare up a few pickup loads of cow manure. But those glorious high meadows where the cows went and where the young ones put on 3 or 4 pounds a day, were far, far away from the garden, on trails that challenge a horse, sometimes. There was no getting manure into a pickup in that country. The only other source, the temporary holding pens through which the cattle were off loaded and separated when they arrived on the trucks, then were set on their way upcountry by the cowboys, might have been an option but that manure, ankle deep on your boot and runny, was from frightened, half-crazed mothers about to lose their calves, and from little guys totally bewildered, demoralized, and disoriented. You don't want crazy manure in your compost pile.

So, for the time being, I was faced with horse manure, buffered somewhat by waste hay and nitrified soil. After the earth moving behemoths left, I had a pile eight feet wide at the bottom, two or three feet wide at the top, 80 feet long and five feet high. That evening, with my garden partner and Herman Warsh, Maryanne's husband, I prepped that pile with four sets of Biodynamic compost preparations from Josephine Porter Institute, explaining the rationale to Herman, who was perhaps more skeptical than he let on. Herman was one of those men who only get kinder as they get older and I thought a lot of him. He wore his riches with grace and poise.

I'd had a wonderful conversation with the dump truck driver during the manure piling work. He asked if I would be interested to have some seeds he and his family had been saving for generations. He brought me some the next day. They were medium tan colored, lima-shaped bean he said were called "Bope" bean that his grandmother had brought over from the high country in Austria 90 years ago and grown out every year. He told me that she had exacted from his father a promise to continue to grow them out and the promise had devolved upon him, even though he confided that his family really didn't care for the taste of them. Turned out that they were fava (broad or Windsor) beans and I have continued from time to time to grow them out myself. (From Wikipedia): *"Broad beans have a long tradition of cultivation in Old World agriculture, being among the most ancient plants in cultivation and also among the easiest to grow. It is believed that along with lentils, peas, and chickpeas, they became part of the eastern Mediterranean diet in around 6000 BC or earlier."*

That fall Maryanne asked me to grow garlic, a lot of garlic, for her to give people, along with a little ceramic garlic roaster, for Christmas, a year later. I put in six 20-foot beds of garlic in October, ahead of the first snows, and mulched them heavily with straw. Then, because strong pre-winter winds sometimes swept the garden and could carry the mulch away, I stretched across that a 25-foot by 40-foot piece of shade cloth and fastened it to the ground to hold the straw in place. Came the winter then and heavy snow cover from November to early April. As soon as I could, when the spring sun allowed, I peeled off the shade cloth and peeked under the mulch to find green garlic shoots just coming through the surface of the soil. To my delight I found that the over-wintering had gone well—quite a coup, I felt, considering that we'd had weeks of sub-zero daytime temperatures with some nights at minus 20 and 25. By July all that beautiful garlic was harvested, then cured, and finally prettified by removing stems and roots and loose outer skins. I never heard how the Christmas gift garlic was appreciated by Maryanne's many friends, but I and the garden did our part.

The Suffolk Punch draft horses at the ranch were wonderful animals, willing workers, beautiful, sturdy and docile. These are not huge, heavy horses like the Clydesdales famous in Budweiser commercials or the Percherons portrayed in old photos of fire wagons, but a medium-sized breed of 15 or 16 hands and well under a ton in weight. We used them in all seasons to pull hay sleds and the chuck wagon and passenger wagon for Friday evening cookouts with guests, to skid logs to the band saw mill in the forest, with the implements in the hay fields. I sometimes had occasion to drive the horses, and to feed and to harness them in the barn, especially in the winter when I wasn't so occupied in the garden.

The harnessing was difficult for me as the harness was complicated and heavy. I was slow to heave it all up on their backs and sort it out, but the horses were very patient with me.

One of my jobs when we were about to hitch them to the hay sled in sub-zero temperatures was to use a long pry bar to break the runners loose from the frozen ground since as Les said, "You never want to let them know that there's any load they can't pull…it'll break their confidence. You have to let them believe they can pull anything." My other task, as Les was bringing the team out of the barn was to kindle a fire in a steel drum near the front of the sled and load up a couple of wheelbarrows of junk wood, construction offcuts and tree branches. The fire would make the hay distribution task less arduous for whoever was driving and for the person busting the bales and kicking the flakes off the sled to the horses out in the pasture. They were fine out in the cold as long as they had plenty of feed. Another of my jobs was to chop ice in the creek where they went for water.

I thought the horses were noble animals, but chickens were more my speed. Maryanne was thoroughly committed to the Suffolks and White Park cattle (these were not raised at the B Bar where I worked but rather at a sister ranch at Big Timber, MT, and at the Seed Savers Exchange property in Iowa), expensive undertakings designed to preserve these endangered breeds.

She listened and approved, however, when I made a case for preserving yet another rare breed, chickens, a more modest endeavor. The reader has seen that I have raised chickens in several places, from my first farm in Kentucky to Claymont and Kimberton Hills and Camphill Minnesota, and that I truly loved birds. We decided on White Wyandottes.

These are a striking breed, pure white, large-sized, brown egg layers, quiet and unlikely to cause problems in the garden. I had three motives in mind beyond the preservation aspects of the project. I wanted to build "chicken tractors" for the garden, bottomless cages designed to allow the birds to cultivate the ground in unused beds and incidentally fertilize them with their droppings; further, I was keen to have them do the same thing in the greenhouse in the winter; finally, they could eat some of the kitchen wastes that accumulated day by day. (My initial idea for to solve this kitchen waste problem, pigs, was not well accepted by Duke who vowed to shoot any swine I brought onto the property, further endangering the breed.)

So I settled for the chickens. While we were raising up the baby chicks in a cage in the greenhouse I was building the chicken tractor according to Andy Lee's instructions in his book called *Chicken Tractor*. It was 3 x 3 x 8 feet made of 2" x 2"s and chicken wire, with a top that opened like the lid of a coffin. My innovation was to put wheels on the thing as it was surprisingly heavy to move around the garden. I've since built much lighter chicken tractors from PVC pipe and light plastic mesh, hoop-style and not so tall.

When it was apparent that the chicken project was a go, Les began building a proper chicken house, large enough to house 50 or more birds during the winter when they would be indoors all the time, insulated and on skids so it could be pulled with a tractor. All of us at one time or another had dealt with permanent, fenced chicken yards so compacted and over fertilized that nothing would grow but the rankest weeds, and we didn't want that. Moving the house around in the pastures near headquarters and using temporary fencing seemed to be an answer, and it was. I constructed hurdles *(Definition 3. chiefly Brit. a portable rectangular frame strengthened with willow branches or wooden bars, used as a temporary fence)* of conduit pipe and chicken wire which were very light and easily portable for this purpose. Further I had in mind an idea which, on the face of it, seemed demented but actually did work when we tried it. This was to place the new chicken house up against the back door of the greenhouse and allow the birds inside in the late fall and winter. At this time of year the plants in there were fully mature and the chickens scratching the soil would not harm them at all. Again, as in the garden earlier, their droppings would fertilize the soil a bit and they would enthusiastically eat any insect larvae and pupae they found. This was a major step up from the alternative, which would have had the birds in their house most of the winter, with deadly temperatures outside and snow 14 chickens high, confined and bored stiff. Bored chickens tend to cannibalize each other and that's no good at all.

Another winter time job I was assigned was grooming cross-country ski trails on the property. Maryanne sometimes had groups of friends to the ranch for ski holidays and deep snow on trails through the forest needed to be compacted after each storm. I was pretty much unacquainted with snowmobiles and got the machines stuck in deep snow fairly often, but was always able to wrestle them free and gradually gained the skills I needed. On occasion when Maryanne's guests were playing in the snow with toboggans, snow saucers and skis on a long, clear slope not far from the lodge, I was there on a snow machine to ferry them back up to the top.

One very practical use to which the horses were put was to snake logs out of the forest to the site where we had set up a portable band saw mill. Les and I and some of the crew had seen one of these mills at a fair in Bozeman where we had taken the draft horses to compete in a pulling event. This portable log cutter uses a band saw mounted on a carriage which moves horizontally on tracks, first to cut slabs from the log immobilized under it, then to cut planks of the thickness needed, one by one. I had made many trips to Livingston and Bozeman and hauled back trailer loads of lumber for various ranch projects so I had an idea how much money was being spent on dimension lumber. I became an enthusiastic supporter for Les's plan to buy a mill and one soon appeared—not the top of the line model, but a very serviceable one that would cut 2x4s, 2x6s, or beams as big as we needed, from logs as large as we could muscle up onto the bed of the thing. Nobody was doing any clear cutting at the B Bar. The trees to be turned into lumber were mature specimens chosen to open to the sunlight at least a few sub-mature trees around them, and only if the horses could get to them and skid them to our little mill yard with minimal damage to the mostly open understory. Les and Scott and the horses worked quite a few days in the forest at the end of the summer. I was mostly in the garden at this peak harvest time but did take one afternoon to drive a 4-wheeler up to the logging site.

Les, as always, was willing to train me to use the machine. He was patient and we communicated well and by now I was catching on fast to these things. He'd already taught me to use the very large, very expensive articulated tractor, with its front loader, snow blower and all the rest; also the bulldozer, the back hoe and many smaller machines. He was tolerant of my mistakes, knew that I knew to ask questions and was never afraid to admit that I didn't understand something. He appreciated, I think, that I was less likely than most city boys to break things, as I was careful and slow; I didn't push engines and gear boxes even close to their limits, nor did I try to show off on horseback (especially not on horseback!) or on all terrain vehicles. I had in mind my own project using lumber from the mill and secured permission from Scott and Les to use certain logs, medium-sized one I could manage by myself to get up onto the cutting platform. Higher-priced models have hydraulic log lifters, but the B Bar's version didn't, so it was a matter of positioning the log with a peavey or cant hook, then working out a way to lift it a foot or so onto the holders that would secure it into position. They were already milling large timbers and thick planks for a project they had in mind.

I was content to engage myself fully with the culture of the ranch and at no time since Kimberton was the distinction between work and life so cheerfully blurred for me. Was it work or life or play to join with guests and ranch hands in hilarious mock barrel racing in the corral—clueless untrained riders on patient plodding trail horses? And my bet of a nickel with Peggy R. (you would recognize the famous family name), a noted horticulturalist, that I had in the B Bar garden a flower she'd never seen (a Cape Daisy from South Africa…but she insisted I show her the seed packet to identify the variety); she made her way with her cane to the garden later in the day with a token of her vast family wealth, her nickel—was that work (schmoozing with the guests) or playful human interaction? But these are trivial examples. On a more basic level—making meat—I also joined with the prevailing culture. It wasn't too long after I arrived at the ranch that I outfitted myself with winter gear, cold weather clothing and boots and, in the same shop a flat-sided Winchester 30-30 lever action rifle, a "'94," the design more or less unchanged for a hundred years. I had the gunsmith put a telescopic scope on it, in rueful admission that my vision was no longer as sharp as it once was. This business of hunting big game for the freezer was taken seriously by every adult male on the ranch staff in the winter. There was no nonsense or braggadocio associated with taking an elk or a mule deer to feed self and family, none at all, and no consumer-cultish frippery about purchasing just the right rifle or hunting knife. Nor was any big deal made of going out into the wildness to find your animal. We lived with these big elk month in and month out. Sightings at a distance were commonplace and we often came across their trails, droppings and tracks. But the animals tended to stay away from the activity at ranch headquarters until their feed in forest and rangeland got scarce in early winter.

I took my first deer not half a mile from ranch headquarters in the forest, when a pair of mule deer bucks passed quietly in front of me not 50 yards away. I chose the leading buck and—how could I miss at that range with a telescopic sight?—fired. He leapt in the air, swapped ends, took three hesitating steps forward and crumpled to the ground. As I found out later when I was cleaning liver and heart in the bunkhouse kitchen sink, the bullet had passed right through his heart.

Later in the winter, in deep snow several miles up in the mountains I waited at the edge of the trees facing a large open area. I needed to pee and, very reluctantly because of the cold, unzipped. As I directed the stream at the base of a fir tree I caught sight of a large group of elk trailing unhurriedly, single file, along the ridge top 100 yards away. There was plenty of time to replace my equipment inside my insulated coveralls, rezip, bring the rifle up slowly, and pick my animal from the line of 30 or 40 elk. I chose a spike bull, probably three years old and 600 pounds, and eased back on the trigger. The animal staggered slightly and disappeared down the other side of the ridge while the others scattered. I sat down heavily in the snow, heart racing with delayed buck fever, deciding to wait a little while before going to look for him. Twenty minutes later I found him dead not far from the trail. He had not been able to go far because the bullet had passed through both lungs, severing the aorta on its way through.

I tell these stories not to brag or to present myself as a great hunter, or even more than just a barely competent one. Rather, to say that the extent to which I thrive when in a new gardening situation always correlates with how well I am able to adapt myself to the social situation and mores in which I find myself. In this case, all four of the men on the ranch staff got their deer and elk that winter. I ate well, I fit in, and I gained credibility where it mattered most, with the people I worked with every day. And—no small point—I learned new skills, always useful and exhilarating.

I had yet to solve the problem of kitchen wastes. The chickens would pick through some of them, but they were definitely picky about what they would consume and leave the onion skins, the citrus peels, eggshells and a lot more. So I decided to build compost bins in the garden. Layered with weeds, spent mulch and waste hay, the kitchen stuff would enhance the compost, I felt, and since the garden had an educational function, the composting operation could add to that. Using two-inch lumber and posts cut with the band saw mill we built a series of five adjacent 4'x4'x5' bins, intending to turn the contents of one into the next on down the line, winding up with finished ready-to-use compost in the end bin. Such frequent turning cuts the time needed for making compost and thoroughly incorporates the kitchen scraps.

But I hadn't figured on the grizzly bear. It wasn't long after I had initiated this scheme that a grizzly invaded the garden, attracted no doubt by the smell of the kitchen scraps. The tracks were there for anyone to see, across the driveway between the ranch manager's house and the garden, through the garden gate, across garden beds and straight to the compost. My boot print fit neatly inside a bear track, with lots of room to spare. Within hours the word came from the ranch manager: no compost in the garden. Period. No appeal. The guest season was about to begin and bears in the headquarters area were an unacceptable hazard. I stubbornly resisted and much of the goodwill I'd built up in two and a half years on the ranch evaporated. Instead of accepting the situation for what it was and gracefully acceding, I became irate and tried to assert my proprietorship. This was my big mistake. I was not a proprietor, I was an employee.

This was the beginning of the end for me at the B Bar and I began looking for another gardening job. I made a flying journey to Arizona—no more Rocky Mountain winters for me!—to look at the situation at the Tree of Life Rejuvenation Center at Patagonia. Dr. Gabriel Cousens was advertising for a Biodynamic gardener and I met the qualifications.

My last night at the bunk house, U Haul out back packed with my things, Maryanne and Herman showed up at the front door to wish me well. I was touched. They were unfailingly gracious, those two, and if I was not shamed by the contrast between my obstinacy and their courtesy, I should have been. Next morning I drove for the last time down the Tom Miner Basin road, headed south.

Chapter 11 –
Tree of Life Rejuvenation Center, Patagonia,
Arizona 1996 - 1997

From the B Bar Ranch in southern Montana I transplanted myself in July, 1996, to Patagonia in southern Arizona, 19 miles from the Mexican border at Nogales. Gabriel Cousens, MD, established the Tree of Life Rejuvenation Center at Patagonia in 1992 as a place to promote his healing work, which involves ayurvedic therapies and live, vegan foods. Gabriel is a high-energy physician with a wide following of devoted and grateful patients, many of whom have been very sick.

Gabriel is a polymath, according to the biography on his website, a learned doctor with certification in conventional Western medicine, in Ayruveda, Holistic Medicine, a physician of the soul. He is a medical researcher, world-recognized live-food nutritionist, psychiatrist, family therapist, homeopath, acupuncturist, expert on green juice spiritual fasting and detoxification fasting, ecological leader, Reiki master, internationally celebrated spiritual teacher, author, lecturer, culture-bridger, peace worker. He is author of ten books on nutrition and healing and is an ordained Essene bishop since 1984, founder of the Essene Order of Light in 1993.

He had advertised for a Biodynamic gardener to provide produce for the Tree of Life kitchen. I was interested for two reasons. I'd never gardened in Southwestern conditions, though I'd visited New Mexico many times. I also wanted to see if Biodynamic compost could be made using nothing but plant materials. There were no animals at Tree of Life, no domestic ones, and thus no manure available. This dilemma is faced by many would-be Biodynamicists: whether you can actually do Biodynamics without raising animals, especially cows. The culture here at Tree of Life was opposite from the ranch I just came from. For instance, I ran into resistance in my first week on the job when I suggested raising bees. The radical vegan cohort of the community, represented by the raw foods chef, Zee, objected on the grounds of "exploitation" of the critters. I let that one go by, having been thoroughly chastened by my recent cockiness at the ranch, though I failed to see how the partnership between bees and their keeper constituted exploitation.

My predecessor gardener had created a round garden at Tree of Life, a little more than 100 feet in diameter. Since the wind blew fiercely at times on the mesa, she had surrounded the garden with a wall of straw bales stacked six feet high, and, since javelina and deer were common, with a double wire fence outside the wall. The intense sun, sparse rainfall, wind and critters made for challenging gardening. As did the surprising cold here at 4,000 feet, even at this latitude. I was astonished at the hard frosts that came around Halloween and lasted well into the new year.

The soil on the mesa was caliche, a surface hardpan, with very little organic matter. Desert shrubs and bunchgrass predominated, with deep-rooted mesquite trees widely spaced. Seriously spiny desert plants abounded—jumping cholla, yucca, prickly pear, century plant with its towering spires and magnificent blooms. I can only imagine what must have gone through folks' minds—the Permaculturists and gardeners Gabriel drew to the place early on—as they contemplated gardening in such soil; their solution was to bring in truckloads of topsoil and compost and build raised growing beds right on the surface. I don't believe the surface was broken up at all, much less double-dug. In this circumstance the gardeners' thinking must have been that the plant roots would eventually work through the hardpan, leaving worm channels and building organic matter. A quick and dirty answer, but an effective one. And "quick" would have suited Gabriel's view of the situation; he was feeding a bunch of people with the income from his doctoring; whatever food that wasn't grown would have to be bought. He would have wanted produce pronto. But raised beds, a time-honored technique elsewhere, were inappropriate in the desert; too much water evaporates from their exposed sides. The indigenous people farming in this kind of country often grew crops in sunken "waffle" gardens, with raised paths or dikes separating them. They knew they needed to conserve whatever irrigation and rain water for their crops. So Gabriel's original gardeners got it half-right—bring in soil—and half-wrong—pile it up. It would have been made more sense to have excavated soil in the beds, made walls or dikes or paths with it, and filled the holes with brought-in soil.

Gabriel settled in Arizona from well-watered northern California and seemed to me not quite to get it when it came to water use in an arid country. I talked with neighbors who were deeply concerned about the center's drawdown of the water supply on the mesa and when I came to realize the scope of his vision there I began to be troubled myself about the center's water use. The vision called for dozens of staff and patients to reside on the mesa, gardening on a much grander scale than now, many fruit trees and hundreds of windbreak trees, a vineyard. There had been a "constructed wetland" installed early on, an acre, perhaps, graded very flat into two diked pools, one slightly lower than the other, and planted with water-loving plants. This wetland was intended to purify the waste water from the Center complex. It was not really functioning during my tenure there as there were too few people in residence to supply the input. My worry was that when the residences, and then the residents appeared, the waste water usage would fill the wetlands' pools all right, until the well went dry.

In addition to the kitchen and garden water usage, a half-dozen interns and apprentices were showering daily. Then there was a wonderful lineup of 300 plus windbreak trees sheltering three or four acres where most of the development was going to take place—housing, therapy buildings, workshops, gift shop (no doubt). This windbreak was made up of carefully chosen varieties of trees and the irrigation line ran from tree to tree over a thousand yards and more. Every tree had one or two emitters. It was my job to figure out how to turn this irrigation zone on, clear the line and the emitters and regulate the pressure so the whole line of half-inch pipe would fill and drip evenly. Most of the trees were alive and some were thriving.

There was only one well tapping a finite aquifer. From this well ran 1½ -inch black plastic water lines all through the property, mostly on the surface of the ground. One run was at least a half-mile long to a shade house where the neglected remnants of landscape shrubs languished, those not used in the initial plant-scaping of the place four years earlier. I sometimes watered this relict collection with water that was very much hotter than my hand could stand, from black water pipes out in the sun all day. This was near the site I'd chosen for a greenhouse and I wondered if sun-heated water would suffice in winter to give a bit of warmth to plants there. After four years or so this initial water line infrastructure was beginning to deteriorate in that relentless sun.

There was a headquarters building consisting of raw foods kitchen and dining area, bathroom and a couple of treatment rooms; also an elegant stuccoed and earth- floored temple building, with pounded earth-and-dung floor Also a sprawling residential structure with space for perhaps 25 people in single-and double rooms. Construction had been halted on the latter building and I was the only person to live there, illegally, I suppose. All of these buildings were of straw bale construction.

Bill and Athena Steen, innovators in the world of alternative architecture and straw bale builders, live not far from Patagonia and they were on hand for these building projects a couple of years before I arrived.

When I came in July the garden was producing nicely, but the spring garden was finishing up. Etoile, apprentice to my predecessor gardener, was doing a good job with the maintenance. Since the climate dictated a shutdown during the hottest months, gardeners most often planned on spring and fall gardens with a break during July-August and December-January.

I needed to learn a lot in a hurry to begin to be able to garden well in this very dicey climate. In summer, from May until October, it's day after day, week after week, of 100° F or hotter. This is relieved somewhat during the July-August monsoon afternoon thunderboomers come almost daily, bringing welcome relief from the dizzying heat and cornea-parching glare.

Outside the margin of strawbale walls and fences around the circular garden was a calamity masquerading as compost piles, a dozen or more of them haphazardly arranged in various stages of decomposition. Other compostable material was strewn about with no attempt to pile it. All of it was dry, dry, dry, going nowhere fast. The piles and piles of garden waste, landscape waste and such strewn outside the garden gate were off-putting and unsightly—terrible feng shui.

Zee, the chef, read about anaerobic composting of kitchen wastes and wanted to try this—his kitchen trimmings sealed in plastic garbage bags. Not to be recommended, but he didn't ask my advice. He kept the bags out of my way and I allowed the airless putrefaction to go forward. Finally Zee abandoned the slimy mess and his helpers and I initiated a scheme for adding the kitchen wastes to the ongoing composting process, right out there where the air could get to it.

I embarked on a two phase plan: 1) to rationalize the whole compost scene, making a series of piles and protecting it all from the wind, providing for regular watering and harvest of the finished stuff; 2) to build a greenhouse, as I began to realize that, however subtropical the climate seemed it was really pretty harsh—temperatures between 30°F and 110°F, severe drought at times, wind and predators. A pit greenhouse covered with shade cloth part of the year would ameliorate most of these problems for baby plants, which could then go in the garden having been pampered at first, grown to a sturdy size, and gradually hardened off to face the reality outside. As it was, as far as I could tell, no one had attempted to grow plants from seed here, except the usual seeded-in-place subjects: melons, corn, beans, peas and such. Tomatoes and brassicas and alliums and salad that I had always grown from seed would do well for us in a greenhouse. The further argument for a greenhouse was season extension; that spring garden would begin earlier and the fall one end later. I could picture almost year-round gardening at Tree of Life, but I didn't get the opportunity to find out.

At about the time of the winter solstice and at Gabriel's request, I went to Tucson to acquire garden starts, a couple of hundred nice plants from a nursery, broccoli, kale, and cabbage for planting in the round garden. We turned the occasion into a ceremony and added a solstice spraying of the Biodynamic crystal spray—BD501 – Horn Silica. Lily was my apprentice and we demonstrated the stirring and spraying and made a ceremony, with drumming, out of the whole thing. With a small group, we were able to organize and do the transplanting of the nursery plants quickly and efficiently. Now in a more temperate garden, I would have seeded these sorts of plants in the greenhouse in February and planted out into the warming garden in April for summer eating. Here, Gabriel assured me, the garden would warm as soon as the days started getting longer and, with started plants in the ground at the first of the year we would be harvesting for the kitchen in April. I was probably a little slow on the uptake about all this, but it validated and clarified my own ideas about installing a greenhouse, so we didn't have to go buy someone else's plants. Gabriel and I were still on the same page here

The Tree of Life Rejuvenation Center was uniquely attractive to folks seeking a holistic, vegan, raw food life experience. I don't mean only Gabriel's patients, who were numerous and loyal, but rather the large number of young people who applied for internships and training, both in the raw foods kitchen and in the garden. At any given time in my 7-month stay there I had up to half a dozen young apprentice types helping in the garden so a lot could get done in a short time.

I was given the task of fielding emails and phone calls from prospective interns, explaining to them the living and working conditions, and scheduling the arrivals and departures of the likeliest candidates. I see now from the Tree of Life website that the community is charging $1,900 for a 12-week internship experience. (It is not for nothing that Gabriel is listed in the *International Who's Who of Entrepreneurs*.) At the time I was there, it was a straight work trade: you got your meals and your tent down there in the ravine and access to the outdoor shower and composting toilet, in exchange for a reasonable amount of work, carried out with reasonable diligence.

So I gave a lot of thought to the internship question while I was there, how it might be when Gabriel's vision really got going, a question I put this way: How could a group of, say, five or six garden learners best be organized in a setting devoted, yes, to training, but also to feeding 25-50 people daily. The needs of the overlighting kitchen presence had to inform all the garden activity. I pictured the apprentices rotating through specified roles, once a month, the rotation completed twice in a nine- or 10-month stay. It would not have occurred to me that 12 weeks, as Gabriel's current program is organized, would be enough time. In my opinion, at least a year was needed to see a garden through a complete cycle in order to provide a meaningful apprentice experience.

The roles, then:

The Tool Guru is in charge of all tools, organizing them, finding them, sharpening and repairing them, making sure they are returned from wherever they are deployed; also responsible for equipment, buildings, fencing; s/he is also Gardener's assistant;

The Watermeister is in charge of all watering, everywhere: landscape, gardens, windbreak, greenhouse, shadehouse, foundation plantings, orchard, vineyard; also Gardener's assistant;

The Gardener is in charge of garden bed preparation, compost, soil making, cultivation, seed sowing, seed saving, transplanting weeding, harvest, labeling. S/he is in tight liaison with the kitchen;

The Straw Boss is in charge of special projects, doing the work him/herself and recruiting a crew as needed. I began to separate out in my mind special projects from "real" garden work at the B Bar, where the gardener was often called upon to do many non-green-thumb things often involving materials handling, everything from a tractor scoop of gravel to a truckload of straw bales; major irrigation setups; bed building in garden and greenhouse; landscaping of all kinds; pruning; mulching; mowing by hand and machine; fencing; building compost bins, cold frames, lathhouse, greenhouse; tree plantings, grape plantings; orchard care.

Woody's Role: Garden Fool – filling in for any of the above, planning, teaching, recruiting, correspondence, accommodations, finances, record keeping, Biodynamics guru, beekeeping, organizing and prioritizing projects, events, trouble shooting. Like the Fool in the Tarot deck, Woody is always about to walk off the edge of a cliff.

Visitors, short-timers, and volunteers would fill *Gopher* roles; running errands, working on crews, small projects.

The program would have worked this way. Each person acted in his or her role for a month, then spent a week learning the next role from the person who has been holding that one for the previous month. The turnover of roles takes place at about five-week intervals. I reckoned that this role rollover would eliminate a lot of problems with people claiming turf and getting stuck in the prerogatives of their roles, such stuckness being spiritually deadening; also problems when people cavil about others' quirks or pettiness in their roles—people would soon see the realities since they would be playing the same role next month. If you stayed the full year you'd get to play all roles twice; what the perspective that would give! I felt with these ideas that I was taking Hartmut von Jeetze's advice and setting up conditions for inner growth as well as fostering outward competence. Once the summer monsoon was over, by mid-August, along with my helpers I embarked on the compost scheme. The piles and piles of garden waste, landscape waste and such strewn outside the garden gate were now as moist as they would get this season and they weree ready to put into compostable form.

Happily, we had a large inventory of straw bales left over from construction projects. We built great bins, four feet high, six feet wide and 30 or 35 feet long. These would contain the compost for aesthetic purposes, protect it from drying winds and eventually the straw itself would be incorporated into the process.

All of the random piles around the entrance went into our bins, thoroughly mixed and moistened. When necessary, we shredded the most woody and fibrous stuff; we did have a monster of a chipper/shredder machine on hand, a gift to the Center, but it was used only sparingly because it was outrageously noisy and disturbing of the peace.

The gardener before me was a Permaculture wizard and she did far more than gardening. The wetlands were her idea, and many swales, complete with water-slowing gabions; the windbreak trees and watering system; and large-scale water directing projects ending in a small but growing pond. All this was needed activity and energetically carried out, but it wasn't gardening; it wasn't feeding the folks.

Gabriel had hired me as a Biodynamic gardener and I needed to take the garden to its next incarnation now. That was going to require ripping plants up from many of the beds in the circular garden. Most of all, strawberries that had been in place for three or four years now, multiplying and matted and yielding scarcely enough to be worth the picking. A third of the bed space in the garden was in strawberries and I had the crew uproot them all to go in the compost bins. We saved enough young plants to renew a couple of beds; now the plants would properly spaced and re-composted to favor good pickings when the time came.

There were perennials which had spread too far and outgrown their usefulness; these we pulled up too.

When all the garden wastes were moistened down in their straw bale piles the crew and I inserted the Biodynamic compost preparations in there. I tried to recapture for them the feelings I had felt when I first did this 20 years before at Claymont. The crew, young and open-minded, took it all in. Whenever we did the sprays of horn manure or crystal, they were be there to see the magic.

This was all happening in early autumn. Meanwhile, Gabriel solicited from a wealthy patron a $5,000 grant to build a greenhouse, and I set about designing an appropriate structure. It was going to want to be a pit-style house, for digging into the ground four feet or so would help to moderate the extremes of the Arizona high desert climate: the staggering heat for four months and the frostiness of the longest nights. The middle of the days, however, even the short ones, were almost always pleasant however, and the spring and autumn were uniformly gorgeous. We needed to re-create that pleasantness as best we could in the greenhouse with the pit and as many passive solar features as I could manage. The budget was the big constraint. After dithering about for too long with notions and drawings of a structure with a concrete block rear (North) wall, met at the top with quarter-hoops of greenhouse framework, a lovely heat-sink in concept, but cost prohibitive just for laying the block. I came to find this out in the process of a delightful conversation out there among the mesquites with the mason who would have done the job. He could picture it, I could picture it, but we couldn't afford it.

Another constraint was that the building code called for a structure engineered to withstand hurricane-force winds of 120 mph. I found a greenhouse kit manufacturer to supply the frame and polyfilm for about $3,000 and paid another $1,000 to have the site excavated, a pit four feet deep and 16 feet wide and 50 feet long. That left the last thousand dollars to cover all the lumber I would need for the end walls, stair steps leading down into the pit, a single long central bed, all the hardware and accessories, including a solar panel setup to run the inflation fan and a vent fan. The site was on a water line, but not an electric line.

The manufacturer's instructions for footings for the eight hoops were acceptable to the county code. We cast 16 concrete piers, using 5-gallon buckets for forms, each with a piece of galvanized tubing centered in it for the bottom of the hoop to slide in. These piers we buried along the two long sides of the greenhouse footprint at roughly six-foot intervals. This required a certain amount of tinkering around, getting everything level, but we did a professional, creditable job, I thought. Since the greenhouse was 22 feet wide, it straddled the pit; walk down the crude stair steps and stand on the pit bottom and there is on your left a shelf of soil at the level of the grade outdoors, about four feet wide, on your right, another to hold seedling flats. The shelf on the north side supported 20 black plastic barrels full of water, 800 gallons worth, as a heat sink, intended to soak up the heat of the day and give it off at night. With closed doors and windows and with the vent system shut down, this heat sink, along with the heat-holding adobe soil exposed to sunlight during the day, would make a decided difference during the cool-to-cold winter nights.

A single solar panel sufficed to run the inflation blower and a second fan that brought outside air into a perforated polyfilm tube suspended from the ceiling—this provided at least a little air movement on a still day, which is crucial. We don't want any dead air spaces in a greenhouse, breeding ground for fungus and such.

As the greenhouse was finalized and outfitted it began to be clear that Gabriel and I had issues we weren't resolving. Issues around water use by the Center, social issues (there were factions, tale telling, backbiting, malicious gossip, confrontational Jews and unimpressed Gentiles) and community issues (mainly my unspoken understanding that the vision was Gabriel's, the money and control flowed through him, and he was going to draw to himself the people who would buy into his ideas. It was not a community, as it looked to be on the surface, an appearance that Gabriel promoted as best he could; it was, rather, his venture and his alone.) I was not alone in my discontent and the very week I left some time later, so did his wife and the staff person who had been there at the Center with him the longest. But Gabriel and his vision prevail and prosper more than a decade later, as far as I can tell from his website. I don't know anyone who has ever worked harder to manifest a vision, especially one that includes peace and healing, nutrition and, again, peace. I honor him as a great visionary.

What a wonder my crew was, the group who hung out down there in the ravine and had their own social scene that I wasn't a part of. I was the straw boss and I treated them with respect and asked of them nothing that I hadn't done innumerable times myself. I asked them to do some endless jobs and they did them cheerfully. Jobs like sifting soil and compost to fill a 40 foot by 6 foot bed in the center of the greenhouse, two feet deep. They plastered the inside walls, helped me build the end walls, mixed concrete, wheeled barrows across planks. They were mostly cheerful and mostly on task, most of the time. I was happy to allow a lot of flexibility. We were in *mañana* country, after all. For example, we were startled one windless autumn afternoon to see vehicles with an odd assortment of trailers attached, moving through Patagonia, some with giant wicker baskets atop. The balloonists had arrived for their annual rendezvous. My crew, enchanted by the prospect of free hot-air balloon rides, went off for the next three days or so from dawn to nightfall to hang out at the balloonists' rallying point to help with the inflations and launchings, ride the chase vehicles to the landing sites and help fold the balloons and package them up for the next day's adventures. They had a blast and I was happy for them. Another side to my benign stance as mentor and workmaster came up when the young woman who came with her boy friend—they were two of the stalwart ones that season—wrecked his truck on one of the nearby roads. They'd had such appealing plans to travel together as a team for a year or two, knocking about on just such assignments as this one and now their wheels were totaled out and they were more or less broke. She was unhurt in the wreck but devastated by guilt. I counseled with them both, celebrated with them the purity and undamaged integrity of their relationship, and rode with them through all the ups and downs of the insurance settlement, with all the phone calls over several days. It turned out that his insurance wouldn't cover the accident, but her dad's insurance would, so the vehicle could be replaced; moreover, their relationship weathered what could have been a real blow and was stronger for it. I just loved working with these young people. Do they remember me as kindly as I remember them?

Meanwhile we had to re-invent the wheelbarrow wheel. The spreading plant called "puncture vine" in the desert regions was widespread on the mesa where the soil surface had been disturbed. Its little goathead seeds lie on the ground with at least two spines upward, sure to skewer the barefooted apprentice or wheelbarrow tire. The guys at the local filling station hated to see me coming with a load of two or three wheelbarrow wheels (not all that easy to unmount from the rim). Finally, I designed and Philip, the on-site handyman, built a laminated wooden wheel, five layers of ¾ inch plywood. We were probably prouder of this invention than we should have been, but it did solve a nagging problem.

We cannot fathom what ancient cultures may have known that we do not. Certainly it is not too much of a stretch to believe that a great deal of important knowledge may have been lost over the millennia, particularly in the past couple of hundred years as materialism has become the reigning paradigm. How did the Egyptians and the Maya work stone with such precision? Did Methuselah really live for 969 years—how? Were all indigenous people able to commune with plants (and the Devas?) in order to learn their uses for healing? Of Course.

Agnihotra is an ancient Ayurvedic practice, a sunrise-sunset fire ceremony. Agnihotra comes to us from the Vedas, mankind's ancient-most body of knowledge. It's not difficult for me to believe that the ancients—closer to the land, the seasons, and all the sources, undistracted by technology's blandishments, would have had holistic understandings about Nature that are denied to contemporary scientific method, and to the dominant materialism that we insist is all there is of truth.

Agnihotra involves preparing a fire of dry cow dung and ghee in a small, truncated and inverted copper pyramid. At the exact moment of sunrise and sunset (there are computer programs for this, as it varies by longitude and latitude, and of course by the day of the year), we chant a Sanskrit mantra and place a few grains of ghee-smeared rice into the fire. The practitioner sits quietly until the fire dies out, meditating, witnessing, and honoring the coming and going of the sun. There is said to be a wave of energy sweeping the landscape and biosphere, accompanying the setting sun. As we make the fire and our sacrifice, as we sing our mantra these energies swirl and intermix and heal as they flow on westward.

I had been aware of this practice since reading *Secrets of the Soil* some years ago, but had never seen the procedure done until early this year, with Gabriel in fact, when I came for my interview with him in April. He sold me a pyramid and I immediately began daily practice of Agnihotra in the greenhouse at the B-Bar Ranch when I returned, coincident with the onrush of seed sowing; there is no doubt in my mind that some of the spectacular growth of plants there was helped by Agnihotra. One quite specific instance of this comes to mind. Toward the middle of May I had about three dozen broccoli seedlings in 4-inch pots, ready to go into beds, but the only space available for them was in the unheated "back" portion of the greenhouse. (It's a measure of the harshness of the Montana Spring that I wasn't even considering transplanting Cole crops outdoors in May.) I crossed my fingers and put the plants in the ground. That night we had a hard frost with temperature about 20 degrees Fahrenheit. Those broccoli plants were prostrated by that frost, laid out flat on the ground when I inspected them in the morning; they hadn't recovered even a little in the warmth of the noonday sun. Recalling that Agnihotra ash is said to have healing qualities, during the afternoon I placed a couple of pinches of ash around each plant's stem and gently worked it into the soil. Within a week the results of this treatment were clear: 80 to 90 percent of those plants were building new leaves and by harvest time each of these was producing usable heads. Now I have seen many times before in my gardening career Cole crops affected by late frosts in the Spring, sometime completely destroyed. But never have I seen plants this badly damaged recover so nearly completely.

Since then I have used the ash from the dung-and-ghee fire to good—if not quite so spectacular—effect in greenhouse, garden, and landscape plantings. The Agnihotra effect is said in the literature to be one of counteracting atmospheric pollution—and where on the planet is any farmer or gardener working in a pollution-free place?

With Gabriel's Ayurvedic predisposition Agnihotra was taken very seriously at Tree of Life. In spite of his high-achieving schedule he almost always made it to the temple for evening Agnihotra just as the always spectacular Arizona sunset put on its show to the west of the mesa. I joined him there, evening after evening, week after week, almost always lighting the fire myself, for sometimes he was little late. I once apologized for being a bit late myself and he said, "Woody, in my world just showing up is rare enough…" Showing up and paying attention were two very strong suits in Gabriel's character.

Sometimes he brought with him patients from his practice in town. Then he would take on his guru mantle and give a little rap about the practice they were about to witness and he would do the fire himself.

Gradually my participation in this evening ritual faltered. I admit this with shame, for my relationship to spirit should have been immune to the growing rift between my boss and me. Gabriel left, as he was wont to do in January with some of his staff, for a three-week intensive fasting retreat with patients in Hawaii. When he returned at the end of the month he met me at the greenhouse where I was working alone, putting the finishing touches to it. He hadn't seen it with the covering on, the whitewash on the mudded walls and the details—the solar powered vent and blower fans and the flowforms functioning. He ignored all that and told me I was fired. That if I performed certain tasks in four weeks' time he would give me a going-away bonus of one-month's pay.

It hurts to get fired. I've sometimes thought in bravado mode: Well, I must be doing something right if I piss off everybody in authority. But looked at from outside, getting fired is a species of failure...

If so, then my response must again be to celebrate these events with Antonio Machado:

> *Last night, as I was sleeping,*
> *I dreamt—marvelous error—*
> *That I had a beehive*
> *Here inside my heart.*
> *And the golden bees*
> *Were making white combs*
> *And sweet honey*
> *From my old failures*

— Antonio Machado *Times Alone*

The sweet honey is the painful self-examination these failures precipitated, the glimmer of humility that was possible once the self-justification and pride that were done away with, at least in the hidden part of me. If gardening and farming is to be a path to enlightenment then there's no reason to expect it to be any less painful than other paths, like marriage or martial arts or yoga or monasticism.

So yes, these experiences of getting fired hurt. They forced me to look at the person I was being within the context I found myself, to examine my relationship with the rules and community mores I had, after all, signed onto when I arrived on the job. To try to figure out, feel out, why I always seemed not quite to fit into the slot designated for me in whatever organization—the ranch, the rejuvenation center, the CSA—I found myself. It's been the same pretty much throughout my life, this feeling of being on the periphery, of being off-center somehow…eccentric?

Who was right and who was wrong in these situations?…irrelevant.

> *Out there past ideas*
> *Of right doing and wrong doing*
> *There's a field.*
> *I'll meet you there.*

> —Rumi

Lessons were learned, no doubt, by all involved. Assumptions were challenged, egos deflated, flashes of insight just on the edge of intuition sometimes, when I witness myself being myself— authority-phobic, maverick, arrogant in my insistence on doing things my own way. Stubborn and guilty as charged. Once I admit all that to myself, and you see it that way…well, then, there we are.

I scrambled some to do the designated tasks—they were reasonable and part of the job and needed to be done—in two weeks. Meanwhile I went on a serious telephone job search and ultimately networked my way into a CSA farmer job in New York, south of Rochester. There, a nine-woman core group with some acreage and equipment did the math with me and I contracted with them to be farmer for a 50-share CSA that year. Oh my. Starting from scratch again.

I loaded up another truck and headed cross country on the tag end of winter.

Family scarecrow contest.

Chapter 12 – Seeking Common Ground CSA, Honeyoe Falls, New York 1997-98

On the way to New York state I stopped at Allan Balliett's place in Shepherdstown, WV. Allan and I had been friends since I was at the B Bar and, having many common interests, we'd corresponded a lot, mostly via email. At the time he was managing editor of the *Biodynamics* journal and gardened extensively in his terraced backyard. He had advised me of the position in New York, and, I'm sure, certified my *bona fides* with Deborah Denome, the point person on the core group. In a cover-your-ass email once Deb and I had come to an agreement, Allan told us he wasn't to be held responsible if the arrangement didn't work out; in other words, don't blame him if, down the road, the deal blew up in our faces. I thought at the time that this was an unnecessary precaution on his part, but of course agreed and I suppose Deb did as well.

On that visit, Allan and I made up some of the Biodynamic barrel compost preparation, the first time for either of us. Allan was well prepared with all the ingredients: fresh cow manure, ground basalt, ground eggshells, a set of the compost preparations from Josephine Porter Institute. The beauty of the barrel compost is that, when you spray it on your garden or a farm field, it's a quick stir, since it's already been potentized in the way I will describe. And it is a wonderful way to get the benefits of all of the Steiner compost preparations on the land quickly in a startup situation, before proper Biodynamic compost is ready for application. This is what Allan and I were doing, mixing and pre-potentizing the ingredients by working with hoes and shovels, stirring and mixing the ingredients in a rhythmic way in a garden cart, working at it from opposite ends, with real intent, for an hour. This was important, we knew; what we didn't know was that this batch of barrel compost would enliven for Allan a series of gardens and CSA farms for years to come.

Allan had a barrel on hand which we half buried, then dumped in the mixture to cure and incubate for a few months. This is the procedure and, as arcane and alchemical as it sounds, it works. In fact, it works because it *is* alchemy. Barrel compost comes from the work of Maria Thun in Germany, who has been doing cutting-edge research in Biodynamics for decades. Barrel Compost is called "Compound Preparation" by Hugh Courtney of JPI and "Cow Pat Pit" compost by New Zealanders.

I much appreciated seeing and working with Allan for a day or so.

I drove on to New York and once again arrived at a place of employment in a snowstorm and managed to get my truck, this time a U-haul, thoroughly stuck in the front yard of Deborah Denome's house. Deb, her husband Bob and their two children lived outside Honeyoe Falls, south of Rochester, in the far western part of New York state, on Lake Ontario. Rochester is not so much of a rust belt kind of place as other Great Lakes cities. Rather, many high tech companies have headquarters or a strong presence there: Bausch and Lomb, Eastman Kodak, Xerox. The Rochester Institute of Technology, the tenth largest private University in the country, is known for its science, computer, engineering, and arts programs. I point out these Wikipedia-like facts because they account somewhat for the makeup of the CSA which the core group had named "Seeking Common Ground." Most members of CSAs are fairly well-heeled financially, yuppies who have the disposable income to pre-purchase food months in advance of its appearance on the table, and who are willing to vote with their pocketbooks for social initiatives of a trendy kind, to take a flyer on cooperative, associative alternatives to the prevailing (i.e., linear, brutal, competitive, exploitive, masculine, conventional) way of doing things.

My first look at the scene on West Bloomfield Road revealed a disconcerting but manageable growing situation. Disconcerting because it was so raw-looking. Bob and Deb had plunked a house in the middle of hayfields on a 12-acre holding. They had moved hundreds of dump truck loads of soil from one area about 300 yards from the house site and literally built themselves a knoll and, conversely, on the other side of the property, a pond. Clever idea, I thought, even if a mighty lot of diesel fuel was expended in the service of terra-forming this place to suit. But the knoll gave the house a fine prospect and a full, walk out basement and the pond even in its first couple of years was a haven for wildlife and people. Without these features the whole 12 acres would have been flat and stark hay ground. The field on either side of the long driveway was left in hay, a buffer from the road. I had about four acres to the west and north of the house to establish a CSA garden. Bob the year before had built a large enclosed pole barn on the back side of the property. The back of the concrete-floored structure was used for storage of supplies for Bob's business, which I'll get to in a minute, and for Deb's bright yellow muscle car convertible from the 70s, her college car, under wraps. The front of the building we kept open for our produce distribution site, for one thing the core group established quickly was that this was to be a CSA where people came to the farm to pick up their produce.

Next to the barn, where there were convenient plumbing and electrical connections, we set up a travel trailer for the farmer, with a portapotty next to it.

Bob was in the portable, pump-able, potty business. As an refugee from the corporate waste management business he had shrewdly built a profitable operation, servicing a need everybody acknowledges and one that no one who is planning an event involving more than a few people wants to screw up. Deb had told me, when I asked over the phone what Bob did for a living, that he provided certain infrastructure support for large events in the area; which indeed he did.

Bob was from the start cheerful and supportive. I don't think he took the CSA thing very seriously; perhaps he knew he'd better go along with it if he knew what was good for him, marriage and family-wise. In the first couple of months Bob purchased a tractor and greenhouse for the project with his own funds, cut the utility line trenches to the greenhouse (steps from my trailer door). He hauled my travel trailer to the site, arranged for rental equipment, knew where to borrow other equipment. Bob and I liked and respected each other, and I'm grateful to him still. Whatever got accomplished in this project, it was due in large part to his initial support.

I selected a greenhouse kit similar to the one I had erected in Arizona and by the first week of April it was up and running. Deb, with blessed foresight, had arranged for a neighboring farmer to bring old horse manure from barns he was cleaning out on contract (the area, which had been home to many diversified farms, was now populated by yuppies with city jobs and pastured horses. Bright new horse barns stood alongside decrepit barns from the former days. The neighbor, whom I came to know as a good natured, helpful sort of fellow, seemed happy to convert his place to growing hay and his equipment was dedicated to moving other people's horse manure around. He was happy to dump truckloads of manure, some of it two or three years old, right where I needed it. I added the Biodynamic preparations and was glad to have the stuff, which could scarcely be called real compost but was at least good, rich organic matter.

On three sides the property was edged by hedge rows, well grown up with many large trees including apples, locust, and a rich brushy understory.

The exposure on my putative garden beds would be all sun all the time.

Meanwhile there were all of the organizational details of a new CSA to work out. Within a few days of my arrival I met for the first time with the core group women. Deb was the obvious leader of the group and the others, seven or eight of them, were co-workers of hers, past and present, or colleagues from high tech businesses she dealt with in her work. Deb, for the present, was a high-level executive in a franchise software business I never really understood. With two preschoolers at home, one of whom had had a major health challenge in the past year, Deb was planning to quit her job within a few months. She and most of the rest were mothers, or about to become mothers and several of them, I could see, were sorely stressed. But they were dedicated enough to the project they called Seeking Common Ground to make room for it in their lives.

We met every Saturday, as I recall, during the first month or two and often enough in between as we came together in various venues in the county to produce our little dog-and-pony show introducing the CSA ideal at neighborhood recruitment meetings. These followed a pattern the ladies had worked out before my arrival, with Deb as chief spokesperson and explainer, then each of the others with a five-minute riff on one or another aspect of the program: the educational events, the festivals, the work requirement, how distribution of the produce would unfold during the season. At some point in the program I was trotted out as the face behind the vegetables and I talked a bit about Biodynamics and the social, economic and agricultural innovations from Rudolf Steiner's thinking that lay behind the CSA concept.

At the first of these recruitment meetings, held in a nondescript meeting room in the building housing Deb's business, there was one sour note among all the effusions of good ideas and high purpose. I had brought along some poster-sized close-up photos of vegetables, pictures I'd taken at the B Bar with Maryann Mott's Nikon, a camera with a truly exceptional lens. I'd had had them enlarged as spectacular images, luscious and sensual. These were mounted on the wall as a backdrop for the speakers. When I called for questions at the end of my presentation, a middle-aged lady asked, with a tone I thought was slightly hostile, where those pictures had come from, implying that we must have bought them from a seed company or something. I explained that I had taken them myself in a garden I'd done a couple of years earlier, but this did little to soften the tone with which she then remarked that we were selling pie in the sky, stating that there was no way we could fulfill our promise of quantity and quality of vegetables in our first year, on ground never before farmed.

Now this lady was Elizabeth Henderson and she's a real farmer. She had an agenda when she questioned publicly whether we could do what we were promising, but it was not hateful at all. She was a CSA pioneer in the area and didn't want the CSA image tarnished by the well-intentioned but naïve (as she saw it) expectations of working-moms-on-a-mission, who hadn't a clue about farming. This was not an unreasonable point of view for Elizabeth to have. (From a SARE publication:) "Henderson has been an energetic — some might say aggressive — advocate for organic farming and CSA for almost two decades, and a second profile could be entirely devoted to her efforts to promote local, sustainable food systems. Through her books — she co-authored *The Real Dirt* and *Sharing the Harvest* — conference appearances, and grassroots organizing and advocacy, she has influenced scores of farmers, other agricultural professionals and policy makers at the local, state and national level."

What she hadn't reckoned with in the present instance was that my loyal and tightly-knit core group had been told before that they couldn't do what they were setting out to do and they were militant in their defense of their ideal. These were tech-savvy women who were used to succeeding. Nor did she know that the farmer they employed had in the last decade done half a dozen startup gardens, most in even more challenging growing conditions than here. I was confident that I could grow quite a bit of food, if not the quantities that would match price-wise what our share holders could buy in the store, but the CSA was going to make up for that, I knew, in entertainment and educational value.

We got better at this, the core group and I, and held five or six such meetings, usually attended by 30 or 40 people, doing it until we had our 50 families pledged and the funds were coming in. This was pretty much a honeymoon period for me and the core group. A few of the gals helped with seed-sowing and Deb worked hard with me to build the beds in the greenhouse. We did several Biodynamic field sprays as the spring progressed, and inoculated those horse-manure piles with compost preparations. At one point a circle of ladies cut up all the seed potatoes, more than a hundred pounds of them cut into pieces for planting.

The things these women did well, they did exceedingly well—heart-centered organization, clearly thought-out plans as, say, for an important festival, brightly executed. And they were generous: one core group lady and her husband bought the BCS rototiller of my choice, a $2,500 item, and loaned it to my use, and the garden's, for the duration. Another arranged to have a friend donate the travel trailer I needed to live in. Another had her husband donate the use of a flat bed truck.

The May Day festival, six weeks after I arrived, brought the new CSA share holders together at the farm, along with families and interested bystanders. At one point there were 40 or 50 cars parked along the drive. And there, across from the May pole was the new greenhouse, up and running and giving the promise of food to come some substantiality. Visitors could see dozens of flats and all the bed space sown with seeds, with some just germinating, a visible, tangible start.

I was harboring a shadowy and alarming suspicion that first week of May, however. As the days lengthened and warmed I thought there should be more robust growth than

I was seeing. Plants, most of them, were germinating in good time but there they sat, languishing in cotyledon or two-leaf stage—suspended animation in the greenhouse, what I came to call during the next couple of weeks the Terror of the Situation. I told Deb about this. We did multiple Biodynamic sprays. We did Agnihotra diligently. We prayed.

Meanwhile I was spending more and more time shaping garden beds with tractor and rototiller. With a two-bottom plow I started at one end of the bed (in my mind it was a growing bed; in reality it was just a sod strip) and turned two furrows toward the middle. Then, from the opposite end turning again into the middle to make a heaped long mound with a dead furrow on either side. Again and again I did this, in between spring rains, until I had several dozen beds of varying length, most 200 to 300 feet long. Later, as the sod rotted, there would be time, I hoped, to apply compost (what passed for compost that first season, old horse manure with its bedding, plus the Biodynamic preparations, and to smooth and straighten the new beds with the rototiller.

In the greenhouse the Terror of the Situation continued through the first two weeks of May until, astonishingly, the preps and sprays and Agnihotra ash took hold and the plants began to flourish. With brave confidence I announced to the core group that the first distribution of produce would take place about the first of July. Given good weather we could do 13 distributions in July, August and September, and eight or nine more in October and November. The last few of these would be weighty with root crops as this looked to me like root crop country—potatoes, beets, carrots, onions—and with exceptions this turned out to be a good prediction.

In June, Dave Peacock joined me as apprentice. Dave was 40 or so, twice the age of the average apprentice and that extra level of maturity was propitious; I had no inclination to deal with teenage hissy fits and ego stroking. Dave's attitude of calm focus and willingness to take on any task to further his goal to learn about gardening was extremely welcome and we spent two seasons together at Seeking Common Ground. Dave was a baker and former restaurant owner, a practical, sensible and cheerful fellow. We got along fine, Dave and I, spending off-work time together at a local restaurant while we did our laundry at the Laundromat and laying in weekend supplies at the Beers of the World outlet.

The first distribution of produce to the CSA shareholders on a Saturday morning at the beginning of July was a small triumph against all odds, I felt, both of organization and of growing. We were able to offer only a small bag of mixed greens, some baby carrots and a bouquet of flowers but people coming for their share could see the promise in several dozen beds running north from the barn—hundreds of staked tomato plants, rows of cole crops, lots of flowers coming on, a big patch of sturdy potato plants.

Distribution day helpers had arrived in early morning while Dave and I were bringing in the produce and we helped them to clean and present the vegetables, keep the produce cool with wet cloths and to instruct the shareholders to take their shares by weight or by the piece.

These helpers were recruited under the CSA's policy requiring eight hours of work at the farm during the season, an innovation not common in CSAs then and probably less so today. Allan Balliett had been skeptical about this from the beginning, telling me that most yuppie couples, even then in the mid-1990s, were already in a time debt, working overtime, ferrying kids between school and orthodontist and soccer practice and music lessons, and would not stand for this, but we had made it clear at the recruitment meetings that this modest amount of sweat-involvement in the project was both necessary and desirable for full participation. In general people were positive about it and many gave more than eight hours of help, happy to be out in the country and doing something practical and meaningful. I cherished these folks for their help and let them know it. In fact I was probably more social in this setting, outgoing and other-directed, than I had ever been before in my life, or since.

Each week I wrote material for a newsletter one of the core group ladies put together, with news of upcoming offerings from the garden, festivals, educational events; and these were available for members at the distribution table.

The distributions continued, on Tuesdays and Saturdays, one-half of the membership on each of the two days. People became acquainted with vegetables and greens they might never buy in the store—kale for instance, and cabbage—but there were plenty of the familiar things, lots of salad and tomatoes, peas and green beans, zucchini and, late in the season, winter squash. Meanwhile the festivals and educational events went on: St. John's at summer solstice, a Labor Day picnic, culinary and medicinal herb workshops.

I caught some flak from the core group, speaking for the members, for failing to provide sweet corn, which was a highly desirable mid-summer expectation in that part of the world. I had planted quite a bit of it in several varieties but I drew the line at hybrid varieties, the so-called "sugar enhanced" or "super sweet" kinds, stubbornly refusing to have anything to do with seeds I couldn't save for following years. Unfortunately, the untreated (with fungicides) open-pollinated varieties I chose germinated poorly in a cool spring and corn was a no-show that first season. I realized, too late, that I should have unbent on this point on the theory that the customer is always right but I had never been that fond of growing corn anyway. It's a space hog and a fertility hog in my opinion, yielding minimal nutrition for all the ground and humus it requires. Even if I was correct about this, I was wrong to be so doctrinaire about it. Deb and a couple of others from the core group met at least a part of the demand by going to a local pick-your-own sweet corn grower on a couple of distribution days to harvest ears for member families. I was grateful for that; it took me off the hook somewhat. The second season I made a much more determined effort to provide sweet corn for the folks, but still refused to plant a hybrid variety. We had a nice corn patch and a fair yield, but the corn was not what our sweet-toothed membership was used to, so the reviews were tepid. Considering the amount of work involved I was no more interested in sweet corn than I had ever been and in the years since I've only grown so-called "Indian corn," for grinding into meal.

Another Terrifying Situation developed. In this case it was about bees.

More accurately it was about the dearth of honeybees in the garden. In the first season I observed few, almost no, honeybees in the garden. Perhaps this was because of the shift in the past 20 years around Honeyoe Falls from diversified farming to rural suburbia, from food crops to hay ground and pasture.

The terror was real. The pollinators were not showing up. Toward the end of the season I presented the problem to the members in one of my newsletter columns and proposed an Adopt-a-Hive program. If several member families would agree to pay the startup costs for a single hive I would agree to manage the community apiary the following season (I'd already agreed to sign up as grower for a second season) and the families who adopted a hive could have the surplus honey for their own use or to share with others. I remember the cost was around $250 per bee colony, including the cost of the woodenware, the bees, tools, two or three bee suits and some miscellaneous items. As it came out we had 10 families agree to this scheme. Dave, always up for learning something new, was enthusiastic about it all and he had agreed to come back for a second year as my garden partner.

I'll have more to say about this Adopt-a-Hive program in a little while.

At the end of the season Dave and Deb and I attended a CSA conference in the Berkshires of Massachusetts. I've never been one to go to these things, or to get a lot out of all the flesh-pressing, catered food and elbow-rubbing, but that's just my typical anti-organization stance. I did have the chance to reacquaint myself with Trauger Groh, one of the founders of CSA in the United States, and to meet Sharon Carson, seed grower and draft horse lady from Delaware, with whom I'd corresponded for years. Then, after a train journey to New Mexico to visit family at Christmas, I traveled to Woolwine, VA, to work for the winter at Josephine Porter Institute with Hugh Courtney, one of my heroes.

(From www.jpiBiodynamics.org*): "The Josephine Porter Institute for Applied Biodynamics (JPI) is a non-profit organization dedicated to the memory of Josephine Porter. With single-minded determination, Josephine Porter carried on the work of making Biodynamic agricultural preparations in the United States for nearly 30 years. Many farmers and future farmers came to her Cherry Valley, Pennsylvania farm to learn about Biodynamic agriculture and preparation making. Hugh Courtney apprenticed with "Josie" each spring and fall season for over seven years. When she died in 1984, Hugh decided to carry on her work by creating JPI. In 1985 the Institute was established in Woolwine, Virginia and is dedicated to making Biodynamic preparations, and conducting Biodynamic agricultural research and education...As taught by Josephine Porter, the making of quality Biodynamic preparations can only be accomplished by emphasizing the spiritual, as well as the practical, aspects of their production....JPI's mission is to serve as a reliable source for Biodynamic preparations for the beginning or seasoned practitioner; as an education center for all Biodynamic practitioners as they begin to make their own preparations; and as a research venue which focuses specifically on the BD preparations."*

The few months I spent with Hugh at JPI stand out as a highlight in my gardening career. For 25 years he has single mindedly, led JPI's efforts with an unmatched dedication. The Biodynamic preparations can not strictly be called arcane, that is, the methods required to make them are not really secret (they are spelled out with quite a bit of specificity in *Secrets of the Soil* by Peter Tompkins and Christopher Bird), but they do require exact and diligent attention to detail, resourcefulness—for instance, just where *does* one obtain stag bladders and cow horns—patience and a meditative approach. These are qualities Hugh possesses in abundance. Further, making these preparations available is a labor of love for him; as far as I know he has never granted himself a salary for his work at JPI.

Hugh is a large man who customarily wears dark blue zip up coveralls; I don't believe I've ever seen him dressed otherwise. He had two careers before starting JPI, as a naval officer and as a librarian. Now, well past retirement age, he carries on with the preparation work and trains the younger people who come to JPI to gain Biodynamic experience.

I was happy to be there also in that role, building fence for the small herd of beef cattle who contributed their manure and, after butchering, their innards. The mesentery and intestines are needed in the Biodynamic method to sheath two of the preparations: the dandelion flower prep (BD#506) and chamomile flower prep (BD#503). I was also tasked by Hugh with feeding the herd, doing some carpentry in the new barn being built to house equipment for the work, cleaning up in various outbuildings.

Meanwhile I kept in touch via email with the core group in New York state. In my last meeting with them I had asked for a 50 per cent increase in salary for the second season, imagining that the group would raise the price per share as well as adding more members. Instead, I was told by email, the membership would double to 100 families and the price remain the same. I was more than a little dubious about this decision. I thought it was asking a lot of me and Dave to double the amount of produce grown, more than double it if we wanted to give more generous share portions than we'd been able to offer the first year, but I was not there to make my case in person. On the other hand we could begin immediately to sow seeds as the season started around March 15 (the greenhouse was unheated so we really couldn't start before that) without all the construction and outfitting time we'd had to spend the previous year.

A rift began to develop between me and Deb during the last couple of weeks I was at JPI. I felt she and, by extension, the core group, was asking for a lot of attention during the (unpaid) months I was away and she felt I was being rather uncooperative; probably we were both right. The upshot was that she asked and I agreed that we have a more or less formal written contract for the second season. As it turned out, though we met a couple of times with a member who was an attorney and worked out an equitable agreement, and I signed it, I never received a copy with her signature and it was never referred to again. This could have been an issue later in the year when the group reneged on the contract, but I didn't press it.

When I returned to Honeyoe Falls in mid-March Dave and I were able to get up to speed pretty quickly and within a month the greenhouse was flourishing with well-started plants in trays and beds. The bee equipment arrived and we, along with volunteers, spent many hours assembling and painting the woodenware, installing foundation, the beeswax sheets embossed with honeycomb patterns that go into each frame. There are 10 frames per super (the boxes, each of which makes up a "story" in the colony) and three or four supers per hive, so this was a big job for our 10-hive apiary.

By mid-April the garlic we had planted the previous fall, 20 pounds of individual cloves, was poking up through the mulch that protected it during the winter and we pulled the mulch back to allow the sun to warm the beds.

* * *

The sequence of seed sowing for our large garden went like this:

- Early as possible, to transplant outdoors later: onions, leeks; early as possible to stay in greenhouse for first distributions, salad crops, peas, baby carrots and beets;   Next: brassicas, early salad crops;
- Mid-April: (in the greenhouse for transplanting outdoors six weeks later) tomatoes, peppers, melons, pumpkins; outdoors as the weather and soil conditions allowed: early carrots, beets, radishes, onion sets, direct seeded salad, peas;
- Mid-May (outdoors): green beans, cucumbers, summer squash, winter squash, peas, potatoes; second succession of direct seeded salad; transplant onions, brassicas;
- Mid-May (greenhouse): sowing fall brassicas for outdoor transplanting in early July;
- Late-May, early June: corn, another succession of beans, another succession of salad crops; transplanting tomatoes, peppers, melons, pumpkins;
- August: direct seeding of fall salad crops outdoors for late distribution.

* * *

In late May I got a call that the bee nuclei I'd ordered were ready and Dave and I drove the two hours to the apiary in the Finger Lakes region to get them. There are four ways to start with bees. One way is to split a populous colony that has begun to create queen cells in preparation for swarming. Not applicable in our case as we were starting from scratch. Another is to catch a swarm, which requires a lot of luck and having on hand the correct equipment to house them. Then there are "package" bees, sent in the mail from apiaries in the South, with two or three pounds of bees in a screened box and a new queen in her own tiny cage inside. Finally, the nucleus hive method, more expensive than the others but the closest thing to a sure-fire startup method. A "nuc" is a miniature hive in itself, already a going proposition, with laying queen, eggs, baby bees in all stages (eggs, larvae, pupae, emerging bees), working bees in all their many roles, and stores of honey and pollen. It consists of five frames in their own miniature wooden bee box with I-don't-know-how-many bees in there, perhaps 4,000 or 5,000 bes. We were told to come and get the nucs at dusk, after the field bees had returned home and the beekeeper had screened off the entrances. Back at the farm the next morning we installed the nucs in the waiting hives, removing the frames from each nuc and placing them in the gap we'd left in the middle of each of the 10 hive bodies. Then there were five empty frames with foundation in each and the five fully populated frames from the nucs. This was a more or less uneventful process and Dave's first introduction to beekeeping, handling live bees. As I was sure he would be, he was brave and careful and deft.

As the warm weather settled in the bees thrived and within a month, as expected, we needed to add a second hive body to each colony, to give them room to expand, and after another month or so, the first honey-storage supers. I had been wary about promising a surplus honey crop to the Adopt-a-Hive families, but as the summer wore on the prospect began to be promising for that. Meanwhile, at one of our late member-recruitment meetings a new member approached me after I'd briefly mentioned the Adopt-a-Hive scheme in my part of the presentation and told me he was an experienced beekeeper and would be happy to help out. Wonderful! As it turned out, I was not there for the honey harvest in September, but this fellow had all the know-how and the equipment to make that happen smoothly and profitably for all concerned.

The second season distributions were somewhat more bountiful for the membership. Even though Dave and I had to harvest more than double what we'd done the previous year, we enjoyed bringing vegetables in from the garden each distribution day by the hundreds of pounds. For instance, we'd planted out 400 tomato plants, four for each family, and by August each member was taking home four or five big tomatoes each week; a couple of big peppers; green beans onions and squash a-plenty.

In mid-summer we were invited to participate as a stop in a garden tour in the Rochester community. For this event, a public relations coup, the core group ladies turned out en masse to be tour guides and I was glad for it as it took me off the hook, though I was, underneath it all, a bit irritated that these gals, most of whom never set foot in the garden from one month to the next, presumed they could do a creditable job as guides. On the morning of the event I took them around and introduced them to the garden and its points of interest. I volunteered to take groups of interested visitors to see the beehives, which were at the far side of the property on the other side of the pond and that trek, repeated several times during the day, pretty effectively took me out of the line of fire.

I admit I was harboring an attitude toward the core group. Understandably, here in the middle of the second season, the novelty had worn off, the honeymoon was over. What had been a sweet challenge in the first season turned into drudgery in the second as the administrative demands of a complex organization took their toll. Deb's leadership understandably faltered as her attention turned inward toward herself and family; she was seriously pregnant in the spring and had her third child in mid-summer. No one else was able or willing or dedicated enough to carry the burden as she had done now for 18 months. The organization was running on momentum and the dynamism of the first year waned. Nobody was learning anything new any more and duty replaced exhilaration. The core group were, after all, volunteers. The only one making any money out of this was Woody.

Meanwhile, I had been corresponding via email with Barbara Scott of Aurora Farm in British Columbia. We'd been aware of each other for a year or so, she from an article I wrote for the journal *Biodynamics* and I from her writings about Aurora's seed offerings. We were both members of Allan Balliett's BDNOW! online discussion group and our off-group messages to each other began to become very interesting to us both. At first we wrote about interesting discussions on BDNOW! Soon she was asking if I might be interested in caretaking Aurora Farm while she and her two sons took a winter journey to South Africa, where they had a friend and, possibly, relatives. I was interested in this possibility because I could already picture that there wasn't going to be a third season for me at Seeking Common Ground CSA and I needed to find a place to be. After a few weeks of correspondence that summer of 1998 the exchanges began to become more personal, then affectionate and finally—as risible as it seems to be to other folks when we tell this story 12 years later—we fell in love over the Internet—that's the way it happened. Email was supplemented by phone calls and we determined that I would head for Canada as soon as my contract with the core group was finished on November 1.

The angels, tickled as they always seem to be with the spectacle of humans in love, contrived to push that date forward.

In mid-August, just as the tomatoes were rolling in and Deb had recovered from childbirth, she called me and asked me to come up to the house that afternoon. I had a hunch what the discussion was going to be about when she told me that Valarie, one of the less-active of the core group gals but also one of the sweetest, would be there. I said to Dave, "They're going to fire me. Are you OK about taking over for the rest of the season?" Dave didn't think it was going to happen, but, confident now with most of two seasons under his belt, agreed that he could finish up for us. When I went to see Deb at the appointed time she began by citing the by now obvious fact that the core group was frustrated with me. Then she told me that the budget was strained—I'd never been privy to the money figures, but I suspected that there was some pressure from Bob to recover some of his initial investments in greenhouse and tractor—and the money was not there to pay me for my last six weeks. Further, that nobody had the energy or the inclination to do the kind of fundraising they'd done last year to cover the shortfall. Rather, the "decision had been made" to let me go six weeks early, in the middle of September. (Don't you just love passive voice?) She could not have known how much I was aching to leave early and get on with my new life at Aurora Farm, and she might have been surprised when I didn't get defensive about being fired, or try to invoke the contract. Instead, my heart singing, I agreed that this would be fine with me and, to make things easier for all concerned, I would finish up September first. I assured Deb and Valerie that Dave was fully up to speed and had agreed to take over.

In those last two weeks in New York I sent quite a few Rubbermaid tubs, mostly full of books, to Barbara as the vehicle I was driving wouldn't take the weight; with Dave I went through all the exigencies of the final distributions he would have charge of in September and October, the details of how the honey harvest would need to happen, and all the rest. He would be living in my little travel trailer there and fully in charge. Happily he could depend on help from the membership, especially from Maggie Tait, an Englishwoman whose husband was working with the Kodak Corporation for the year and an avid gardener. Maggie and I had picked beans together for many hours and she was a gem.

At four in the morning on September 2 I headed down the driveway and turned toward Niagara Falls, for I was determined to drive the whole way in Canada and experience the vastness of my adopted country, holding in my heart the whole way my new loves, Barbara Mary Victoria Scott and Aurora Farm.

Barbara M V Scott, founder and Guiding Light at Aurora Farm,
and the author.

The Compostmeister.

Barbara and helper shaping a spiral garden at Aurora.

Chapter 13 – Aurora Farm, Creston, British Columbia, Canada 1998-2005

Barbara led me to her seeds…or her seeds led me to Barbara, either is true. She came to this magical piece of land in 1989 to make a place for her two boys, toddlers then, to thrive in Nature alongside the prevailing culture but not immersed in it. With great energy, courage, imagination and entrepreneurial spirit Barbara did what needed to be done: put new roofs on the buildings, learned to live with a milk cow, created gardens where none existed before, became trained in the Biodynamic techniques, created markets among chefs and others who wanted good fresh food and finally, shaping the future of Aurora Farm, learned to grow, harvest and market garden seeds.

This, the fact that Aurora was a seed farm, was probably the major attraction for me initially (before I fell in love with the lady), as Barbara and I corresponded in the spring and summer of 1998. I was in the midst of my second season as head gardener for Seeking Common Ground CSA and was expending enormous energy—my own, my helpers', and tractor fuel—moving produce from the fields to the distribution barn. Vegetables are *heavy*. A partly-full 5-gallon bucket of tomatoes weighs 30 pounds or more, of green beans, 12 pounds. On distribution day at the height of the season, 50 families would take away some 500 to 700 pounds of vegetables and that happened twice a week.

Seeds, in contrast, are light and easy to move around. I liked that.

Another factor: If we harvested 250 pounds of vine-ripened tomatoes for distribution they had to go out of there pretty much the day they were picked or they would spoil before they could be eaten. That's one reason store bought tomatoes are so awful—they are picked green and allowed to ripen, forced to ripen, on the way to the eater. Green beans go limp, lettuce wilts, peppers pucker. Fresh produce is an ephemeral thing.

Seeds, in contrast, keep for years. Some forever.

Talking with Barbara via email I became inspired with the idea of growing seeds for the reasons I just outlined. And for another: The seed business—like so many other aspects of our culture—was becoming dominated by corporations. Even Seeds of Change, which started out as a high-minded organic seed company, had been taken over by M&M Mars, the candy conglomerate. Small family-owned seed companies with their unique flavor were rapidly going down. Those who grew all their own seeds, as Barbara did, were a tiny minority. As always, I was opting for the underdog situation by throwing in my lot with Aurora Farm.

For some years I had been saving seeds, but never with the intent of selling them and never in any systematic fashion, just as the opportunity presented itself. Barbara, on the other hand, had years before made the observations I was now making and had come to the conclusion that growing seeds on a small scale could make a viable business. In fact, she was the first person in North America to grow and market Biodynamic seeds. This lady was and is a visionary.

By noon, I'd crossed over the Niagara Falls bridge into Ontario. Lord knows what the Canadian Customs guard thought of my outfit—I'd strapped all my long-handled gardening tools to the outside of the camper—but he accepted my story that I was touring Canada for three weeks as a gardening writer and consultant. It would be several years before I'd set foot again in the U.S., and ultimately I would receive a Canadian Permanent Resident visa.

I'd determined to drive across Canada from the Niagara crossing to British Columbia, just to get the feel for the country, 30 years after I'd last spent some time there, in New Brunswick. By and large, I liked what I saw. As I drove the blue highways—no freeways for Woody—I found reasonably friendly people, though Americans are more affable, it seemed to me. For days I reveled in the immense landscapes of Ontario and the prairie provinces. By day seven on the road I had crossed into British Columbia and was within a few hours of Aurora Farm. Barbara and I had agreed that I should arrive in the morning so we'd have a few hours together before her boys, Nathan, 11, and William, 13, came home from school, so I stayed overnight in Yahk, just an hour or so away.

Aurora Farm is 31 acres of hilltop land overlooking the Creston Valley in southeastern B.C., just a few kilometers from the U.S. border at the tip of the Idaho panhandle. The view to the west is the Selkirk mountain range; to the east, the Moyies—the western ramparts of the Rockies. To the south the view ranges all the way to the Moyie mountains in Idaho; to the north Kootenay Lake recedes into the far distance. The Kootenay River winds through the valley heading north into the lake. Before it was settled and drained by white farmers in the last century the mostly marshy valley was hunting ground to the Txunaha band of First Nation people. It's one of the largest and richest agricultural areas in B.C. Potatoes and hay, orchards and dairy farms. Plus a few organic farms.

From the valley floor I drove up the long, switch backed driveway to the top of the Aurora hill and into a new life.

Barbara greeted me at the barn, as we had arranged beforehand. Serious hugs and deep gazing into each other's eyes were called for at this point. We'd already used up all the words in torrents of emails and phone calls these past months. When we came up for air she took me to the fence corner by the pasture gate to introduce me to Bessie, the home cow, her partner on the farm for all these years. It was in fact Barbara's relationship with her cow that opened her to an understanding of Biodynamics and made possible her practice of the art, for Bessie provided the raw material for compost, the manure. More than that, Bessie was a preceptor. Barbara's piece, "Bessie's Teachings at Aurora Farm" comes up later in this chapter.

I wasn't long in adapting to life at Aurora and much of our way of life came to be written up as articles for Biodynamics the mostly bi-monthly journal of the American Biodynamic Farming and Gardening Association. I'd published three articles in that journal before, about my time at the B-Bar Ranch, and about subtle energies in the greenhouse there. The first piece from Barbara's farm was

Aurora Farm: Biodynamics in a Powerful Place

The road is a first-gear climb, featuring several switchbacks, from the Kootenay River Valley floor to the hilltop where Aurora Farm lives. If you'd known where to look when you crossed the Goat River bridge a few miles earlier you'd have seen a remarkable solar house on the hilltop. Now, at close range, it's not the home that catches your eye but rather the vibrant gardens Barbara Scott has been tending for nine years.

Barbara, her sons William and Nathan, and Bessie, the home place cow, are the crew that has worked to put together the first commercial Biodynamic seed initiative in North America and a sister project, Dawn of Chiron Biodynamic herb products.

Drawn by the good energies of the people, the place, and the products, I joined the Aurora Farm endeavor in September. Aurora Farm is located in southeastern British Columbia, just across the border from the tip of the Idaho panhandle. This valley is a real banana belt, with an almost 200-day frost-free growing season, very unusual at 49 degrees North latitude. While there are some medium sized dairy operations and conventionally managed agribiz potato and hay farms in the area, there are many diversified smallholdings and small fruit orchards as well. The Kootenay Valley, glacier-gouged and flat as a floor, lies between the Selkirk and Moyie ranges of the Canadian Rockies at 2070 feet elevation. This Aurora Farm hilltop, 260 feet higher, is a monadnock—apparently escaping glacial erosion—and the rock outcroppings here seem very ancient. Everywhere you look soil is in the making, with the rock crumbling, lichens and mosses doing their work and larger plants rooting.

Barbara worked Biodynamically from the beginning, having learned of the technique from her reading. She purchased her first preparations from Magic Mountain Farm in Quebec. A year later, returning from Vancouver, she turned off Highway 3 at Oliver, B.C., in the Okanogan Valley, to buy some apples. She was attracted by a sign offering fruit "Grown by the Biodynamic Method," and met Sophie and Otto Rothe, who became her mentors. She knew she was on the right track when, as she says, "the taste of that first Biodyanmic apple just exploded in my mouth!" Sophie and Otto helped her make her first Biodynamic preparations.

On slopes and formerly bare moor-like areas, healthy conifers—pines, firs, tamarack—have sprouted in large numbers in the past nine years; the non-arable land seems to want to reforest itself since this ground has had Biodynamic care.

Barbara began, as so many of us do, in the exhausting routine of selling perishable vegetables, marketed to resorts, restaurants and sometimes door-to-door on the road that runs along Kootenay Lake. "One day," she says, "I went to the garden in early summer to harvest spinach for sale and the whole patch had bolted overnight. That got me to thinking and within a few months I was in the seed business."

Aurora Farm vegetable, flower, and herb seeds have been sold via mail order and store displays now for nine years. Last year Barbara added an Internet webpage to the marketing and information effort and 1999 will see a new initiative added: a seed CSA. Here's what the webpage says about that:

"CSA, Community Supported (or Shared) Agriculture, is a fast-growing movement in North America as more people choose to involve themselves directly with the food they consume and the farms that supply it. The Japanese word for CSA translates "Food with the farmer's face on it." There are about 1,000 CSA farms and gardens operating in the U.S. and Canada to supply quality produce to member families who purchase a share of the harvest with an initial payment that frees the farmer from arbitrary and capricious market forces. At Aurora Farm we are offering an Internet-based CSA for seeds based on similar principles: involvement of the home gardeners in the process that ends with high quality Biodynamic seeds of your choice delivered to your mailbox. Your share price supports the ongoing financial life of one of the very few Biodynamic seed initiatives in this hemisphere. It's not only money and seeds that flow in this system, but also information and goodwill. You'll learn more about

Aurora Farm, about seed saving, about Biodynamics, from our email newsletters. You'll have free consultation from us on gardening and seed issues—if we don't know the answers, we'll find out for you, or at least help you hold the questions..

In the runup to the new millennium we MUST seek new ways to cooperate, to magnify our good intentions, build community. Join us."

Herb-based tinctures and oils are a growing aspect of Aurora Farm's business. Barbara was making St. John's Wort oil long before the current popularity of this herb as a treatment for depression. "I knew intuitively that echinacea and St. John's Wort were going to be important herbs for our times," she says. "St. John's Wort has an affinity for sunlight. The flower and leaf absorb and store solar energy. We've become afraid of the sun and try to block it out for fear of skin cancer, but we mustn't lose sight of the fact that the sun is a wonderful healer and father of all life."

In addition to St. John's Wort oil and echinacea tincture, Aurora Farm produces skullcap. valerian, and peppermint tinctures and arnica oil.

Now come the devas. Twelve year old Nathan talks with them regularly and their guidance has been crucial for the farm in recent years. The landscape angel Shevacalon oversees life force activity in the whole of the valley. She hangs out, according to Nathan, underground beneath a granite boulder in the middle of Aurora Farm's main garden. Shevacalon's advice is very specific. Not long ago we were finishing up a perimeter spraying of BD#500, the horn manure preparation, at "The Peak," the highest point on the Aurora hilltop. We asked Nathan to contact the devas and tell them what we were doing. He sat down on a rock and calmly went into a trance for a couple of minutes. Then he turned to us and said, "The devas are happy we're doing the spraying, but they really don't relate to our idea of property lines...it's all the same to them, one big landscape. They say they'll answer questions now."

I asked about a water source on The Peak. We've been hoping to develop a water source higher than the house and gardens, so gravity could supply our water in the event that electricity failure made the well pump inoperable. Dowsing had shown that water was there, but where is the best place to tap it?

Nathan reported, "They say the water here on The Peak is the best and purest on the farm. Shevacalon will show you where it is. It's very close to the surface."

Shortly after, we went to the spot, at the head of a steep slope of very loose shale... tricky climbing and not a place one would go without a mission in mind. No well drilling rig could make it up here. Nathan carefully moved a few pieces of shale, reached back into a crack and came up with a handful of very moist soil. We'll develop that spring gently, with devic guidance. (END ARTICLE)

SIDEBAR (w/ photo)
WEATHER COMING IN...
SUCCESS WITH SEQUENTIAL SPRAYING

WOODY:
"Well, Nate, here it is raining
and lots of weather coming up
the valley. Whatd'ya think...are
you surprised?"
NATE:
"What's so special about that?
It's what the preparations are
supposed to do..."
WOODY:
"I guess I should take a picture,
to show people it worked."
NATE:
"You mean there's people who
know about Biodynamics who
don't believe it?"
WOODY:
"Well, Nate, some people just
need some encouragement...
wanna be in the picture?"
NATE:
"Sure!"

It's just 34 hours since we sprayed the last in a sequence of four Biodynamic spray preparations. After 11 weeks of almost unremitting drought here in southeastern British Columbia, last night we got enough light rain to dampen the ground well another shower at morning barn chores. All day I watched the clouds come in from the south; now, later in the afternoon we had a 20-minute downpour and, as I write, a light soaking rain, with thunder rolling like foothill-sized beachballs across the Kootenay valley. Tuesday afternoon (September 15) we talked with Hugh Courtney at Josephine Porter Institute and settled on the following sequential spray schedule to invoke soaking rains:

Tuesday evening: Spray BD#500 (horn manure) mixed with a good handful of Aurora Farm BD compost. Nate, William, Barbara (the compost maker), and I each stirred for 15 minutes and sprayed about half our arable ground in the falling dusk. Wednesday morning: Stirred and sprayed BD#501 (horn crystal) in a fine mist over the entire garden, orchard, compost, and landscape areas. Wednesday evening: same as Tuesday evening, on the other half of the growing area. Thursday morning: Cooked, stirred, and sprayed BD#508 (equisetum) as the last spray in the sequence.

The entire routine was underlain with prayerful, strong intent on the part of the humans involved to invoke rain...soaking rains lasting for days. We believed it would happen. We made plans to burn brush; we brought the mattress in from the deck; we used rainbarrel water in the stirring crock. From Wednesday, we accompanied the spraying with Agnihotra, the Auryvedic sunrise/sunset atmospheric clearing ritual. Wednesday night: a few drops, enough to send the deck sleepers scurrying indoors. Thursday morning: BD#508 Thursday night: light rain much of the night Friday morning: light rain at choretime Friday morning and midday: clouds rolling, rain in the distance Friday late afternoon: downpour with soaking rains following.

With gratitude, we acknowledge the work of all the non-humans involved.

(Editor's Note: the sequential spraying technique is detailed in the JPI newsletter *Applied Biodynamics*, Issue No. 6, Winter, 1993.) [End *Biodynamics in a Powerful Place*]

Next came a piece for the journal about trees. The editor was very receptive to down-to-earth, practical articles coming out of direct experience on the farm...

Trees at Aurora Farm

Chainsaw in hand, I gazed up at the charred larch trunk. Gnarled and weathered, from my viewpoint it resembled a totem pole thirty feet high. I scrutinized it for signs that it might provide wildlife habitat but I saw no woodpecker holes, no critter homes. I pulled the starter rope on the saw and dropped the tree trunk, remnant of a fire that passed through these woods maybe twenty years ago. It would again be fire- wood, this time in our cook stove.

There are blackened stumps and trunks spotted throughout the landscape and the woodlot behind the barn, some upright, some fallen and returning to the Earth, evidence that this Aurora Farm hilltop has experienced fire many times in the past. With this in mind, one of our tasks this late winter season has been to remove lower limbs from isolated conifer trees most exposed to wildfire on hillsides and grassy, brushy areas. A quick moving fire line feeding on dry grass and light woody stuff could ignite conifer needles on low branches causing the whole tree go up like a Roman candle. By taking off the branches whose low hanging tips would catch fire, we hope to save these trees. And there are hundreds of them.

It's also tree planting time. There has been a population explosion of young trees since the biodynamic preparations began to be used on this land ten years ago, with certain treeless areas seeming to want to reforest themselves. Many of the younger trees are much too close together and are ideal candidates for transplanting. So far this season we've dug and replanted two or three dozen of them—white pine and Douglas-fir—placing them mainly in places where they'll provide windbreaks for garden and pasture. In the right place and with the right care such transplanted trees grow rapidly. A line of knee-high white pine treelings put in along the north garden fence eight years ago are upwards of twelve feet high and six or seven feet broad. And a couple of weeks ago I cut forty or fifty willow twigs and put them in the greenhouse in a bucket with a few inches of water. Root and leaf buds are breaking now and they'll go out soon to fill in the windbreak line between the conifers.

Trees as Givers

"Trees are the highest and noblest plant form, whose giving is universal and unconditional." - Callum Coats

Our trees give so much. They are the soil holders and water conservers. . . they are the oxygen generators, the lungs of the planet. . . they are the regulators, protectors, cleansers of our ecosystem. When we bend ourselves beneath the conifers with pruning saw and long-handled lopper, taking those lower limbs gently, judiciously, we breathe in clean, vivified air- heady stuff.

The trees shade us and our livestock from the intense mid-day sun. Yesterday we cleared out the underbrush from beneath an Amabilis fir that graces a sharp bend in the drive-way, about halfway up the hill. . . a good stopping place for an unhurried walker; maybe a rustic bench will go there. From our woodlot behind the barn we take firewood and larch posts, and we eye coppice material—wattles and rods and wands and poles—to make trellises, shelters, and fences in the garden. Willow shoots are an obvious choice for basket making, and larger pieces are for bentwood furniture. We trim the soft tips from those conifer limbs we cut and use them for bedding in cow stalls and pig pen. Cows eat the fir needles from limbs we hang in their stalls. What trace minerals are they getting from those needles? I don't know, and the cows can't name them but they know they need them.

The windbreaks and woods provide wildlife habitat. There are owl holes, squirrel nests, woodpecker holes in the snags we leave standing for just that reason. Under sheltering conifers whitetail deer wait our storms and rest in midday, and nearby under the largest firs there are sometimes huge anthills. We are fortunate there has been no logging on this hill in recent memory, and firs measuring more than two feet at breast height are not uncommon. And then there are the nuts and fruits and berries and medicines for ourselves.

At Aurora Farm we have the following native species: Douglas-fir, Amabilis Fir, White Pine, Larch, Balm of Giliad (Populus tricocapa), Quaking Aspen (Populus tremuloides), Willow, Vine Maple, Rocky Mountain Juniper, Birch, Hazelnut, Chokecherry, Saskatoon Berry (Serviceberry) and the following brought-in species: Locust, Black Walnut, Chopaka Walnut, Butternut, Shagbark Hickory, White Oak, Sugar Maple, Horse Chestnut (Buckeye), Mulberry, Apple, Apricot, Pear, Plum, Northern Pecan

Each year a few more trees are planted in the fruit and nut orchards and in the landscape as such, for we can think of no more optimistic endeavor, no more lasting legacy, no more positive, life affirming act than that of planting trees to celebrate our lives here.

Unless they are the selfless, mighty deeds of Anna, Ferdinand Vondruska's wife. Ferdinand, a preparation maker and pioneer in Biodynamic forestry practices, and frequent contributor to the BDNOW e-mail discussion list, wrote from the headquarters of the C-Dar World Forest Team, Garibaldi Highlands, British Columbia:

> *It is wonderful to see what is happening in the forest, when my little wife is working for months out there, with a small hatchet, making forest compost. The trees towering above her and the work, truly, seems overwhelming. Nobody would do it, though there are hundreds of miles of forest around here. But there she is, making this tree (branch) compost, stacking finely chopped branches, twigs, and other stuff onto a pile. She then covers them with moss and inoculates them. You should see the elementals - it is mind- boggling. They physically pop into and out of it and can not believe that a human being has come to create an island-of-peace for them.*

> *At the beginning I was very reluctant, thinking (see: thinking and not feeling) thinking that this does not work. Too small, too insignificant, too labor intensive, too. . . whatever. Excuses, brain-cheese, me falling into the thinking trap. And then, at the bottom of that trap, seeing the light at the end of the tunnel.*

> *God, if you would know how the forests are yearning for mankind, for communication, for an embrace, for help and a story. It could make your heart*

bleed. Perhaps, there are a few people who can spare a few tears, sometimes, and shed them in the forests.

Let the trees be consulted before you take any action

Every time you breathe in
thank a tree

Let tree roots crack parking lots
at the world bank headquarters

Let loggers be druids
specially trained and rewarded
to sacrifice trees at auspicious times

Let carpenters be master artisans

Let lumber be treasured like gold

Let chainsaws be played like saxophones

Let soldiers on maneuvers plant trees

Give police and criminals a shovel
and a thousand seedlings

Let businessmen carry pocketfuls of acorns

Let newlyweds honeymoon in the woods

Walk, Don't drive

Stop reading newspapers
Stop writing poetry

Squat under a tree and tell stories

—John Wright

Biodynamic Tree Paste

Very soon it will be time to apply the biodynamic tree paste to our fruit trees. In lecture seven of the Agriculture Course, Rudolf Steiner sails forth on one of those astonishing insights that makes the reader gasp: the only part of the tree that is plant-like, he says, are the small branches that bear leaves, flowers and fruit. The great mass of trunk and large limbs is really "mounded-up soil, soil that is simply in a more living condition than the soil in which our herbaceous plants and grains are growing."

The plant-like parts, he says, "are rooted in the twigs and branches of the tree just as other plants are rooted in the Earth. " Etherically rooted. Thus, in biodynamic practice, we care for, fertilize, and cultivate the tree trunk, that mounded-up, much enlivened soil.

Ehrenfried Pfeiffer says :

> For the treatment of tree trunks, especially to keep the bark smooth, to protect it from splitting and to heal any injuries, the trees should have once a year, during winter, a coating of sticky fluid paste, up to the lightest branches. This paste consists of equal parts of clay, cow manure, and sand. Herr M. K Schwarz tells us that this coat prevents the sap from rising too soon and thus wards off danger from frosts. Pfeiffer goes on to say that he has modified this recipe by adding BD#500 (horn manure) preparation and BD#508 (equisetum); also, as remedies, he recommends an extract of oak bark (disinfection and "preventing pests from breeding"), extract of nasturtium (American blight), extract of calendula (injuries). He also suggests a routine washing and brushing of tree with BD#508 in autumn or winter.

Hugh Courtney gives the following recipe for tree paste:

> 6-9 parts betonite
>
> 23 parts BD Compound preparation (Barrel Compost)
>
> 4 units BD#500
>
> 1 part rock dust
>
> small amount of linseed or castor oil
>
> BD508, fermented, enough to make the paste liquid for brushing or spraying

Above I wrote, "Very soon it will be time. . ." and the time came even as I face the editor's deadline for this piece. Today, with moon in Sagittarius and approaching the new moon, was the day to apply tree paste. . . a bright, dry, sunny day in Blackberry Winter in the second week of March, one of the last few days of dormancy for the fruit trees. Earlier it would have been too cold and cloudy; later it would have been too late. In the greenhouse we ground native clay to a talcum consistency in a hand grinder, sifted sand through seed screens; in the kitchen we simmered equisetum tea; in the cow stalls we collected fragrant manure; we took a handful of Agnihotra ash and a good pinch of BD#500 (horn manure). After stirring the tea for twenty minutes in a three-gallon crock - in the sunshine outside the barn - we assembled all the ingredients, squeezing the lumps of manure through our fingers to make a wonderful, medium tan mud pie slurry. All morning and part of the afternoon we painted the tree paste by hand on tiny treelings and well-grown trees, paying particular attention to cracks in the bark where insect larvae hide and to wounds from our pruning a few weeks earlier. What a satisfaction, working our bespattered way through the fruit trees, leaving behind us as the paste dried gray-ghost trunks and limbs. . . what a joy to serve the trees! (End of *Trees...*)

Soon after I arrived at Aurora, Barbara and I talked of bringing in more cows. Despite several artificial insemination attempts Bessie had not "settled," i.e., had not conceived a calf, and there was the question whether she was beyond motherhood, too old for it. So perhaps a younger cow should come to the farm, preferably one who was lactating, for Barbara and her sons had been without fresh milk from Bessie for a year or more. And, as we discussed the matter, it might be that a bull would be a good idea, since neither we nor any cow we knew was much in favor of artificial breeding. Out of these conversations came the experiences I wrote about in

A Cow, A Calf, and a Bull Come to Aurora Farm

It's well past the 24th of the month and Bessie hasn't come into heat. This is likely very good news. If she has settled with a calf that means Danny Boy did his job, earned his keep. Rosebud has missed two heats, so it's likely she's pregnant too. And Dexter's doing fine, he's growing fast and he's good natured to boot. All's well in the barn at Aurora Biodynamic Farm.

++++++++++++++++++
DRAMATIS PERSONAE
Rosebud: Dexter cow, 2 years old (horned);
Dexter: Dexter steer calf, 4-5 months old (horned);
Danny Boy: Kerry bull, 2 years old (horned);
Bessie: the Aurora Farm home cow, Jersey-Brown Swiss cross maybe 12 years old, (etheric horns).
Barbara }

Woody } Herdspersons
+++++++++++++++++++

When I arrived at Aurora last autumn Bessie was due to freshen, to have her 8th or 9th calf. When two weeks went by with no sign of imminent calving, we called in the AI guy, Jordy. Jordy does artificial insemination with cows all over the Kootenay River Valley and he'd been here nine and a half months ago to impregnate Bessie with sperm from a donor bull. (How do they get that sperm anyway? You don't want to know...) After an examination that had him sweating and grunting armpit deep in Bessie's rear end, Jordy declared that he didn't believe she was pregnant at all. He was sweating and grunting not so much with the exertion, but because this was the second year in a row Bessie had failed to deliver a calf after his ministrations.

Though Jordy had some ready explanations having to do with possible mineral deficiencies in the feed and his experience that Brown Swiss sometimes take a year or two off in the middle of their calving careers, Barbara and I began talking about getting a bull. Artificial insemination, with all its advantages, seemed to us a chancy thing, and, well, a cheap shot frankly, at least from the cow's point of view. Nothing, we figured, would get Bessie back into breeding shape quicker than the hormone-pumping sight, sounds, and smell of a bull nearby, and the ensuing...er, activities. While we were at it, we figured, we'd get another milk cow with a calf by her side.

+++++++++++++++++++
DIALOGUE
Woody: "Barbara, I have an imagining of a little herd of these black cows on this hilltop...I can just see 'em here...with calves...and a bull. Wha'dya think? We need a bull here..."
Barbara: (hesitating) "We need a NICE bull here..."
+++++++++++++++++++
DIALOGUE
Woody: "Ralph what do you think about this mineral deficiency thing in the local hay?"
Ralph: "You people grow herbs here, don't you?"
Barbara: "Biodynamic herbs, Ralph..."
Ralph: "Feed 'em herbs. They'll take what minerals they need out of herbs."
+++++++++++++++++++

In *The Family Cow*, Dirk van Loon tells how he approached a local Vermont extension agent with questions about family cows, only to be told: " 'Family cow's a thing of the past...there's no money in a family cow...Only work.' He...looked me sharp in the eye and challenged, 'Fifteen tons of manure a year! You going to tell people that?' " Well, your average Biodynamic farmer sees things a little differently than the average extension agent, and that 15 tons is exactly what we're looking for. It's Bessie's manure that has brought increasing fertility, burgeoning life, to the Aurora Farm seed and kitchen gardens these past several years, via Biodynamically prepared compost. Far from being a liability on the farm balance sheet, manure is an asset. In peasant times gone by you measured a farm's wealth by the size of its manure pile.

In a rural community like ours you ask around to the neighbors when you're looking for a cow, and it didn't take long to find Ralph. Ralph keeps some cows, a few jennies, a jackass, and a huge brood sow a few miles up the Goat River from here. Ralph had for sale a Dexter cow with calf at her side, and a Kerry bull. Now the Dexter, from Ireland, is noted for its small size (Rosebud can't weigh much more than 600 pounds) and ability to do well on poor forage. Small size works for me; I'm no longer young, never was much for upper body strength, and there are times when you just have to manhandle a cow a little bit, establish your dominance. And rough forage is something we have plenty of on our 31 acres here.

Lady Loder writes of Dexters in Newman Turner's 1952 book *Herdsmanship*:

"Being a mountain breed they are extremely hardy and can with advantage be kept out of doors all the year round...they are capable of thriving on the closest grazed pasture....I found I could keep five Dexters with the food required for three Jerseys."

That sounded fine to me.

The Kerry is a little larger than the Dexter, also from Ireland, also black all over. Since we aren't committed to "purebred" stock, but rather to a breed or cross-breed which will do well here, Danny Boy, the Kerry bull, looked like a good candidate for sire of the expanded Aurora Farm herd.

Rosebud's calf, whom we named Dexter, is a sturdy little guy. I pictured him with a buddy, under yoke. We haven't yet found a suitable yoke partner for him, but we will; or we can work him alone. There's plenty of work to be done around here that would suit a small ox team: moving logs, carting manure, compost, and firewood.

DISCLAIMER

My major qualification for writing this piece is my willingness to stick my neck out, make plain that I don't know it all, but will do it anyway. There are many readers of *Biodynamics* much more qualified and experienced to be writing about cows than

I. True, I've kept a cow or two from time to time on smallholdings, and spent much of the last year of my Biodynamic training in the dairy barn, which gives me a lot more experience than most folks, but I'm not an expert stockman by any means. I'm a guy who likes cows, the routines of milking and mucking, and, of course, manure.

Not just any manure. I've used horse, but not happily; I've messed with goat and rabbit and worm manure, and with purely plant-based compost; but I've always come back to cows. In 1921, speaking to a group at the Research Institute in Stuttgart, Rudolf Steiner said, "In point of fact, the only really healthy fertilizer is cattle manure....the only ideal fertilizer....This must be the basic principle." (*Agriculture*, pp 244-245}

In the Lecture Four of the Agriculture Course, he elaborates:

> *What is this manure in reality? It is outer nourishment that has entered into the animal, that has been absorbed to some extent and give occasion for the dynamic development of forces within the organism, but which has then been excreted, rather than serving primarily to enrich the animal with substance. In passing through the organism, however, it has become pervaded with astral and etheric activity. It has become permeated with nitrogen-bearing and oxygen-bearing forces. The mass that emerges as manure is impregnated with all this. (Agriculture, p 71)*

He then goes on to present the rationale and method for making Biodynamic Preparation #500, Horn Manure, perhaps the most significant and far reaching passage in the lectures, arguably the foundation of fertility management in Biodynamic agriculture.

With this in mind, the mucking out of stalls becomes less a burdensome chore and more a ritual in service to the Planet, a reversal of the trend toward extractive, poisonous agriculture. Driving a wheelbarrow of manure and soiled bedding to a compost pile and offloading it become a celebration of life, an affirmation.

For the first time in 10 years now I have the chance to build a manure pile by hand. The winter manure from four large animals—-150 pounds a day, 3 cubic feet more or less—is a meaningful but not an overwhelming amount. Unfrozen and with the right moisture content, it's a malleable material and, forkful by forkful, I can construct a nicely shaped pile outside the south end of the barn, six feet wide or a little more at the base, sloping up to about shoulder high. I've used dump trucks and front end loaders and manure spreaders to make piles, but this is the best—forking out of a wheelbarrow, sculpting to a pleasing and efficient shape, retrieving the odd turd that rolls down the side and finding a place for it in the grand scheme of things, with a sense of its preciousness. Before the Spring Equinox this pile will be ready for the

Biodynamic compost preparations, another ceremony evoking fertility. We'll apply a skin to it then, a thatch of waste hay that will protect it as it matures, and when we put the gardens to bed next fall, this is the compost we'll use, gratefully, with thanks to the animals and the forces behind the preps.

"Practice Conscious Love on animals first...they are more responsive..."

—G. I. Gurdjieff

We *owe* these animals, comfort, feed, bedding, and good water. We owe them our attention and our love. We owe them thoughtful consideration.

Sure it takes a lot of time. For us, with four animals, it takes about an hour to do the chores that need to be done, twice a day, every day. That's not counting the occasional morning's work fixing fence, repairing stall doors or mangers, and those other odd little time consuming jobs that crop up every few days around the barn and pastures. I'm guessing that nine of 10 readers—at least among those who don't keep large animals—are saying to themselves, "Well, that's too much time; after all, TIME = MONEY." I strive never to criticize what someone else has to do to earn a living, but the equation around here is more like, TIME = FERTILITY = RIGHT LIVELIHOOD. The best investment we can possibly make toward a sustainable productive life is in the fertility of our land. Economy of scale? We're not interested in eight cows, even though eight would be scarcely more trouble or time; our interest rather is in the number of cows this land can support, and we're still finding out what that number is. (End *Cow, Calf and a Bull*)

Cow, Calf, and Bull...Update from Aurora Farm

Our two cows freshened in quick succession, 10 days apart. Rosebud gave us Danny Boy II, a bull calf; Bessie, the home cow, presented a beautiful sorrel heifer we named Venus, born on Friday the 13th of August. For the first time in three years we have home-grown milk on hand and the barn is burgeoning with new life.

Danny Boy, the bull, is no longer with us...or rather, he's with us but pretty thoroughly cooled down in the freezer. We bless and thank him every time we eat a hamburger, or walk by the compost piles to which he contributed so mightily, or smile as his namesake, almost a month old now, scampers about the North Field. We celebrate Danny Boy when we lead Venus ahead of her mom from the stall to the South Field...the likeliest looking heifer you've ever seen...sweet, calm, gorgeous, feisty on the lead rope. And we most especially exalt Danny Boy because he brought Bessie back on line as a mother. Our instincts told us that after two barren years of failed artificial insemination pregnancies that the bull's presence would get her hormones flowing...it's a juicy, lively thing to have a bull around and the calves are the proof of the breeding that took place two or three weeks after Danny Boy came to Aurora last fall. We honor the bull too whenever we clack his shinbones together for music making at the sweat lodge fire. We sent his hide to the tannery and his 8 hoof-halves, ebony shells shaped horn-like, mollusk-like, hold crystals on the windowsill and may be used sometime to make Biodynamic preparation #500, if I can ever find the reference for the procedure.

I ended my last piece on cow-keeping at Aurora Farm with the statement: "our interest is in the number of cows this land needs, and we're still finding out what that number is." (*Biodynamics* #222) The story of why Danny Boy went out of here belly up in the back of the butcher's truck is one of those bittersweet reminders that prudent planning in farm life should not assume the best weather, or even normal weather. We had a dry, cool spring this year in southeastern British Columbia and the pasture grass never came on as it would have in a year of normal rainfall. As summer approached, the normal late afternoon thunder storms were many fewer than usual and our two pastures were slim pickings indeed for the two pregnant cows, and for Danny Boy himself and Dexter, the fast growing steer calf. By mid-June, the bull, who'd been content to stay behind a single strand of electric fence, began getting out, seeking better feed out in the landscape...and the gardens. Now coaxing a hungry, formidably-horned 1,200 pound bull back behind his fence is challenging fun the first couple of times, but only the first couple. While Danny Boy was not a fractious animal and on the contrary was very nice—for a bull—the sight of him kicking up his heels, pleased as punch that he was where he oughtn't to be, was a daunting one. Equally problematic was the sight of the massive dents his platter-sized hooves could make in a soft, well composted garden bed. We had three options: feed him hay through the rest of the summer and on through the fall and winter, with no guarantee that he still wouldn't go looking for more luxuriant stuff; sell him for less than he was worth; or slaughter him. Unhappily, economics dictated the latter choice.

Feed

We are striving for a self-contained farm organism here. We grow a very high proportion of the food we humans eat; we grow practically all our own seeds; we cut firewood as our main fuel source; the astounding fertility of the gardens comes from 10 years of BD composting, mainly with cow manure and garden wastes. We need no further inputs for the garden.

The next step for us is to stop buying in grain for chickens, pig, and milk cows. In the quantities we have to deal with, we can do this with human powered-methods. Hay will be more of a problem. Two or three adult bovines will eat a big bale of high-quality hay every day during a long winter off pasture...180 bales, say, or 6+ tons. Currently, we have to buy this in from neighbors. This year we are experimenting with mangles, the huge fodder beets that have been more popular in Europe than in North America, not so much as a substitute for hay, but rather as a supplement, mineral-wise. So far so good—they seem to grow very well here; chopped into chewable chunks, they will make an excellent feed, especially in late winter.

Scythe-cut grass and clover from road edges and pastures (in a good year), stored loose in the barn or stacked in the field, is a definite possibility to minimize the quantity of bought-in baled hay. We haven't been able to do it this year, but we will be cutting a good deal of dry stuff later in the season for winter stall bedding.

Other supplements for the animals include wheelbarrow after wheelbarrow of succulent summer weeds and thinnings from the garden; cull garlic, chopped, roasted and ground up as an immune-building garnish for their grain; homemade apple cider vinegar; various herbs. We grow seeds for our livelihood, so there are large quantities of dry seedstalks from herbs, vegetables, and flowers that go to the animals as well.

SHELTER

The first building to be constructed on this hilltop by the architect who purchased the land 22 years ago was the barn, and it's a barn to die for. The guy knew how to do it right: concrete floors, wide doors, roomy stalls, plenty of ventilation, a wonderful drive-in, roofed dogtrot between the north and south sides for hay and tool storage. The center of farm life here, this well-laid-out, comfortable barn is home for the animals, working space for our seedwork, curing space for garlic and onions.

In one pasture we have a sun and wind shelter, an open shed with roof and two walls; in the other there are trees for shade and windbreak.

Water is available in both pastures, pumped now from a deep well but by year's end gravity-fed from a spring.

What a joy it is to have fresh, whole milk! When I was a child, a city kid with farming aspirations even then, I spent a few weeks on a friend's farm and there drank home-grown milk. When I came home, I just could not stomach the store-bought version. My parents compromised on chocolate milk, which I would drink, but I stopped consuming milk entirely as an adult until I came to Kimberton Hills Camphill Village where I had my training in Biodynamics and where everyone consumes fresh, unpasteurized dairy products in quantity.

Conventional thinking in nutrition says that adults don't need milk, and the medical establishment hoopla over cholesterol makes consumption of dairy products a guilt-ridden indulgence. We ignore the conventional wisdom around here and drink milk with meals and snacks and take cream with coffee. We make and happily consume tapioca, soft cheese, hard cheese, yogurt, and butter. Here's some of our rationale:

Stephen Byrnes is a nutritionist and naturopathic doctor. He wrote an article, "Politically Incorrect: The Neglected Nutritional Research of Dr. Weston Price, DDS" in which he says that "Price noted that all peoples had a predilection and dietary pull towards foods rich in the fat-soluble vitamins. Price considered butter from pasture-fed cows, rich in these vitamins as well as minerals, to be the premiere health food. Fat-soluble vitamins are found in fats of animal origin, like butter, cream, lard, and tallow, as well as in organ meats." Price's research focused on dietary habits of the world's most healthy indigenous people. The details are available from the Price-Pottenger Foundation, and from Sally Fallon's book *Nourishing Traditions*.

Danny Boy Goes Down

Ross, the butcher, arrived at our place at 6:15 AM, about the time Danny Boy and Rosebud are let out of the barn. We opted to have a professional's help with this job both because the bull was so large and because it was high summer, not the usual time for on-farm butchering. The carcass would need to be cooled down quickly. But the killing was not something I was going to offload on anyone else. I entered the north side of the barn and opened the big door to the outside, talking quietly to him all the while. As always, he was happy to go out in the morning air and headed toward the flake of hay I'd put out by the fence. He didn't notice that Rosie wasn't with him. I had a wordless, regretful moment with him as I raised the 20 gauge shotgun, eased the hammer back, and sighted along the barrel.

Ross said later that he'd moved his head a bit to the side as he looked up at me and that's why the slug hit his forehead a little off center, but it might have been a tear in my eye. It was about the hardest thing I've ever done on a farm.

Epilogue

Venus, the heifer, will replace Bessie when she retires in a year or two to live out the rest of her life here free of mothering chores. Danny Boy II will make a yoke partner with Dexter and we'll have our ox team. Rosebud, who's never been happy here where she can't be boss cow, is up for sale. (End *Update*)

During my second winter on the farm I wrote a piece for *Acres USA* which tried to address questions of proper or reasonable scale for a family farm. In an era when all of the pressures of the agricultural markets and government subsidies favor the mega-farm, monocropping and industrialization of agriculture, was it even possible to make a living on a diverse family farm? I made my case and the reader is free to judge whether it was merely a wishful one.

Enough Is Enough: Right Livelihood at Auora Farm

> *"Steiner was himself asked about size of farms and so on and said clearly that if he were a farmer, he would farm the smallest possible acreage so as to get it right, do the most good, etc."*

> —from a BDNOW! posting by Andrew Lorand.

Scale is like timing—sometimes timing is everything and sometimes scale is everything.

I'm not advocating necessarily for small scale here, rather for right scale.

People like Gene Logsden and Wendell Berry can wax philosophical about abstractions like right scale much better than I. My way is to talk of direct experience, to present examples showing how right scale translates to right livelihood for us at Aurora farm. If it's small scale too, then we're in the same camp as the Amish farmer Berry writes about, who, when asked why he didn't farm more land since he was so

166

prosperous, said, "I guess I'm just not smart enough to farm more land than this…not and do it well."

These slices of our life are not meant to be instructive. Farms and farmers are too individual to admit of direct transfer of one farmer's methods—much less of feelings and understandings—to another's farm. The examples and experiences I recount are meant to be evocative; the word means "to summon or to call forth; to call to mind or memory; to create anew, especially by means of the imagination." Evocative, perhaps of what the reader already knows.

Our Farm Is So Small…

That I spent part of a morning today hand-cleaning milk thistle seed, putting it up for drying and packaging. It took maybe an hour of prickly work to garner enough seed to fill, probably, this year's demand—a dozen or two packages. That's how small this operation is. Now, milk thistle is a comparatively low-demand item.

On the other hand, it took maybe 100 person-hours to grow the plants and harvest and process the tomato seed we need for sale this year—1,000 packets of eight different varieties. Not much by Burpee or Seeds of Change standards, but plenty for us. We don't want to get much bigger or richer, we just want to do it right.

Our Farm Is So Small…

That our first chore this morning was finally to get Danny Boy II into his halter, the blue one with bells. He'd fought us horn and hoof and wildly twisting contortions when we'd tried to get his mom's old halter on him. It was only when we decided to take Venus's halter and put it on him that he accepted the idea. But that first time the buckle was twisted and it had to come off again. That was a chance to glue holiday bells on it. And Venus's new halter has bells too.

Venus and DB II have been together for most of a month now and they're so sweet with each other. Weaned at the same time, they comfort each other over loss of their mom's teats. It's precious to see them lying side by side, hips touching, chewing their cuds, half-sleepy, half-watchful, ready to jump up and investigate any change in the surroundings—a leaf blowing, the herd dog Lotus passing by on some errand, the outside door closing up at the house.

They're like bookends, those two, born 10 days apart in late summer. DB II, half Dexter and half Kerry, is black as the gates of hell. Venus is sorrel, going darker as she approaches heiferhood. They're never more than a yard apart, it seems, awake or asleep. We've lavished a lot of time on these calves during the past four months and expect to expand on that considerably, because we like to do it, because we'll add value to calves and farm thereby. But does it make economic sense to have spent this many hours dealing with these calves? And to contemplate spending even more? Not if you count the time and figure that time equals money. But why would we count the time if our aim is right livelihood (support…substance…subsistence…vocation") We don't raise cows for money, we raise them for fertility. The Biodynamic compost we make with cow manure is like black gold.

Our Farm Is So Small…

That, by hand I grind the grain for the 30 Aracuana chicks we have brooding in the workshop. They get barley, rice, wheat, buckwheat, rye, corn and some eggshells, and a bit of Azomite in there. I was grinding, just cracking the kernels, not grinding to flour, using the Molina hand grinder set up at the end of the storage area. It's a bit strenuous, and my body gets into the rhythm of the thing, smelling the warm meal, and I become aware of a memory evoked here. I'd done just this same thing before, or something very much like it , in a peasant lifetime. I had the same sensation, the same feelings. In Bohemia? Or Alsace? I had forefathers, great-great grandmothers in both those places. Ancestors. I began to be able to tap the instinctive wisdom, coming down from them. I think from my mother's side.

Rudolf Steiner says, "Before any science of these things existed, everything people did was guided by instinct, and those instincts were often quite specific and reliable… Remarkable wisdom they expressed in clear and simple terms."

After 35 years of taking care of chickens, I have figured out the feed formula for baby chicks; whatever you've got on hand in the way of grains, assuming your pantry is well equipped, ground to suit the birds' age. Minerals in the form of clay, garden soil and compost. Celtic salt, Azomite, alfalfa flakes hand screened from the cow's hay, fresh clover. Equisetum tea (for feather-promoting silica) chamomile tea (to mellow them out), some suet and fat scraps from time to time. Lots of variety. Don't let them get bored or they're liable to start pecking each other.

I didn't get that formula from an extension handbook or from Joel Salatin. It got it from my ancestors.

Another memory evoked in recent weeks: I was milking Bessie, saying those soft soothing things I say to relax the scene and encourage her to let down her milk: "So Bess, easy girl, that's good, now Bess, let go. Whoa now, moveyourdamnfoot, this is good, now Darlin', easy, almost done…" and Bessie's response comes in soft groans as she snuffs the hay and licks up the last of her grain ration. There are soft groans and rumen rumbles and gassy sounds at my right ear. My hands seek out the rhythm that's there in the milk flow, and my body rocks in time with feel and sound of spurts into the steel bucket. There's the heady, warm smell of milk in my nostrils. Here we go again, a certain rhythm, a certain balanced effort, a particular fragrance, together calling out a remembrance of having done this before, said these things, felt this comfort hunkered against the cow, and pleading with her, pleasing her, courting and cajoling her to get the milk to come freely and with ease. What a warm knowing it is, how to care for a cow and be cared for by her—and the knowing is there underneath, in my cells.

Similar memories arise again and again in the daily work, always when the rhythm, the effort and an aroma of some sort set off something deep inside; in digging a bed or stirring Biodynamic preparations or hoeing a long row. Not just a deju vu feeling, but a knowing too, a confidence, a connectedness.

Our Farm Is So Small...

We are the customer-service people, the seed acquirers, the CEO, the CIO, the CFO, the growers, harvesters, manure shovelers, bed diggers, long-range planners, soothsayers, herdspersons, firewood rustlers, egg gatherers, chroniclers, chefs, errand runners and apprentices—the same two people, with a bit of help here and there.

By the day and by the season, we dance through these and other roles, with each other, by ourselves, on the telephone, with visitors, over the Internet, in the kitchen, the seed room, at the barn, in the woods. There are a hundred decisions to be made in a day, domestically, agriculturally, business-wise. Much of the time—when we are most in the flow of things and operating harmoniously—our work is guided by memories, intuition from outside our ego-selves. If we can get out of our own way, solutions appear, questions are answered, and the way to do what needs to be done becomes clearer. I claim no special status in this regard, since a century or two ago most human lives were led along these lines, the unbroken, unspoken memory of the ancestors informing the actions of the descendants. It was the commonest of things, this feeling that you already know how to do something, or how to be, in your heart, toward the land, the soil, the other creatures. We sought and seek our power from the Earth, not from culture. Sometimes we ask outright for guidance; sometimes the guidance is there unbidden, in our hands. The juice of our peasant heritage flows most freely there, in our hands.

Regard Steiner's wistful evocations of the peasant intelligence. You know he already has seen, in grief-stricken moments of clairvoyance, how the capitalist dollar mindset debases ancestral knowledge and crams modern ideas into its place; how corporate propaganda supplants ancient and true values with gadgets, rape of spirit and wage slavery; how slogans like "economy of scale," "the bottom line," bigger is better," and "time is money," become unexamined axioms underlying the industrialization of agriculture, the despoiling of land, the bureaucratization of experience, and the perversion of education.

But memory remains. We operate under what Andrew Lorand calls "a metaphor and encouragement for thoroughness, depth and presence of personal, spiritual involvement over the more industrialized version of more is better..." Our ancestors were pretty much ignorant of affairs outside their own village or region, but within the circumference of their attention they were all "depth and presence." Depth and presence and faithfulness and devotion and reverence for all life. More and more, at Aurora Farm, in our daily routine of observation, attention to detail, care for rooted brothers and four-footed sisters and the soil that nourishes us all, we are gifted to live by light of memory, shedding some of the baggage of the present.

"Bigger is better" becomes "enough is enough." (End Article)

Still pondering the economic question and focusing down on the family level, I wrote "Bessie has Always Paid Her Way at Aurora Farm." (as published in *Biodynamics*, journal of the Biodynamic Association)

Bessie Has Always Paid Her Way at Aurora Farm

When I went to let Bessie into the barn tonight, she was standing right at the gate and the strobing red light from the solar fence charger, mounted on the latch post, was reflected in her great brown eyes. No reproach in those eyes for all the standing and waiting she'd done while I got her stall ready. Rolled grain, three kinds, with apple cider vinegar and a dusting of roasted garlic powder...a fresh flake of hay to go with what she had picked over during milking this morning, two buckets of water from hose coiled in the water tank closet. Tonight's a little shorter night than those early in January and back around the solstice...yet long enough for Bessie to pretty much clean up anything edible there in her stall—odd bits of hay and grain and alfalfa flakes that sift through her feed table. In the morning—we don't much believe in early, early milking around here—after daylight, when Barbara and I have had coffee and bundled up for morning chores, Bessie will be there at her stall gate. Again no reproach; she just lets you know that she's been waiting for a while. Another scoop and another squirt and dusting and a honkin' big flake of alfalfa hay to hold her interest during milking. A short shank with a snap link tethers her to the table for her breakfast, while I clean out the accumulation of cowpies. She's likely sleep-squashed one or two of them. A five-gallon bucket of sawdust gets spread out under her business end, and I turn to the wash bucket and udder rags.

"Whoa, Bess. Washin' up." I have to hold her tail out of the way, but I talk to her before I do. "Eh, girl, warm water." Last thing to remember before leaving the house is to fill the wash bucket with hot water. Scrubbing her udder I feel the old girl letting down the milk, front quarters more taut than the rear. The udder swells twice its size before I've finished the washing.

"Little bucket now, Bess." The first bit of milk goes into the pet bucket for the dog and maybe sometimes a barn cat. I put it down for the animals and come back to Bessie with the stainless steel, this-means-business bucket. "Big bucket, Bess, stand steady." Now Bessie hasn't once stopped snuffling and tonguing and chewing during all these ministrations, but her eyes see everything happening except directly behind her. Certainly she's been aware of me coming in and out of her field, but she doesn't have to attend to anything at all except her feeding, unless I do something out of the ordinary, which seldom happens. It's my job as proprietor of this one-cow dairy to keep the routine to Bessie's liking for things to go smoothly and predictably. Bessie rewards us by keeping her tail more or less quiet and stepping nicely aside with a rear hoof when required. And of course by letting that milk down easily.

Today, January 13, is Venus's five month birthday, so we're entering into Bessie's sixth month of lactation. For the first three months Bessie's primary job was nourishing Venus toward heifer-hood. We milked her mornings, after we separated mom and calf at nights when the calf was a month old. During the day they roamed the pasture together and Venus nursed at will. At night they went into adjacent stalls and Venus had to wait until morning. There was some milk for the family during that next two months, but Bessie held much of the cream for the calf.

So the first item on the paying-her-way balance sheet is: 1) Venus: as a bred heifer in a year or so, worth at least $1,000; she is a russet/henna beauty and if she has all the good-nature of her pa, Danny Boy, and the productivity of her ma, Bessie, she'll be worth even more to us. 2) And then there's that milk for the family for the first three months—one gallon a day for ninety days—$450 at five dollars a gallon (fresh, whole, raw milk for table use, cooking, cheese, yogurt, cream).

The ninety-day point in the lactation was when we separated Venus and Bessie formally. The just-weaned calf joined Danny Boy II, her half-brother bull calf who's just ten days older. The milk fat calves go into winter on a bit of grain and plenty of hay, comforting each other over loss of mom's teats.

After the calf is weaned, the quantity of milk Bessie provides the family doesn't change much. It's winter now and there's little in the pasture for her. She too is getting by on hay and a little grain. But the quality of the milk goes way up. Since Bessie in no longer holding back cream for the calf, we now find four to five inches of cream at the top of the wide-mouth gallon jug in the fridge. Add to this two more months of cream-rich milk, gallon a day for sixty days—$300.

3) Then there's the manure. The daily deposits of manure Bessie leaves for us add up. In winter, when she's in her stall from dusk to well past dawn, about half a wheelbarrow goes out from her stall each day; half a wheelbarrow of manure and sodden bedding. Say two cubic feet every day, or sixty cubic feet a month—two yards. Twenty-four yards in a year's time for Bessie spends nights in her stall in spring and summer too, and we often clean up the heavily used pasture corner by the water tank and her shelter as well. That's a decent-sized compost pile, say twenty feet long, six to eight feet at the base and four to five feet high. Twice a year her stall gets cleaned right down to the concrete, though we leave a foot or so of the trampled, soaked bedding and manure around the edges as microbiological "starter." This adds up to another good-sized compost pile. We're talking TONS of compost from one cow toward the fertility of Aurora Farm gardens; an arbitrary figure is $2,000.

4) Now Bessie is getting on in years. She's what I'd call a matron cow, not yet finished with calf rearing, perhaps, but she's already mothered six calves in her eight years at Aurora Farm—Whiteface, Rose, Buffy, Easter, Blue, Venus—six calves at an average $500 value, divided by eight, since we're going to add these items up on a per year basis. That's $375 per year in calves (a low estimate).

5) Now that we're into the sixth month of lactation we can still expect a considerable quantity of milk, diminishing to be sure, over the next three or four months, say one-half gallon a day for ninety days at five dollars per gallon: $220.

GRAND TOTAL: $4,345 this year.

Holy Moley, Woody's cooking the books! Is he trying to say his milk cow makes him four grand a year? One cow?

Okay, there are costs, but fewer than you'll believe. We bought in $300-$400 worth of hay this year, for Bessie, the two calves, and for a while Danny Boy II's mom. We buy in forty dollars worth of grain maybe ten times a year for feeding calves, chickens, and sometimes a pig, as well as Bessie. Her share of feed costs—maybe $500. There are no other costs. No vet bills. Bessie gets pasture, hay, grain, supplemented by garden wastes, herbs, garlic, cider vinegar, Agnihotra ash, a little Azomite.

Here's the killer question: what about LABOR? You're spending as much time with that cow, putting her in, taking her out, washing her bag, milking her, fixing fence, hauling manure, as most men do with their wives. Count the labor in there.

All right. Total labor per day, about an hour and a half, all told. That's seven days a week and 365 days a year. Call it 600 hours. But don't tell me I could make seven dollars an hour clerking down at the 7-11 and therefore the cow business is a wash.

You see, I apply Amish economics here. For example, where a cost accountant would charge against the farm to time, fuel and equipment wear expended, say, in hauling manure, the Amishman considers the manure spreading a benefit to the farm; the soil in improved for next season's crops, the horses get exercise and training, and the driver gets fresh air and a look at the field.

I don't consider the labor expended for Bessie's care as a commodity, rather, it's a service. It's a service to the farm, to Biodynamics, to the planet. As a service, it's my choice to render it and no cost accounting can touch it. The exercise keeps me healthy; the morning and evening rhythm is grounding; the attention to detail sharpens my perceptions; the nurturing character of the work allows me to express my feminine side. I am a better person for taking care of animals, and who will account for that? Who will tell me what that is worth?

Leaving aside the financial figures, we come to the intangibles, the interesting stuff. In a way, Bessie represents, calls forth the spirit of the place, the farm individuality. In her single-minded metabolic nature she *is* the biosystem around here. Her energy, her presence, her connection to the great cow oversoul, knits the place together. As she grazes or chews her cud, she's aware of everything going on, seldom reacting with more than a looking up in the direction of the disturbance. But she knows. When the dogs got into the poison a clueless neighbor set out for coyotes, Bessie knew. When the bull was slaughtered Bessie knew.

Bessie's calm being, her knowing, permeates every corner of the farm and, through her compost, enlivens especially the garden beds. When we contemplate more that the material details of our daily lives, when we take time to consider the layers and webs of existence in which we are enmeshed, when we remember what it's like to be a peasant and to be possessed of the instinctive wisdom Rudolf Steiner spoke of so wistfully, we are grateful to know Bessie and to have our lives enriched by her. (End Bessie Has Always Paid Her Way)

Barbara added her voice to the journal with "Bessie's Teachings at Aurora Farm."

Bessie's Teachings at Aurora Farm

Barbara M V Scott, MSc

Morning Chores. "Okay Lotus let's go to the barn for Bessie. Oops, I mean Bessie's calf, er, I mean Venus." Lotus , the little Aussie girl dog doesn't respond any differently even though Bessie is no longer physically present at Aurora Farm. All the animals seem to respond and act on a soul level with all the kindred spirits. And on a soul level it was and is with Bessie, Aurora's home cow for many years now. She came to us with her grounded manner of being and departed in that same manner, steadfast and always with much grace and ease toward her responsibilities for the land and all those she looked after. One of the biggest hearts and greatest beings I have ever known. She incarnated as a cow and displayed the intelligence and sensitivity of many a great being.

I had never had a cow, only smaller animals: dogs, cats, chickens, rabbits, goats and domestic birds; the idea of a milk cow was somewhat formidable. Before Aurora Farm I had spent many years in the wilds of Vancouver Island studying Timber Wolves to fulfill credits for a Master's in Wildlife Biology. Although that program was associated with the ivory tower, spending timeless time in the deep woods helped shut down my thinking brain and let me open to the heart-mind and intuitive wisdom truly inherent in the hunter-gatherer phase of human evolution. So the idea of going from a hunter-gatherer existence to agriculture related activities with a cow was somewhat foreign and seemingly like a brand new lifetime. One doesn't often here mention of the Horned Goddess in Evolution courses either, so that connection was still to be made.

One of the requirements to become certified BD farm was to have a cow and having worked away at the compost with a cross-section of chicken, sheep, pig and goat manure, having had relatively good results, there was still a voice inside that said "something is missing here". So when a friend and local Mennonite farmer said "You need a cow." I instantly asked, "Where can we get one?"

And that is how Bessie came to us. A three way trade—Walter, the Mennonite farmer got a windmill we had acquired for our homestead up North, Keith, another farmer got a small tractor, and we had Bessie came to Aurora Farm. She had been roaming with a herd of range cattle and she arrived without a name and no record of her age or breed. Coming to Aurora with no labels and fitting into no pigeonholes, wonderful! (We determined later that she was a Jersey-Brown Swiss cross.)

On a warm July day the horse trailer carrying our first cow winds up the switch back drive. I wait at the barn in anticipation and with some trepidation. I had prepared a large stall in the barn and had the newly made halter shank hanging conveniently for her arrival. The horse trailer stops in front of the barn and I notice first off that she had spattered the back of the trailer quite thoroughly with dung and I flashed, "What am I getting into here?"

Out she comes and I take her on her right side by the halter. I am at ease and my heart is drumming. I feel for an instant through the cow/halter/human hand contact that a bolt of gentle lightning has passed through me. There are no words; the feeling is one of grace and ease and that this cow and I have been together at another time. There is gratitude from her, and total adoration and opennesss from me. My teacher in animal form has arrived at Aurora and I walk her into her stall to introduce her to the first of the "patterns that connect".(1)

Up to the house, Nathan and William are waiting, having watched her arrival from a distance. "Come and see the cow Boys," I call, "she is a real beauty." Down we go to see the cow in the stall. Nathan was probably 5 years and William 7. " Oh, she's BIG," says Nathan. William stands silent, a boy of few words with tremendous sensitivity. "What do you think, William?" I ask. "Yea, Big". And begins to head out of the barn. Off to the sandbox. I let Bessie out in the field that has been fenced for her. Easy, everything is easy with Bess. It is like she has come home to help me discover that homeless, nomadic part of myself.

Cow days and cow nights , morning and evening chores are the best and most sacred parts of my day. "Good morning, Bess." I utter as I approach the south barn side door. "Oooahh," she responds. Like a morning snapshot Bessie is hanging her head over her stall gate…those soft Jersey almond eyes! My heart leaps and I am at once contented and feel the ground of my own being.

Grain with powdered garlic and apple cider vinegar is given and she always says thank you with her being. When there is grass outside the barn she goes out there to feed while I clean her stall and receive my morning farm duties. Who is transmitting the daily duties? It appears to be a cooperative effort. Through listening and receiving the inner workings of her manure into the heart mind I begin to Show-up, Pay Attention, Tell the Truth and Be Open to Outcome. I'm in life/ land skills training and the teacher, through the land, is Bessie. Who would have thunk it? Is this really happening to me? How will I ever tell anyone what is really going on here and that I (we) actually know nothing and it is the best place to be. Shut off your mind Barbara and just get still and ready to receive the incoming information. She's out in the pasture and you have work to do.

My first attempt at "showing" Bessie something resulted in more "humility training." I take her on the halter shank to explain the electric fence to her. As we move along the fence line she looks at me with an air of "You figure I can't sense that electric field? Remember, I'm an etheric being and furthermore you are under my tutelage. Go do some real work." Shades of embarrassment come over me and I begin to get it.

As it turned out she was in calf when she came to us which we realized about 3 months later and so got the lowdown from Walter how it would all look close to the calf's birth. One day in early February when things are looking pretty calf ready Bessie heads to the bottom of the 30 acre field in front of the houses and I sense an air of immediacy about the situation. Fill her milking bucket with warm water and bring along a soft rope and pray for protection, grace and ease. Down we go, Ruffie (Lotus's predecessor) and I, to the very farthest part of the field. Bessie is lying down and well into the birthing, everything looks good. I see a nose and two baby hooves and as Bess appears to be struggling I hitch that soft rope around the hooves. As she pushes I pull, and after about 4 of those the calf is born and Bess is immediately on her feet licking and mooing and making sure all is alright with her baby. A Mother of all Mothers—no dysfunction here, just pure love and intimacy. I try to work the two of them up toward the barn and then realize that is not my place to control their situation. Ruffie and I go happily up to the barn and greet our family with the good news. Everything is easy with Bessie.

For some time we kept on the goats, sheep and pigs and mixed all their manure together and then used Bessie's alone (per R. Steiner) to create those wonderful alive organisms that steam on wintry days. Gradually we let go of the initial farm animals, at Bess's recommendation, and as we realized the quantity of manure that was actually coming from the cow. Not to mention the superb quality of it—sometimes it had formed compost before it left her stall! She snorted and turned her nose up (literally) at the pigs and sheep while basically ignoring the goats, as if to tell me that their manure was not in any way, shape or form fit for this farm and besides the smell was all wrong. So, gradually all the other animals were let go . Bessie very confident in her new role communing with the cow oversoul, teaching me how to love this land, and the virtues of human, humus, humility and being humble in the face of it all.

Her first calf at Aurora was a Hereford cross and we called him Whiteface. We had been hoping for a Heifer and when Nathan was sorting out boy/girl calves in his own mind he rang out one night at the dinner table that Bessie would give birth to a "hoofer." We never quite understood whether he couldn't pronounce heifer or was simply being truthful of the situation. Whiteface grew into the summer and one day in August as I was tying him out to feed on the fence line he eyed me up as fair game as a mate and tried to mount me from behind! After we got done with that nerve racking incident and he continued to jump his fence, he was looking very good in freezer paper for the winter meat supply. We hadn't known Bessie had been in calf when she came so this was an extra bonus—meat, along with milk and manure. What a Blessing and a Gift. Thirty-three acres and a sensate cow initiating this rocky outcropping and all her beings into a fertile, living sentient being.

The next calf Bessie birthed was a heifer,-Rose a dual purpose Shorthorn. Sold to a local part time farmer once she was in calf. He left her roped while he was at work and one day came home to her dead on the end of her lead. He phoned us in despair, telling us what a wonderful animal she was and didn't we have another like her to sell to him.

Then came Buffy,- an Ayrshire bullock who was as gentle as a lamb. When I told the local dairy farmer we had an Ayrshire bull he explained " Oh that breed can be very nasty." His words shocked me as Buffy never displayed any meanness at all and was a true joy to be around. I guess in a large dairy operation the bulls are considered only for one purpose and that wasn't what we were doing at Aurora Farm. When George Baumann of Lofstedt Farm came to certify us Demeter , Buffy was part of the meal. As he had been checking the fields he noticed that Bess had come to visit he and his partner. This had impressed him and he had very much felt her presence. She always checked out everyone who came to the Farm and impressed on them her unmistakable presence.

Bessie's next calf was born on William's birthday in early April and she too was a dual purpose shorthorn. Another beauty who developed a limp in her ankle which made her progressively more lame until the neighboring Jersey collector who bought her felt he had to ship her. To date, Bessie has birthed alternating male/female calves . Neither Bessie nor I liked the idea of this artificial insemination and did our best to achieve the best of possible outcomes.

Along comes Blue, a beautiful shorthorn, born on a blue moon at the last of June. Another heifer. Then two years of some dysfunction probably arising from the non-virtues of artificial insemination. We decide to get a real Bull (the first full grown at Aurora) And Danny Boy helps Bessie become fertile again.

On Friday the 13th Bessie begins that low moo that signals a birthing is imminent. I take her to her stall and let William know (now 14 years) this is an ideal opportunity to view the birth of a calf. He stays by her stall , while doing some other chore and then comes down to see Woody and me in the south field. "Hey, Mom, Bessie has some blood and stuff coming out of her." We go up to check and she looks comfortable so we decide to leave her alone and go up and have lunch.

A new cow spirit in the stall, Venus, who was not at all what we envisioned as calves usually take on the characteristics of the bull who was a black Kerry. This one is a throwback and has been blessed with her Mother's jersey face and the henna color of her Father's ancestors. A very ethereal calf and with no skittishness of some . Oh happy day, everyone is well and we are all feeling blessed with the Gifts of Fertility.

We finally heed Bessie's unspoken advice and keep one of the heifers. Venus, the last of the calves is home cow at Aurora now and she will freshen at the end of March.

Last year in the late winter it became apparent that life was no longer easy for Bess. A developing limp and a kind of sad aura. She told me she would not make it through the year. Although one doesn't expect the home cow to live on forever there is a big difference between expectations and the reality of acceptance. This was almost more than I could bear and combined with a difficult soul period and all the delights of two teenage boys life was somewhat strained.

In early April, I spoke with a friend who knew Bessie intimately and came to understand that although this was painful it was actually perfect. I began to work with Bessie on a deeper level, letting go with as much grace and ease as I could muster and presenting Bess with compassionate choices for her best possible outcome. A lot of sound and cleansing and being with her in gratitude as she had always done for all of us at Aurora. She's got me meditating again and she appeared to be in one steady meditation calling on the spirit's that she needed at this time of no sound from within her.

On several occasions Bessie woke me up to the ground of my own being. Although somewhat rough she acted out of compassion.

During the summer months she was often out in the field and I needed to go with the Aussie dog Ruffie, to bring her in to the barn. This time, it was late in the day and as I was stumbling up the hill Bessie planted her head between my shoulders just hard enough to wake me out of my slumber and not enough to knock me over.

On another occasion, as two apprentices and myself were working in the garden, she was mooing a different kind of sound than I had heard before. I kept feeling that I wasn't understanding her sound. As it turned out she was asking us to pay attention to the fact that the dogs were down at a neighbor's hayshed eating strychnine-laced bait.

Bessie knew the whole story and with just one sweep of her tail or watching her chew her cud one could sense her state of being.

She came to me the day she physically left and she hadn't been in her normal spot late in the morning. I could feel she just wasn't present. That same day there were water problems and Woody and I were down at the barn for some time with the water man.

As I was stirring Apricot jam , I heard the back door open and Woody come in. I knew what he was coming to tell me. "Bessie's dead". he says after he got me to sit down. "Oh, oh, oh, oh…." was all that would come out from inside of me.

After making arrangements for her burial the next day I was sorting out the feelings that had come over me. It was like everything and nothing had happened here at Aurora Farm. Neither her life, nor her death would she have made into some kind of big deal. Another day on the farm…

Now Venus is home cow due to freshen in the Spring. She is quite a bit younger than her Mom, and born on the place and we are appreciating her being. So let's go Lotus, let's go to the barn for Venus.

Thank you Bessie for your great and immense being. Gratitude from all at Aurora and elsewhere with whom you have shared your teachings.

Sometime after Bessie's parting the news of the 9th White Buffalo Calf's birth came down the wire. Bessie's birth and death coincided on the same day.

Barbara M. V. Scott, M.Sc., is a Biologist by formal training and a farmer, pagan and artist by direct experience. She lives with her husband/partner,- Woody Wodraska and two teenage sons,- Nathan Nass and William Scott, at Aurora Farm. Their livelihood is the production of seeds, herbal remedies, teas and a training program where others come to learn Rudolf Steiner's methods of Agriculture. Barbara and Woody give workshops in composting internationally. (End "Bessie's Teachings")

The last article was the most difficult one to write, as the economic question began to come to a head. We felt ready to call on outside help:

INVOKING ANGELS—AURORA FARM IN TRANSITION

Fern, our home cow, presented us with a bull calf this morning. Fern is in prime condition from feeding on new grass, prime for making milk and being a mom. This year we had blessed rain in August and September and she's out in the pasture with her baby enjoying new autumn grass, the first we've had after five years of drought. Each of those drought years we were feeding hay—scarce even in this hay-growing valley—by July and the rice crispy crunch underfoot when you walked in woods or field was enough to break your heart.

We live in grateful and mutually appreciative cooperation with our home cow, who is ultimately the source of fertility on our small acreage.

And so are the turkeys thriving, outdoors on grass most days in their moveable turkey tractor, which is getting a bit small for the 10 of them, half-grown now.

Seeds are coming in too. This morning I harvested by hand cosmos seed and broadleaf plantain. That's what we do at Aurora Farm—raise seed for backyard gardeners, high-vitality, authentic, un-tampered-with seeds of vegetables, herbs and flowers. Heritage seeds, open-pollinated old-time tried and true varieties. We market over the Internet mostly. Lettuce, carrot, parsley, spinach, calendula, lavender, pumpkin…the seed-gathering season starts in July with chives and ends sometime in December with the harvest of the last leek seed heads. Timing is everything.

We grow probably 80 percent of what we eat, counting meat, eggs, dairy products, potatoes and other veggies, salad, lots of fruit. We live a lifestyle that is closer to that of our ancestors than most people, closer to the land, more dependent on Nature, in tune with the seasons. An anachronistic life, perhaps, but it has suited us.

The milking, and all the tasks that go along with it—feeding and persuading Fern that we're only taking our share, mucking out, straining the fresh, raw milk into jars for the fridge, yogurt making, cheese making, butter making—it's a rhythm of life, a morning and evening pulse in our lives.

So there's the cow and a calf and welcome milking chores; a flock of chickens, the turkeys, the gardens, the harvest, maintenance on four big buildings and stewardship of 31 acres…

And it's all gotten to be a bit much for Barbara and me. She's been doing it for many years and is feeling destiny's push to do something new and different; I'm well into my seventh decade, past the time I should be doing this much grunt work. The boys are grown now and we don't require this big a place or this much responsibility We could do with partners. We should to begin to back off. But there are questions arising in us during this age-old process of passing on the legacy of the land.

We have been holding these questions for years and should share them, on the chance that readers may have suggestions.

How does it go when it's time to turn over to the coming generation—read a *Stronger, More Clever, More Enthusiastic, and Younger set of people*—a farm and business we've worked so hard to manifest, in co-creation with the land and unseen allies; and the corollary question since we could hardly just leave and hope for the best: How to realize at least some of the value of what has been accomplished here, in the form of those abundant dollars we all must have? If the elders need to get out of the way and give the outfit over to the youngsters, how do the elders step into the real world without at least an illusion of security?

For many months we've advertised for people to share the farm with us. Keeping in mind Question #2 above, we've had to restrict serious negotiations to those who have some capital to invest, who can buy into the situation, and there have been some of those folks interested from time to time. People who have had a presence in the community or corporate world and made money. But those who have the money also have ties and obligations and a certain level of comfort in their lifestyle; the dream is one thing—the actual shift to living in the country and heating with wood and being earth stewards for a living seems just too much for them, at least for those we've talked with. Another category of responders to our offer of sharing are the young, strong, clever, well-intentioned inquirers, plenty of them, but all more or less penniless.

For both kinds of interested parties who contact us, invariably via email after visiting our website, the Aurora Farm presented there is a virtual reality, an idyllic one, as attractive as we can make it. Then, some visit and the on-the-ground reality affects diverse people each uniquely. Some the land embraces and uplifts. Others not.

It's time for us to take the next steps. We need to become elders. Barbara can teach, I can write. Together we expect to share with a community of like-minded, supportive people. We have been isolated too long, in quiet and honorable service to the land and the seeds. Our light has been under a bushel. We have been in service to the Earth mother over decades, striving for an ideal of right livelihood on the land, living respectfully and responsibly on the land.

Aurora Farm, the landscape, is old, old beyond our imagining; Aurora Farm, the farm and business that Barbara created, has grown up and requires parents no longer, but partners. Our notion of a partnership is exceedingly flexible and offered on generous terms, we think. There are many unusual elements in this transfer of stewardship, this process that starts out looking like a real estate deal and soon becomes much more.

For Aurora Farm is an organism, a living, growing being not so easy to pin down. "31 acre hilltop property" doesn't even come close to the reality. Aurora is a place where beings of many species, including quite a few invisible ones, make a living and a life together in co-creation. It's forest and mossy outcrops and gardens. There is a legacy here to transfer to new owners, a legacy of fertility and right livelihood, of appropriate scale and heartfulness. Any transfer has to be a land-based transaction, not a culture-based one. A value-based deal, not a money-based one.

But here is what we're up against when we put it up for sale.

The real estate guys have heard it all before. In the eyes of the owners, who have melded their lives with a farm over decades, every place is unique. Where we, the stewards, see history and family memories, the real estate brokers see shabbiness and care-worn proprietors. We hope for a price that reflects values we hold dear in our lifestyle, that validates our work; they want a price that will move the "property." They know the market, we know what went into the place, every hard decision, every outpouring of love.

They have no interest in chickens or compost or milk cows, the woodlot or the gardens. Their mindset centers on the properties they know have sold in the area in the past year or two. So-and-so much per acre. Buildings? Even better, but they'd rather sell a ranch house with a modern kitchen. These are idiosyncratic houses and workshop structures and nowhere near new. The price they quote insults and saddens us. Don't mistake. These are good people, these brokers. We shouldn't expect them to be other than who they are, realists. But we have been living ideals all this time, and there's no fit here. We may wind up selling outright, but not with the help of these guys.

However, we haven't looked at all the possibilities, when we've tried 1) farmsharing and 2) the real estate route. Let's get creative here.

Let's turn Aurora Farm into something it hasn't been before. Let's repackage it. It has been:

ANACHRONISTIC FAMILY FARM FOR SALE

In a spirit of thankful and awe-struck acknowledgement, I want to say here that Barbara has always been the guiding light and will behind this place. As she learned to be guided by the spirit of the land, she took a neglected, property and saw only its promise. She eased it toward its potential as a nurturing, family-centered gem of a farm. She worked and worked, whether she was in the moment daunted or exalted by the task. I admire her and love her for that. By now Barbara speaks with the voice of Aurora and manifests its being in her own.

Like the farm and like Barbara's blooming confidence in the early years as a co-creative gardener/farmer, the seed business grew as an organism, from an inspired observation...to the germ of an idea—selling righteous seeds, grown right here...to the skill-building needed to transition from herb and salad grower to seed gatherer...on to all the marketing issues: printing seed envelopes, advertising, selling, the website. The business grew as an art form, idiosyncratic and quirky as its proprietors, all bound up with our lives financially and otherwise. We are the eaters, growers, gatherers, stewards, herdspeople, entrepreneurs, educators, compostmeisters, seedspeople.

What we have never been is business oriented, and this entity which has a web presence as a business, and various appurtenances that make it look real, is really kind of a shirt pocket affair. Can we rationalize and legitimize it, transform it into something recognizable, say, to the money people? Angels, donors, investors, grant givers, contributors, fellow travelers. What would the alternative to ANACHRONISTIC FAMILY FARM FOR SALE look like?

- A Land Trust?
- A Non-Profit Corporation?
- A School? (of Life, of Seeds, of Healing, of Biodynamics)

- An Intentional Community?
- A "real" Corporation? i.e., a profit-making one
- A Co-op?
- A Partnership?
- A Preserve, or Refuge of sane agriculture amidst the industrialization of our food supply?
- Absorbed, perhaps into a larger, well-funded entity.

Maybe one or more of these would work for us, and we've even done a bit of web research on some of the options listed…Land Trust and non-profit status mainly. Here's the rub.

We are already busy enough with day to day duties of stewardship. At this stage, when we should be moving into the role of elders, we just don't have the juice to create something entirely new out of what's here. These are new tricks and we're old dogs. We don't really want to learn the vocabulary, the social and legal parameters of something so complex as a corporation or trust.

This outfit needs an angel…several angels.

- Calling a lawyerly angel who will sort through the options and advise;
- Calling a spirit-in-business angel who will gently point out what we have overlooked amongst our resources;
- Calling a reality angel to matchmake the dream and the real world;
- Calling garden angels and stewardship angels to share the responsibility for the health of this land and all the beings on it;
- Calling financial angels, for all we have is wrapped up in this place;
- Calling marketing angels, for there are many seeds waiting for a garden;
- Calling patrons, participants, supporters—people who appreciate the value of the seedwork, the worthiness of independent, family-sized initiatives like ours;
- Calling Co-Conspirators and Accomplices, for this almost-subversive activity we're engaged in, this revolutionary activity: growing our own food and sharing the seeds.

Above all we call for someone to come and learn from us so we can move gracefully into retirement in a win-win social environment with a sense that the legacy will go on.

Meanwhile we do get validated: we received last month a grant from the Angeles Arrien Foundation in recognition of our seedwork. We have a greenhouse project underway and requests for our catalogue come in pretty steadily.

We have been ahead of the curve for a few years, but more and more folks begin to understand that there are alternatives to the industrial approach to agriculture; never mind the irradiation, genetic manipulation, sterilization, and hybridization of seeds…we'll do it ourselves. A few even realize that seeds are too precious, too sacred to sell at all. Our business is a paradoxical enterprise all together, for our attitude can be Nature's: seeds should be dispersed freely, given away to the gardeners of the planet, passed on as gifts and legacies, bits of *now* presented in faith and fond hope to *then*. The price we charge is not for the seeds themselves, but for the service of bringing them to the customer.

And when Barbara went to Olympia, Washington last spring to do a compost workshop for a few friends, the event cloned itself and she wound up doing three workshops in four days, one to students in the eco-agriculture program at Evergreen College. People are thirsty to understand fertility, to learn the techniques of soil building, to grasp the details and experience of the Biodynamic preparations. The building of fertile soil, our daily task in cooperation with the worms and the cow, the microbes and micro fauna, is second nature to us, but its practical application is a revelation to less experienced gardeners. There is no worthier endeavor than to teach compost making, no greater gift to the planet, and Barbara is a master teacher, one of those whose profound understanding of her subject on every level of her being—as a farmer, an artist, a mother, a cow person—inspires confidence and fosters competence in her students.

There are angels out there, and answers for our questions. We know this because we see many worthy endeavors funded and thriving, and this transitioning of land and livelihood has been a feature of the passing of human generations for eons. It's no mystery how it's done. In service to the things that count: family, Nature, fruitfulness, All Our Relations.

I paused in the woods today to look closely at the stump of a big larch we'd cut a few weeks ago, which has mostly made its way to the firewood stack. I started to count the rings, but my eyes and patience both failed me and I resorted to an estimate: It's been 200 years that this lightning-battered tree had stood on that spot before we felled it. The crown, some 80 feet above the ground, was shattered by lightning at least once and there grew from that blasted top a half-dozen raggedy limbs, each searching the sky ungracefully, gallantly. The stump, just above the butt swell, is juicy with resin and those 200 or so rings testify to the transitory nature of our tenure here on this land. When this tree was a sapling in the first decade of the Nineteenth Century Lewis and Clark passed by a hundred miles south; Hudson Bay Company trappers had yet to penetrate the Rockies to this area; the place itself, this flat valley, was a rather unwelcoming marshland, visited by the indigenous band later called the Kootenai, but no-one's homeland. This tree witnessed all the changes: the draining of the marsh, the logging, the influx of farmers and cowmen, greed and progress—and the irreverent slash of a national border just south of us. That historical backdrop even I—short-lived next to this tree—can comprehend. But the tree is short-lived next to the mossy rocks and the overlighting Deva of this landscape, and our 15-year tenure less than an eye blink to them. For us, 15 years is a great chunk of a lifetime; for the tree those years are brief seasons, but at least recorded in the rings; for the spirits of the place, our tenure will be unremembered except maybe a tiny blip on the long eons made by our halting attempts to co-create with the spirits of the place.

How It Is That We Can't Just STOP What We're Doing?

There is, as we have said, a greenhouse project underway...a turkey flock, raised from poults...a chicken flock, raised from chicks...all begun this year. And we continue to honor catalogue requests and seed orders.

You see, what we have been about here all the while is developing potential; nurturing while we are being nurtured, growing while we're growing ourselves, finding ways for the land to fill human needs, while the humans balance the energies and call in the good, true and beautiful.

And then there are these two young men: William, almost 20, and Nathan, 18. While they may not be ready to take over, they deserve a shot at the legacy held by the land they were raised on, and to make their marks. For William, his building skills in stone, timber, and his calm approach with animals. Nathan too is a builder, of relationships and trust and his own leadership skills. He's now a lead lift operator Vale Resorts in Breckinridge, Colorado.

And the seeds. How can we NOT gather the seeds as they come? Since they are presented to us freely from Nature, an obligation is upon us to disperse them.

While we hold in trust this land and heritage for whoever will be the new stewards we can allow free rein for everyone's imagination, gifts and talents. There is a momentum stirring here and we aim to flow with the energies wherever they take us. (End Chapter 13)

Dome Greenhouse from www.growingspaces.com.

Chapter 14 – The Mountain School, Wood River Valley, Idaho 2005-6

It was a rough spring for us that year. Aurora Farm was up for sale at a realtor-advised price far below what we knew it was worth. There was not the usual springtime joy and anticipation in the garden, for we'd decided not to do much this year, being pretty clear that we'd not be there for harvest…we were depressed in spirit and Barbara's blood-iron level was so low she'd consented to go to the hospital for an all-day "total dose" intravenous infusion of pharmaceutical iron-dextran recommended by a physician we really didn't trust much. A sad state of affairs for us, to be guided by real estate people and medical men. We were not, as Barbara said later, in our right minds. The expectation of leaving the farm and the sheer uncertainty over what to do next, these unmanned me, further weakened Barbara, and clouded our judgment.

I wrote just now, "far below what we knew it was worth." The crux of the matter. Our understanding of farm "ownership" is incompatible with what is normal in our culture. We try to work with and within the economy of the land, recognizing that we are just passing through as stewards and that our tenure is no more than a blip in the life of the land, even if it is a large chunk of our own lives. The best we can hope for is to leave the place a bit better than we found it. The real estate folks will nod knowingly if we tell them this and try to bring us back to what to them is the issue: how much properties similar to this one have recently sold for.

Compelling reasons underlay the decision to sell: there were health challenges; the maintenance of four large farm buildings had become burdensome, money-wise and energy-wise; diminishing financial reserves. Barbara had been on the farm for 16 years and while the seed business provided a vital service, it did not pay all the bills; while the gardens and animals were a joy, neither did they yield much income; and while the farm lifestyle had served as a nurturing environment for Barbara's sons, William and Nathan, they were fully grown now and on their own. As we waited for the realtors to bring us qualified buyers, the only thing that kept us from all-out despair—for Aurora had sustained us and nurtured our souls in so many ways that the grief of leaving was already upon us—was to picture a life away from the farm that would be equally nourishing. We had been looking for opportunities for months, but none really fit our situation until in March we came across this announcement on the website of the Biodynamic Farming and Gardening Association:

> **Idaho Waldorf Kindergarten Seeks Garden Program Director** *Start-up opportunity for creative grower! The Mountain School of Bellevue, Idaho, in the scenic Wood River Valley near Sun Valley, seeks a Garden Program Director to establish a new garden program for a 20-student Waldorf-inspired Kindergarten in its initial year. The recently acquired 1.4 acre property has no existing preparation so this is an opportunity to be creative in designing a model educational biodynamic garden where the children and community participate and learn. Property includes a 24' x 12' greenhouse.*

Qualifications

1. *motivated and creative, self-directed and able to organize time*
2. *willing to locate in the Wood River Valley (Bellevue, Hailey, or Ketchum)*
3. *record of practice and study of biodynamic agriculture*
4. *experience in biodynamics including: soil preparation and cultivation; growing and harvesting vegetables, herbs and flowers; small greenhouse management; irrigation; composting; seed saving; biodynamic preparations; pest management; beekeeping; and managing chickens, goats, bees, and llamas.*
5. *ability to explain biodynamic concepts (seed saving, soil prep, crop rotation, rhythms, biodynamic preparations, composting, etc.) to adults and children ages 4-12*
6. *interest in or experience with young children in an educational setting*
7. *ability to acquire and organize educational materials related to biodynamics and farming*
8. *familiarity with professional organizations*

Benefits

1. *part-time or full-time negotiable on program design*
2. *on-site apartment*
3. *monthly stipend negotiable on experience*
4. *life in beautiful Wood River Valley*

Visit www.themountainschool.info to learn about the school program; find out more about Wood River Valley at www.sunvalleycentral.com. Send resume to Katharine Woods, Head of School, at xxxxxxxxxxxxxxxxxx or call xxxxxxxxxxxxxxxx.

Barbara perked up when I told her about this job listing. Somehow the notion of teaching little guys, kindergarten kids, about gardening struck a chord in both of us. We talked with Kate Woods, head of the school, who made it clear that it was she and her dad, her deep-pocketed dad, who were behind the endeavor, that a property had been purchased, that there were problems with community support including the nearest neighbors—a large ranch to the north and a subdivision to the south. Both were hostile to the idea of a school. There were also problems with building codes, those in the Valley being super-strict. These difficulties seemed to us at the time to be not-so-serious, maybe even typical for such a startup venture. The lure was the modest scope of the job itself, the fact that Barbara and I could share the responsibilities, and the appeal of knowing that we would have a place to go after the farm sold. We realized later that, while there may have been a few parents in the Wood River valley who welcomed Kate's plan for a school, that plan was not emerging organically from a deep need felt by an organized group of parents seeking an alternative, but rather was arising almost solely from Kate's entrepreneurial and pedagogic energies.

We talked with Kate a couple of times in the next two months and I went to Idaho in June, after driving Barbara to the Buddhist monastery near Kamloops, B.C., for a retreat, low iron and all. A couple of weeks with the monks would help, we felt.

Though at Aurora Farm we were just a few minutes' drive from the U.S. border at the northern tip of Idaho's panhandle, I knew only that one facet of the Gem State, the Panhandle. Sun Valley is quite another Idaho, several hundred miles south. Hints of the difference showed with a few upscale homes as I drove south from Stanley, when the view of the Sawtooth Mountains first presents itself. There on the lower slopes are properties designated as ranches, and even some cows grazing, with trophy homes situated just visible from the road. Bragging-rights homes, adorning the stunning landscape. Cross over the Galena pass, going south toward Hemingway's Ketchum, and the ranches are fewer while the ostentatious homes increase in number and variety, sprinkling Papa's beloved upland shotgunning country; if this had been happening in the 1950s he'd have turned surly and maybe shot out a few picture windows. The owners mostly weren't here anyway. These are, by and large, second or even third homes.

Ketchum has more banks per capita than most other places, with another two or three a-building during the whole time we were there. I crept through the almost solid tourist traffic on Main street in my 20-year-old Vanagon.

I called Kate to let her know I was nearly there. "Oh, I have a friend here," she said, "but I can make time for you."

On to Hailey, with the swanky homes getting thicker, but also past the Sawtooth Botanical Garden, a sweet place, and along the Big Wood River, which was becoming a little more impressive with each mile. Technically, it was not Sun Valley where we were to live and work; that town is located just next to Ketchum where many of the brighter lights of local society live. Ernest Hemingway was one of the first. He visited Ketchum in 1939, moved there two decades later, and died there in 1961. Nowadays, Clint Eastwood, Bruce Willis and Demi Moore, Arnold Schwarzenegger and Maria Shriver are all homeowners there. Jamie Lee Curtis has hit Sun Valley's slopes, and Teresa Heinz—the Heinz food heiress and wife of Massachusetts Senator John Kerry— has been an active community member for years.

Where we really are is the Wood River Valley, which is the watershed running due south from Galena Pass. The proximity of the Wood River and the wildness along it (one thing the building codes got right—no houses on the riverbank) those things enhanced our lives immeasurably in coming months. I walked its bank twice a day, took my son fishing there, watched in awe as it flooded in the spring and saw 60-foot cottonwood trees washed from the banks and float by in full leaf.

Hailey, where even the most modest of homes is valued at half a million dollars plus and the population is predominantly ordinary folks caught in an upwelling of real estate valuation and tax increases that would drive many away in the long run. A wry comment in Sun Valley is that the billionaires are driving out the millionaires.

Immediately south of Hailey is the Friedman Memorial Airport, with its 7,000-foot runway and, on summer and winter weekends, dozens of private jets parked wingtip to wingtip on the tarmac.

On past the airport to the Flying Hat ranch, whose owner was turning out to be Kate's nemesis, obstructing the forward motion of the school in county planning and zoning procedural wrangling. This guy has a multi-multi-million dollar piece of property which for some reason is threatened by Kate's little school.

I pulled into the circle driveway. It's literally just on the other side of the fence from the ranch. There's a grass mound in the center of the drive topped by a Maypole, a nice touch for sure, maybe a little defiant.

Nobody home to greet me. I went up the front walk to knock and get a close view of a log home with big front porch. All I could see through the glass front door was a country kitchen with a formidable restaurant-sized gas range. Just off the veranda, across a little lawn, was a three car garage and above that, I knew, was the space Kate proposed to make into an apartment for Barbara and me. The entrance to that was around the corner of the building and I scoped out for the first time the tapering triangle of land that went west toward the river, where the agricultural activities would be. In fact, there was a load of brought-in topsoil heaped in the likeliest garden spot.

Comes the Lady herself, in from a long run in the June afternoon, all aglow with sweat and endorphin delight. Between smiles and gasps after her final sprint into the driveway she welcomes me, suggests where I can set up the camper van for the night, introduces Zack, her running mate who's just rounded the Maypole, and suggests we have a walk by the river when she's had a shower. I am dazzled, as much by the sudden warp in the pace of events—I'd been traveling, after all, in Woody time, slower than most—as by Kate's thousand watt smile. A sturdy lady of the 35-ish vintage, she transmits such exuberance at close quarters that I needed to distance myself pretty quickly. Okay, a walk. After all, there can be more truth revealed in a walk taken together alongside a river than in all the boardroom meetings at corporate headquarters. While I waited for her one of those jets screamed by, not that far overhead since the runway touchdown point was only a mile away. This happened repeatedly during the afternoon and once, when Kate saw me wince, she said lightly, "Oh, you'll get used to that." I didn't tell her what I was thinking: that nothing in me *wanted* to get used to that.

Kate had told us that her father, Ward Wilson Woods, was wealthy, a retired investment banker. He was underwriting the purchase of this property and the startup costs of the school—renovations of an existing building, legal fees, and the garden/minifarm—with loans to Kate personally. She told us time after time when we were working with her that he expected repayment from her, that the project needed to become a paying proposition planned, promoted, and administered by a pedagogical whirlwind named Kate Woods.

She had also told us that her dad had not been very understanding about the need for a gardening program, but was on board with it now. She'd somehow convinced him that nutrition and education might have something to do with each other. For her part and to her credit, Kate is committed to that. Not all Waldorf people would be. She plans to run a kindergarten, an after-school program, and summer camps right here. Being with the animals, working in the vegetable beds, preparing and eating food from the garden—along with walks by the river and hikes in the hills—Kate was going to keep these children moving, hanging on to her comet tail.

What she needed from us, she explained, was to be there, doing our gardening thing for the children to observe and imitate, even help us. Barbara had raised two sons doing just that, and I had worked with handicapped adults in the garden, so we felt comfortable with this.

The second part of our mission, Kate told me, was to teach her *everything* about Biodynamics. She would apprentice herself to our experience and, she fully expected, become a competent Biodynamic gardener in a year, even six months if that was all the time we had for her and her project. Again, because Barbara and I had both trained many apprentices over the years, this presented no problem for us, though the timeline seemed a bit hasty. The lady was clearly motivated, undaunted by the scope of things that must be learned, and bright enough, we thought.

We didn't realize, though we should have, that the person who assumes the role of boss is unlikely to be able to humble herself enough to take on the mantle of an apprentice. This, it turned out, was a deal-breaking miscalculation though we didn't realize it until much later.

Kate was obligated to waste incredible energy, time and money dealing with the legalities of the school startup and the neighborly objections. She also went twice to Burning Man, an adventure requiring several days to get ready, two days plus to travel, 10 days on the scene, and probably a week to recover. She went to India for a couple of months, Europe for a shorter period, and to California six or eight times. She took instruction in Permaculture and sessions called The Art of Living; in firedancing and Yoga.

In other words, she was *busy*. She missed so much of what a serious apprentice should not miss. When Kate was working in the garden, she was truly there (after we banned her cell phone) and, being a robust lady, she could do a lot of work, especially if it was on her own initiative. For example, inspired by the Permaculture workshop, she dug two nifty spiral raised-beds in the garden, with help from whoever she could Tom Sawyer into it. She did that job with vision and diligence and goodwill. Also an extensive wild flower planting along the Flying Hat fence row. But she missed so much otherwise, the plantings and prunings and transplantings and planning and decision-making, seed saving, harvest and food preparation that an apprentice would normally participate in. We could rarely corral Kate to be with us long enough in the garden, in the greenhouse or with the chickens to impart to her a sense of continuity, a feeling for the exquisite timing required by the garden and livestock.

But we didn't know at the time we were beginning to talk about the job that the two roles, boss and learner, were incompatible. In the flush of goodwill and her dazzling vision—*children who know where their food comes from!*—we overlooked that in the beginning. Though we'd worked year after year with apprentices we'd never had one who also wrote the checks. The ones we knew had some humility, could be corrected, could be kept to task, could be asked to curb their native creativity in favor of what the garden truly needs, could be counted on to listen to instructions, could above all be there on the ground with us, that is, to show up. These apprentices were able to learn that there is a big difference between having and tending, between doing and being, between activity and progress.

From the beginning Kate had envisioned a cow for the project. She knew on some atavistic level that a cow would ground the place, provide fertility, force the rhythm of care-taking to emerge. Also, that for the children a cow would embody all that is best about farm life: gentleness, productivity, selflessness. She wanted the children to witness the milking chore, to drink raw milk, to make yogurt and cheese and butter... all those things. I didn't have the heart to disabuse her of this latter part, for raw milk is verboten to state health departments and, while we could certainly have a cow on the premises, there was no way the children would be allowed to consume raw milk products. But very soon it became clear to us that Kate's lifestyle did not have room for cow care, for the inescapable routine of feeding, mucking out, milking, turning out to pasture and late in the day into the stable, fence-fixing—all the day-to-day chores. If Kate wanted to be a cow owner, clearly someone else would have to be the cow caretaker.

All these understandings were to come later. Now, Kate and I were walking back from the river with a plan. We would leave things as they were, with no commitments, until I returned with Barbara in a couple of weeks, so she could see the situation.

Barbara asked, when I was telling her of my visit with Kate, "How well do you think she will take care of the people who are supporting her?" What a far-seeing question, I thought at the time, but I had no real answer. Her other question was: "Did she offer you a meal?" No, I realized, she hadn't. That first evening, after our river walk, Kate was expecting some friends, one especially, who was going to teach firedancing, so made it clear that she would not be able to be with me. The following day her morning was taken up by some event, but I was fine with that for I wanted to explore the Valley a little, including a visit to hot springs I'd heard about outside Ketchum. In the early afternoon we would meet again. Barbara's questions spotlighted issues that would become important later in the year, issues having to do with hospitality, the warm welcome that might have been offered to a respected guest—but wasn't—and the regard which a potential apprentice might show for a mentor.

Meanwhile I would return to Aurora Farm where there had begun to be some extraordinary interest in the farm, real estate-wise.

I showed the house and land that Saturday to a couple from Invermere and later in the week to a neighboring couple and their son. Shortly after, I went to the monastery to fetch Barbara and very soon we went to the Wood River Valley together to let her feel the place out.

After my visit I'd told Barbara that Kate lived in the midst of chaos. The large shop building that was to become the school was pretty much stuffed with her possessions, mainly, it's true, with Waldorfian impedimenta: costumes and fabric to make more, classroom furniture, books, craft and art supplies. A large room on the first floor of the house was set up as a kindergarten classroom, a lot tidier. Kate had been preparing to open a school for some time and acquiring many of the appurtenances. When Barbara, a person who believes firmly in keeping her surroundings orderly, saw all this, she remarked to Kate that she would need to unclutter things a bit. Kate's response, "Oh, that'll be a hard one for me…" We soon understood that Kate found it much easier to acquire things than to find a place for them. What we didn't understand right away was that the chaos was symptomatic.

This time we met Ward Woods. I'll reiterate and say that neither Barbara nor I was in a sane place. The stress of selling the farm, the place of our own growth and that of our sons', was almost too much to bear. We were leaving home, burdened with decision making, and inevitably we made some very questionable ones. With our self-confidence at a low ebb, I don't believe we presented ourselves very well to this worldly and successful businessman who routinely judged and pigeon-holed people pretty quickly, I'd guess. He volunteered nothing. His questioning of us was not at all probing or by way of getting to know us on a human level. He did want to know which mammal Barbara had studied for her Master's thesis work—wolves on Vancouver Island—and then informed us that he was on the board of directors of some wildlife conservation group. He was convinced by Kate that we were the best candidates for the job and he was here to make the best deal for her. What we settled on was this: Barbara and I together would hold a half-time position called Farm and Garden Director; we would create a garden with Kate, establish animals, be present to teach the young ones; we would work 10 months of the year, taking time off in winter; for this we would be paid $1,000 per month and have the use of the apartment above the garage with all utilities paid for.

Two things stand out in my memory from that wimpy negotiation. Ward Woods told us that "Kate is on a tight budget here," and "Just because the hillsides are still green in June, don't forget that it's basically a desert here.

Done, we agreed after a half-hour conversation. There were lots of twists and turns in that agreement. For instance, Kate and her father clearly felt that the apartment and utilities were worth about $1,000 a month, making our in-kind compensation equal to our cash salary. For their part they felt they were paying us $2,000 a month. I did not press our case on this point: that in all the gardening positions I had held, housing was included on the understanding that the gardener needed to be on hand, close to garden, greenhouse and animals in order to exercise stewardship, to hold the consciousness for a living system.

What we had to live on was the thousand bucks and my three-digit social security check.

Another twist that was later acknowledged by Kate, was the ten-hours-a-week-from-each-of-us fantasy. Nobody punches a clock on a farm. We do what needs to be done, and stay with the job until it's finished.

Never mind, done deal. This was late June. We figured to close the sale of Aurora Farm in early August and come here to move in and begin gardening before the Valley winter set in. We did try to insist with Kate, after Ward left, that we keep business and personal matters separate, which never really happened. We began our land work with a spray of Biodynamic Barrel Compost preparation and if a bit drifted over the fence onto the Flying Hat Ranch, well, we couldn't help that. Kate participated in the stir and the spraying and we left her with an Agnihotra pyramid and taught her how to do the fire and Sanskrit chant.

The agonies of that hellish July, getting rid of stuff, deciding what to do with the few precious things that would go with us, I will skip over. The reality of the leaving process was manifest a thousand times everywhere we looked on the farm, in nature, in the houses, barn and shop, the grief that would continue and only grow.

By the second week of August we arrived at Kate's with a U-Haul truck tightly loaded. We knew from talking with her on the phone that she was working hard (and spending a lot of money) to make the apartment habitable, but it just wasn't done yet, and wouldn't be until the first week of September. This was fine with us. We unloaded our worldly goods into the garage and took the U-Haul back. Then we headed to the Oregon coast in our VW van for a respite.

Under the circumstances we enjoyed our tour, even at the height of tourist season. We found lonesome beaches and decent campsites and covered the length of the coastline from one end to the other. Found a wonderful forest campsite at the top of California and stayed there a week. We were thoroughly zombied out, Barbara and I, especially when we found ourselves in the midst of the culture, in the towns or on the freeways. In nature we were pretty good, still in deep grief, but the trees understood.

About this time we began reciting to each other Rudolf Steiner's "For the Michael Age" and to use it as a grace before meals:

FOR THE MICHAEL AGE

We must eradicate from the Soul
All fear and terror of what comes towards Man
Out of the future
And we must acquire serenity
In all feelings and sensations about the future
We must look forward
With absolute equanimity to everything that may come
And we must think only that whatever comes
Is given to us by a world directive full of wisdom.
It is part of what we must learn in this age,
Namely to live out of pure trust
Without any security in existence.
Trust in that ever present help of the Spiritual World.
Truly, nothing else will do
If our courage is not to fail us.
And we must seek this awakening within Ourselves
Every morning and every evening.

—Rudolf Steiner Nov. 1917

We have occasionally been told that Steiner never said that. Our answer is, "Well, if he didn't he could have and should have!"

We needed this reminder, for on top of the grief we were, whether or not we acknowledged it, living in fear. Fear for our future beyond Kate's project, fear of being landless, having lost sovereignty. Our acceptance of Kate's offer was based on having a place to live at no cost to us and the ability to do a garden to feed ourselves and other people. The more Biodynamically-grown food we could absorb, we knew, the lighter our spirits would become. Further, we needed to begin the shift in our mindset from entrepreneurship toward teaching, toward taking what we had learned in our decades of experience out into the world.

We returned to Bellevue the first week of September and found the apartment ready to move into. Kate had done a very nice job and did not stint on the details. She'd made it as comfy and functional as she could for us. For a very small space, 700 square feet, once we'd moved in and discovered how best to arrange ourselves, it worked very well, and was warm, something we needed in our stressed state.

By the end of September Kate and a friend had brought in a load of old cow manure and we spread it along with the heap of topsoil on the garden space, only 30 feet by 60 feet, right outside our front door. We seeded and mulched this space with annual rye grass which would set a strong, worm-nourishing root system by the time we needed to dig in spring. Barbara and Kate went to get strawberry plants from a friend's garden and installed a big bed of new runners. We built a compost pile in Biodynamic fashion and did another spray with Barrel Compost, which brought the energies of the preparations to the ground, even before anything else was planted there. Another spraying, I remember, on Michaelmas, September 29, about the time a large bed of garlic went in.

Just before Michaelmas I worked with Kate to sow seeds in flats. By then we were fairly sure we would have a greenhouse up by winter (the 12'x24' house mentioned in the employment ad was in the plans for the new school building, but those plans were on hold) and we would need to stock it with well-started plants immediately if we hoped to have greens to eat, a little at least, at the first of the year and a nice amount by early spring. We sowed seeds of two or three different lettuce varieties, spinach, kale, Swiss chard, parsley—all of which are fairly cold-tolerant. Kate was earnest with the task of planting seed, a little clumsy, but willing to follow my suggestion that she do it silently and visualize the healthy, mature plants that would come next spring from this seed sowing. Of the two instructions I gave, not talking seemed to be the hardest for her. We had no place in the apartment to situate a half-dozen seed flats where they would have sun and warmth and be able to be watered, but finally solved that problem by setting up a half-sheet of plywood over the stairwell, under a window.

Meanwhile I was researching greenhouses and came up with what I thought was a great design for our purposes, a geodesic growing dome from Growing Spaces in Pagosa Springs, Colorado. The growing dome comes in sizes from 12 feet in diameter to 52 feet and seemed from the website to be functional and elegantly simple, if pricey. Of great importance for us, the design seemed ideal for our area of heavy snows. We marked out a 26 foot circle just at the edge of the garden plot and began talking with the folks at Growing Spaces about pricing and a possible delivery date. Construction projects in the Valley pretty much come to a halt by November first when the cold and snow set in, so we were anxious to go forward with the greenhouse.

True to form, the people who passed, or didn't, on building projects in the Valley treated Kate's inquiry about our greenhouse with skepticism. We had detailed plans and material lists, and Growing Spaces had hundreds of these greenhouses in place, a number for 10 years and more, in some of the heaviest snowfall areas in the West, including in Crestone, Colorado, at 8,000 feet. I had photos of intact Growing Spaces greenhouses with three or four feet of snow on top. Kate made valiant efforts to find an Idaho engineer who would pass on the structure and write a favorable letter to the Planning and Zoning guys, with no success.

Finally, with the window of suitable construction weather rapidly narrowing, in early October we decided to go with a 12-footer, which would come out under the 150 square foot cutoff that requires a building permit. Better a small greenhouse than none at all.

Within a week the kit arrived and two carpenters, friends of Kate's, began putting it together. By Halloween, it was pretty much finished and it was used as a performance space for Kate's (the school's) Halloween party. With this event we learned that Kate, with her strong sense of self, was never happier than when she was on stage, directing or performing. The party was an elaborate affair for kids and parents, with dramatic sketches, fire dancing, extravagant costumes and exotic music.

Another few days after the party went by until we had the waist high soil beds inside the greenhouse assembled and filled and the six-week old baby plants installed. Lettuces like Marvel of Four Seasons, Winter Bloomsdale spinach, Red Russian kale—all chosen for their cold hardy nature. The greenhouse became Woody's little kingdom and we would all be eating salad in March, I knew.

At one point when Kate was stressed out over the bureaucratic nonsense with the building code people, she complained, forgetting that the greenhouse would provide all the garden starts the school needed for the following season, "Why should I have to go to all this hassle just so Woody can have something to amuse him this winter?" True, with Barbara gone to South Africa for January and February (and Kate gone to Thailand and India), I would have little more to do than plan for the garden and keep an eye on the greenhouse. The plants would languish until the days began getting longer after December 22, above ground at least, but below ground root systems would slowly and inexorably expand. During the crystallization period, January 15 – February 15, if I could keep it above freezing inside, growth would be happening, and by Spring Equinox, salad aplenty. But for Kate this was not the reality it was for Woody, and even for me a reality with "Inshallah," God willing, appended.

There were also chicks to tend that winter. Around the middle of October a little flock of 25 mixed pullet chicks was delivered to our post office (though 3 or 4 turned out to be cockerels)—Buff Orpingtons, Aracanas, and Barred Rock, like the salad varieties, chosen for cold weather hardiness. These we raised in the garage, then moved to a shed the greenhouse carpenter guys converted to an insulated, cozy chicken house in late fall. They were under a heat lamp much of the winter, grew to pullet size by spring and, shortly after, began to lay.

By spring, this was the most troublesome batch of 25 chickens I'd ever dealt with, and I'd been raising chickens, off and on, for almost 40 years. Hens and roosters, both were bullies, many of them, viciously ripping out each others' tail feathers and sometimes a bird with a bloody butt was so put upon by the others that we had to separate him or her out from the others. A couple of the victim birds, including a favorite beautiful Aracana cockerel, were killed; a couple of others died for no particular reason as chickens do sometimes. We killed one cockerel for soup because the hens were so hard on him.

I pondered deeply about this nasty behavior but came up with no definitive answer.

By late May the greenhouse was overflowing with garden starts: melons, tomatoes, peppers, winter squash. These were warm weather plants we'd already been told that you couldn't grow in this high, mostly cold, valley but we'd ignored such nay-saying. These would go outside in the first week of June and the direct-seeded warmth-loving plants like beans and corn would be seeded a few days earlier.

Kate had arranged with a fellow we called Rock Wall Jeff (not be confused with another Jeff, who helped her rustle cow manure) to build a series of dry stone walls of river rock nicely placed between the strawberries and greenhouse, and near the chickens, running in quite beautiful curves laid out by Kate. We brought soil and compost to the beds created behind these low walls and sowed in one section the Three Sisters—beans, corn and squash. In tribute to Native agriculturalists most of the varieties were Indian: Hopi Pale Grey squash, Rainbow Inca and Mandan Bride corn, Anasazi beans. Another rock wall bed, facing south, we reserved for tomatoes since they were going to need all the help they could get, warmth-wise.

By June it had become clear that we were working far more hours than a split half-time position would warrant. I approached Kate for a raise, citing the hours worked, the fact that she routinely paid carpenters $25 an hour, and that we were holding the greatest part of the consciousness for garden and mini-farm since we were there all the time to oversee things. Kate objected briefly to my arguments, "But a carpenter's work is so *hard* and gardening is healthful and fun..." In the end, however, she raised our salary to $1,750 per month. She continued to insist that the apartment we lived in was worth $1,000 a month. We occasionally thought about taking a rental in town within bike riding distance and coming to Kate's place, say, from 8 am 'til noon, five days a week. Perhaps we should have done that, if only to give her a taste of the consciousness needed to oversee a garden.

Kate, in private, did acknowledge our teaching and our role as mentors and student...in words, sometimes extravagant, she was able to recognize our knowledge and eldership and her need to learn from us...but life, as she configured it, got in the way. Kate wasn't able to spend the time with us, in the garden, together, to gather from us the subtleties of being a gardener. As the summer wore on it became clearer that she expected us to be the gardeners and stewards while she owned the garden. Of course she had been flexible enough to grant us a substantial raise and she likely felt she had hired herself some gardeners; her stance shifted in late summer from being apprentice toward being boss.

At one point in late summer Kate sat Barbara down behind the house by the potato beds and harangued her for two hours. Barbara reported later that Kate had a lot to get off her chest: She felt we weren't worth the money she was paying us; that all her friends thought we were ripping her off and not doing anything to earn our salary. Kate felt we insulted her every chance we got, interfered with her personal life and independence. Barbara was away too much. She accused us, in a nutshell, of enjoying a life outside her control. Perhaps she expected that we would shut down our life's work to devote all to her shadow Waldorf-inspired school. Barbara, as I understand it, was quite passive during much of this tirade. What Kate didn't say, but had said earlier to me, is that it was a disappointment to her that I was physically unable to be involved in the heavy work around the garden.

By late summer she had withdrawn mostly from the garden. She rarely came there even to cut salad and never to ask a question or seek instruction. At one point I was hand winnowing some garden cress seed when she came by. I tried to show her how very simple the seed-gathering was, and how bountiful the plants were being, shedding thousands of seeds for us to gather. Kate didn't really seem to be that interested. Her agenda was to ease further into ownership of the situation, with us running the garden and doing the harvest. Never mind the details.

She got very interested in the details, however, when by fall she began to understand that seeds worth potentially many thousands of dollars were being harvested from her garden. Toward the end she demanded at least half of the seeds for herself. She had come to see the garden and the seed-saving in terms of the monetary value of the produce. She had made some efforts, under Barbara's tutelage, to preserve produce, making tomato sauce and learning to save tomato seeds. But Kate was so far alienated from the garden that she couldn't honor the process, she was so distracted by her life—by the many people who passed through, attracted to Kate and her vision, and then left under not-so-happy circumstances; by the machinations of the neighbors; by her new boyfriend, who was the caretaker for the southern end of the next door ranch; by her frequent journeys; by the legal upheavals, and by drama between her and her family. So far alienated was she that the abundance of the garden was lost on her. She could take no account of the miracle of plenty before her. She knew however, that I was happily gathering seeds and she wanted her part of that wealth. We had no intention of keeping all these seeds for ourselves. We would gladly share them and gift a portion to her as Nature's bounty because it was the right thing to do, not because she demanded it. Kate had no inkling when we were talking garden last fall that a seed crop would naturally come with that. She didn't understand that there is no way for a seed gatherer not to gather seeds, so collect them we would, and share them.

It's very true that Barbara was away a lot. Our employment understanding called for us each to be off for two months in the winter, and I had not been away at all save for a single retreat to the Monastery of Christ in the Desert. Four months, then, for Barbara to carry on her outside activities—a trip to Africa for composting workshops, Reiki initiations, attending training. Maybe she took a little more time than that, from September to September. When she was in the garden however, she often worked in high gear for five or six hours at a time.

The only question that made sense at the time was this: "Just what was it that didn't get done during the times that Barbara was away, Kate? What is it that's been neglected, what do you observe?" The garden was munificent, food enough for twice the number of people eating it. There could be no complaint about neglect there. And the seeds were a pure bonus.

I worked at a much slower pace than Barbara, but kept up with the seed gathering, which required keeping consciousness for the maturing of a couple of dozen varieties of flowers, herbs, and vegetables at a time, harvesting them when they were ready, and caring for the seeds. Seedpods (say for soybeans or peas) could be too moist in the morning to shell out the seeds, and just right in the afternoon. Seed gathering needed close timing and knowledge of what to look for. Kate missed those lessons. I wrote a plaintive account of her apprenticeship at the time:

While the garden was spectacular and productive, the teaching just didn't happen in the way it needed to. There's no blame, only disappointment...

I wanted to show you, Kate, something about this mullein plant here at the center of the garden. You'll remember that it's a volunteer. We didn't plant it; it just appeared in the middle of this round bed of herbs, in a place to teach us something about striving and generosity. Rootedness. Now in this mullein, nearly at the end of its life, the ultimate act of Nature's great-heartedness unfolds. I want to inspire in you a sense of wonder about what's happening here; I am in awe of a plant that can uplift itself with such grace in such a striving as this. Never mind that it's grown seven feet tall in its central spire, and added half a dozen subsidiary spires. Never mind that it's provided enough velvety leaves for poultices and tea for a small community. Never mind that it's been such a source of inspiration for us as we've worked around it and glimpsed it out of the corners of our eyes a dozen times a day. For now in frosty November, beyond all those gifts, this plant presents us with Mother's astonishing generosity: her seeds.

Each spire by now has seedpods the size of a large pea. I did a rough count and there are about 32 pods for each inch of stem. Another rough estimate: there are about 12 feet, 144 inches of stem, so four and a half thousand pods. The seeds spilled out in the second picture here are those from one pod. There are 500, more or less.

Kate, this mullein plant is prepared to shed for us more than two million seeds. If your sense of wonder is kindled by this, so much the better, for Steiner tells us in this week's chapter (of our reading Love and its Meaning in the World*) "that all philosophy, all deeper contemplation on the secrets of existence, proceeds from wonder, from amazement. In other words, as long as human beings feel no wonder at the phenomena of life around them, their life is vapid and thoughtless and they ask without intelligence about the why and wherefore of existence." Steiner links awe and wonder with compassion and conscience as "powers whereby human beings transcend what they are in the physical body."*

But I also want to make another point, since we're often at loggerheads about money, and counting carefully: 2,000,000 seeds equals 100,000 thousand packets. At $3.50 per packet that's a third of a million dollars. Now you wrote a week or so ago, as an addendum to our contract, that seeds should be divided equally between us, as well as the edible produce of the garden. You're quite clear then that seeds have value and we think accounting of our worth to you needs to reflect this. Note too, please, that by far most of the seeds with which we started this garden came from our Aurora Farm inventory, with never a mention of payment. Not only the value of the seeds themselves—and we have many, many more varieties saved here this season to offer you openhandedly—but also the techniques for gathering them, the appreciation of their special qualities, these could have been yours if you could have made yourself available for our teachings these last few weeks.

*   *   *

I hope there is a wistful feeling communicated there for that is what I was experiencing at the time, two weeks before we left in mid-November. Wistful because I had come to Kate's to teach—didn't much matter to me if it was teaching little guys or grownups—and it hadn't happened. Sixteen months after my initial visit the school was no closer to opening, and Kate had proved to be less suitable as an apprentice than we might have wished. I wasn't really angry with Kate, rather with my own naiveté for not seeing this coming.

I prepared a photo book of the garden, including a flattering picture of Kate, and had it professionally printed and bound, as a gift for her and presented it to her explicitly as a peace offering.

During the last six weeks we were there, we exchanged frequent emails with Kate around the possibility of signing up for another year. It's a measure of the estrangement we were feeling with each other that we negotiated in such an impersonal way, but it also made sense to have in writing all the proposals and counter-proposals, both to refer to and to pass on to Dale Bates, the architect, who had agreed to mediate with the three of us. Mediation had been Kate's idea earlier in the year, but she had proposed a professional mediator, with whom she'd had other dealings. We demurred on that occasion, but Dale, we felt, was someone known to all of us. He had enthusiastically taken part in one of our Biodynamic stirring sessions, and in a reading group we had initiated to discuss Rudolf Steiner's *Love and its Meaning in the World* . We'd enjoyed his and Peggy's hospitality several times. Dale's business and relations with his large staff seemed to prosper and to reflect high ideals. Prior to our first and only meeting with him as mediator, Kate outlined a set of terms for our employment.

The terms she proposed were so larded with legalese that we responded:

What is it that leads you to seek remedy in a legalistic, heartless, inhuman, ugly contract and lease agreement like this? What makes you want to kill the spirit of co-creation that brought us here? Why replace cooperation with coercion?

Now, when we try to reduce this experience of ours to hours and timecards in some convenient/conventional way as it's done in the wider culture of jobs, we run into problems: 1) We ourselves in our role as stewards are reduced by this reckoning and we won't stand for it; we've paid our dues and deserve more respect than that; 2) When compensation for stewardship (as opposed to a job behind a counter or tending a machine) is reduced by this kind of reckoning the sacred is disrespected as well.

What we have experienced as our sacred duty, here in this place with this garden, you have considered a job. Perhaps it was the only way you and your dad could conceive of what was happening, and you confused offering an opportunity for stewardship with offering a job. When you offered money you saw it as binding us to the task, no matter how ill-defined; we saw the money as allowing us to be here, the means we needed to be able to apply ourselves to the mission, the stewardship.

On October 25, we met with Dale and Kate in our apartment. Dale had a certain protocol he wished to have followed regarding his role as mediator and, by and large, did a good job as listener and commentator, but the procedure did not allow for any discussion of the sources of the difficulties between us and Kate. What was allowed was dialogue about how we might continue our relationship into a second year, the contract points that might need to be clarified. By this point Barbara and I were quite sure we would leave within a month and Kate, who had been discussing job terms with a Waldorf-trained teacher and had apparently offered this apartment to her, was happy for us to go. At one point Kate said, "I would like to consider today your last day on the job here." None but Kate took this seriously (our original contract called for termination by either party with one month notice), but as it turned out our last paycheck from her at the end of the month was for precisely 25 days of October and no more. Though we tried for our remaining three weeks on the ground to make this right with her, Kate stonewalled about any further pay, even though we had expended considerable effort in saving seed, cleaning up in the garden and making things orderly in the tool shed.

How did compassion and dignity fit in here? We felt under-appreciated and disrespected by Kate because of the disconnects between her dismal view of economics and our idealistic one; we had from the beginning wanted to bring into our discussions the premises of associative economics—the principles of good will, selflessness, and generosity that might prevail in the way honorable people could work together for a noble goal, in this case Kate's own goal of combining nutrition and education in one seamless curriculum.

Kate's view, all bound up in counting hours and dollars, amounted to wage slavery; ours exalted human freedom and cooperation. Thomas Carlyle coined the description of economics as "the dismal science" in a tract entitled Occasional Discourse on the Negro Question, in which he was arguing for the reintroduction of slavery as a means to regulate the labor market in the West Indies. He argued that slavery was actually morally superior to the market forces of supply and demand promoted by economists, since, in his view, the freeing up of the labor market by the liberation of slaves had actually led to a moral and economic decline in the lives of the former slaves themselves. (Thank you Wikipedia for that explanation.)

As it happened, we exited Kate's place on November 16, all our chattels in a 4-horse trailer destined for storage, and ourselves back in that VW Vanagon, headed for a Christmas reunion with Barbara's sons in the Kootenays.

Chapter 15 – Meadowsweet Farm, New Hampshire – Summer, 2008

The mismatch between our values and Kate's was echoed a year and a half later when we found ourselves again entering into what we hoped would be an innovative Steiner-style associative economic arrangement with a landowner. Given exorbitant land prices and the expenses of startup equipment, housing, and so forth, I had held for some time the notion that we could best re-enter the farming life—as teachers—by offering our talents and experience in a partnership arrangement with an already-existing enterprise where the infrastructure was in place. To do this in a seemly way Barbara and I would need to occupy a status on the farm somewhat more elevated than that of a renter or hireling, similar perhaps to that of elders in a tribal society, and take on serious stewardship responsibilities. A measure of trust would be required on both sides, trust on our part that our needs would be taken care of and on the part of the landowners that their farm's life would be enhanced by our activities there. Ideally, ultimately, there would be no "sides" at all. Again, could the economy of the land be the reigning paradigm?

From http://www.arthuredwards.net/associative_economics

Associative economics constitutes a new paradigm in economic thinking. It stems largely from the insight of Rudolf Steiner's 1922 course in economics, and is based on awareness of the true nature of economic relationships.

Associative economics seeks to open up a new path into a new landscape, from competition to association as a mode of co-coordinating economic life, seeing individuals, not market forces, as the true agents of change.

And from Jeff Poppen in Biodyamics, Spring, 2008:

People can associate economically in a cooperative manner; Rudolf Steiner wondered how to set a price value on goods. Nature plus labor creates goods with a value, such as farming some potatoes.

The true price of the crop is when we receive enough to enable us to satisfy all our needs until it is time again to produce the same product, another crop of potatoes. Ideally, we need to be clear that we don't get paid for our labor or the potatoes, but simply to satisfy our needs until there are more potatoes. When grandpa grows several bushels of potatoes for his family, we have an example of associative economics. The family wouldn't consider paying him, just as they wouldn't consider letting him go without something he needs. Food, although necessary for human existence, is a transitory wealth. The potatoes will soon be worth nothing. But the farm that grows the potatoes is the means of production, and insures the future. Food and labor need to be taken out of the marketplace; farms and other means of production need community support. When an objective community spirit is working in associations of people providing for each other, a wise intelligence appears; we feel good when everyone gets treated fairly. CSA has its roots in the recognition of the fundamental difference between growing something and selling it. By juggling around a farm's organic material and livestock, food pours like manna from heaven on this earthly paradise. Plants, powered by the sun, can't help but create food and feed from the air and rain, and each year the animals reproduce. These resources, the farm's cornucopia, are a result of nature; the growth processes are a production economy. There is more every year.

On the other hand, what happens after harvest is no longer a result of nature or growth. People are involved in transporting, marketing, and consuming the farm's production, making this a human process in a reduction economy. We use it all up. These two economies are mutually dependent and make a whole, but work best autonomously. Farmers have no business in the market economy, where excess production creates problems. The marketplace has no bearing on the processes occurring on the farm. When farmers can make decisions from the needs of the farm itself, rather than from monetary concerns, farms thrive. Marketing is not the farmer's forté, just as farming is not for most other people. "Farmers' market" is an oxymoron.

What wise words coming from this Tennessee farmer: *"Food and labor need to be taken out of the marketplace; farms and other means of production need community support. When an objective community spirit is working in associations of people providing for each other, a wise intelligence appears; we feel good when everyone gets treated fairly."*

When we placed the following advertisement on the Forum of the website of the U.S. Biodynamic Association we knew we were expecting to break new ground.

Biodynamic gardeners and teachers seek opportunity to share life's work

Barbara M. V. Scott and Woody Wodraska wish to share the rich diversity of our life's work in a heart centered, human based community motivated to leave a life affirming legacy for the children and the Planet. We have lived and breathed Biodynamics for many years and wish to be with people who take Rudolf Steiner's spiritual impulse for agriculture to heart in their lives. We uphold a vision focusing on education, nutrition and right relationship with all beings. We need congenial housing and modest salary. Read our biographies and about our work in the world at: www.soulmedicinejourney. com 541-535-1786

On Leap Day, 2008 we received a response from Bob Bernstein at Meadowsweet Farm in Antrim, New Hampshire. He wrote, *"Susan and my property is 100a in Antrim, 25 miles northwest of Wilton and northeast of Keene. We've been 'homesteading' here for 15 years, are 52 and 56 respectively and seeking.......well, seeking. We have no job to offer but perhaps the makings of one.*

The farm is old, viewsome, ever more fertile and offers similar potential to the 17 others you've known and loved. Empty cottage 6/1/08 with view of Mt Monadnock. More later, feel free to call or write."

No job to offer, even at our modest salary stipulation. The next day he wrote again. Among many details of his farm, his work, his farm work, he said, *"Typically we rent\ barter the cottage for 750\mo less 10 or more hours @12\hr barter rate for help with chores etc. That includes water and electricity but not heat which is gas and wood. We are open to rent\lease\sale options."*

And much later Bob sent a copy of the lease agreement he'd used with prior renters of the Cottage. His "10 or more hours at $12/hour barter rate" became 20 hours ($250) discounted from the rent of $750. To my mind, 20 hours per month between the two of us, Barbara and me, working land and animals was laughably little time—40 minutes a day. One would use that up just feeding and watering chickens, collecting and cleaning eggs. If Barbara and I were to undertake serious land care, gardening, and Biodynamics practice at Meadowsweet Farm, if we were to be considered stewards of certain aspects of the place, then our needs at least should be taken care of, and, I thought, this will become obvious when we're actually on the ground there.

If the reader detects a typically Woodyesque naiveté and lack of foresight in our impending decision to carry ourselves and all our possessions from Oregon to New Hampshire on the strength of such a weak assumption, I will own that. But the nitty-gritty of such an association could only be worked out in practice, it seemed to me, and we were already well into spring. A summer of no gardening loomed before us and that would be unsupportable. Rather go, we thought, than stumble over details. Rather trust good will, flexibility, the farm's abundance, and the economy of the land to prevail as events unfolded.

Further, Bob seemed to be somewhat flexible about the terms surrounding housing. He wrote, "farming and such could probably offset rent...much-yes, most—maybe..."

I wrote back: "You mentioned that the cottage usually brings in $750/month for you, less an unspecified amount of work/chores available at $12/hour. I'm sure the $750 is a significant adjunct to your household income but *paying rent would not be in the cards for us at all*. Garden work, animal care, wood cutting, driveway plowing, building maintenance—all those things and more—certainly would be, however. Our souls ache for such work. *We will be taking a significant risk, bringing ourselves and our household across country on speculation, as it were, no matter how much we are propelled on good will and positive planning. We hope to be received into a nurturing place*."

Bob talked at some length with us about preparation of much more Meadowsweet land for gardens than had been done before: the best part of an acre across the road from the cottage, in addition to a sizable kitchen garden in his back yard that had been cultivated for some years. The new ground had been cover cropped for several seasons and the light, sandy soil was in fine tilth.

After a good deal of emailing back and forth Barbara and I determined to go forward with this admittedly risky proposition, investing some $6,500 as it turned out, on travel and moving expenses, first to get Barbara there to New Hampshire at the end of May when the cottage became available and gardening could begin in earnest, and me a month later, with all our possessions in a rental truck. Summer 2008 gas prices were hovering around $4 per gallon, but we proffered the plastic all the way across country and figured we'd pay the piper later. Our intent was to spend three years at Meadowsweet, about the time it takes to transform a cared-for farm into a Biodynamically-nurtured one. If we could have rent and utilities covered, and eat mostly garden produce, we figured we could pay down the credit card debt in a timely way, especially since we had been doing without a vehicle for a few months and thus had put a tourniquet on one of the typical American family's great cash hemorrhages. The three years could also be the building-up time for our educational endeavors whose shape we had yet fully to envision. Would we try to run a school where students came for a few days or a week or two, several times a year? Would there be opportunity in southern New Hampshire to bring the gardening impulse to the three existing Waldorf schools?

During the month Barbara was at Meadowsweet and I was still in Oregon, preparing to move our possessions, she told me by phone of her daily activities, her writing, the garden work, potato and 3-Sisters planting with Waldorf school students, how it went with the goat milking. A quarter-mile of potatoes went in, and 100 tomato plants. The cottage was comfortable, though sparsely furnished, and she'd be happy to have our furniture and such. The view was spectacular, the soil was lovely, and Bob and Susan and family were welcoming. Already in those first weeks Barbara had supervised the spreading of Biodynamic preparations on the gardens on two occasions. She was making yogurt and ricotta cheese

When I arrived at the end of June and we'd gotten fully moved in I was able to make my own observations.

To my delight farm life at Meadowsweet was centered on one of those great New England barns, just across the road from our Cottage, a three-storied structure probably about 80 by 40 feet, built of weather beaten boards but in pretty good shape overall, except for the roof which was due to be replaced, a $19,000 job, we were told. The ground-level storey was dedicated to the animals and their stalls, feed storage, tool storage, milking setup.

When I arrived there were four sheep, three donkeys and maybe a dozen goats—two milking does, one superannuated doe, four or five adolescent does and bucks and a group of little guys born this year. Too many goats for my taste, but I've never been an enthusiast. There were about four dozen chickens, a couple of adult turkeys and 15 baby turkeys at the ball-of-fluff stage.

My first full day on the farm was marked by a crisis in the Meadowsweet animal realm. I was exploring the barn and came into the ground floor animal section to stand by the gate that separated the feed and tool section from the critters when I saw one of the sheep lying down under a manger and in obvious difficulty, breathing hard. I went to find Barbara and tell her about this, as she was very much in touch with the scene in the barn. Still discombobulated from my cross country trip, I withdrew, to hear later that two of the four sheep had died, apparently from getting into grain stored in the milking stall and overeating. Barbara told me later that she sat on the barn floor with a sheep's head in her lap, applying Reiki energy, to no avail. At first, Susan had speculated that grass clippings she had fed them might have something to do with the deaths. Then, since Barbara had milked that morning, the finger of blame pointed to her—gently and tentatively, but nonetheless pointed—as the one who may not have secured the latch on the milking stall gate properly. This was important because at least one of the goats was latch savvy. No mention was made of whose decision it was to store grain behind a single, waist-high gate.

The barn was a delight from a distance and closer up in the part that sheltered the animals; when you entered the level above, however, having shoved aside one of the giant sliding doors, you encountered a filthy, chaotic shambles. No single family could have accumulated so much stuff—some of it useful, some of it pure junk with the dust and pigeon poop of several decades layered on. Room after room was crammed full of obsolete and broken furniture, odds and ends, usable materials, good lumber, items of unfathomable function. Up in the hay mow, it was the same story, except that here you could find yourself falling through missing or busted floorboards if you weren't very careful. Thousands of dollars worth of lumber, though, neatly sorted. Two more rooms up above, one crammed with hastily rolled pieces of fencing and the other, you could just barely see how, with a day or two of cleanup, it could serve as a teaching room.

For one of our foremost hopes in coming to Meadowsweet was to inaugurate a school for conscious agriculture; we had already talked with Bob and, by extension the Land for Good people, about finding funding for such a project through their organization.

Earlier in his life Bob had been a general contractor, so he had a fine collection of power tools, portable and floor mounted; the planer, band saw, table saw, compound miter saw lined up in the central bay among various projects-in-waiting, including an 18 foot wooden boat in need of renovation. At one point Bob spent a Saturday cleaning up that working area in preparation to attack one or another major project, perhaps that boat. I was able later to take advantage of the lumber and tools to build a top bar beehive. Bob's history as a contractor had an unforeseen ramification later. He felt, and said out loud, that this professional experience gave him a keen judgment about how long tasks subcontracted by careful workmen should take. This became an issue when Bob insisted that Barbara and I keep a record, time- and task-wise, of the activities for which we expected to be compensated, as work-trade for rent. I told him:

What is not clear is how our work for Meadowsweet translates into income that might allow us to honor the agreement. You have encouraged us, several times, to keep track of our time in certain categories, categories which would then presumably be parsed in relation to ongoing work for the farm, work for our own food, work for your food, work that has nothing to do with Meadowsweet, work for the future of the farm. Barbara agreed in principle to do this; I did not, because I cannot see my life in these terms. It would take a Talmudic scholar or a Medieval scholastic to sort out my life in the ways you imagine.

This subtle point is one of the rocks on which our ship of associative economics was to founder: the notion that stewardship was something that involves counting or measuring of the spreadsheet sort. This is how it seemed to me: for Bob, if you couldn't count it—hours or dollars—it didn't really exist. And, further, the notion lurked behind this discussion that the landowner—the fellow who requires rent of his helpers—is best suited to decide whether, say, a gate latch shall be repaired (*Says the peon—Let's see: 15 minutes at $12.50/hr = $3.125...but wait, I've already earned my $250 discount from rent this month*) or be left until next month. Do you see the trap here? Either every single task has to be analyzed like this, with the hireling trying to guess what the "Boss" might decide; or none is so analyzed and the job to be done is prioritized in a more organic fashion within the large picture of the needs of the farm. Our position was that the roles *Boss* and *hired hand* are immaterial and obsolete. We felt we could all be equal before the economy of the land, all be supported by the farm and all be working toward its health and well being. Strange as it sounds in a culture founded on ideas of property ownership, our position was that the very idea of humans owning land was preposterous. The time of any one family's tenure on a farm, a few decades, at most a century or two, is infinitesimal compared to geologic time or the life of the planet. We denizens of Meadowsweet are there by grace, we felt, by fate and destiny, no matter whose name appears on the deed, and in the long flow of time will be as forgotten as those who built the rock walls we see wending through these woods, walls which once bounded sheep pastures, now taken back by the forest.

But the Lord-of-the-Manor-to-serf relationship was close to the surface at Meadowsweet and the Landlord-to-renter stance firmly in place. Old-paradigm stuff, but sanctified by law and custom. *We never dared to question it.*

Rudolf Steiner might have wept, to see how far we were in the summer of 2008 from the ideal of threefold social order at Meadowsweet farm.

Try as we might to pry Bob and Susan out of the old paradigm the more stuck they were in their preconceived picture of their relationship to us. We were valued for the rent we would pay, devalued when we didn't pay it. In the Bernstein scenario the inhabitants of the Cottage helped bolster the farm's bottom line. It had been this way for the 12 or 15 years Bob and Susan had been there, and that was the only way they could conceive of the relationship. Never mind that Barbara and Woody were there as full-time stewards; never mind that our talents and experience, added to their resources, could make a model Biodynamic teaching farm there; never mind that the gardens during the 2008 season would generate food far beyond the needs of the farm's folks, and that this had a great deal to do with Barbara's timely work in the first month, our ongoing Biodynamic practice, and the viability of Aurora Farm seed that had been sown with no compensation for *our* bottom line.

In many ways these folks were very kind and understanding. They allowed us occasional use of one of their vehicles. They shared meals with us and jars of apple sauce they'd canned. They picked up our mail at the distant post box as they went by. As frustrated as he must have been about our rent balking, Bob never once raised his voice when we talked. But on this point of rent-paying they were unyielding. They were under no obligation, of course, to buy into our idea of how an associative relationship might work or to think differently than they had about ownership.

In August Barbara left for an extended teaching/learning journey to New Mexico, Ohio, and Tennessee. We were both feeling less than enthusiastic about our future at Meadowsweet. We had failed to establish trust. Steiner said in the lecture *The Individual and Community,* "...social morality is then founded on the only basis upon which the social life can be based, that is upon the basis of mutual trust. This trust we must be able to win even for the big concerns of life....And without this trust—a golden word—without this training for trust, for faith in the individual, not only in the nation or in humanity, but in the individual, nothing can be done."

We may sound sour-grapey if we note that there was a class consciousness on both sides here, with the land owners lording it over us, but the top-down flow was definitely present, along with a lack of communication among equals. Invariably when there was a need to talk over details of every day life and work, Bob would say something like, "Well, I just have a few minutes here to tell you this..." or "I have a conference call coming in five minutes." And *never once* did the four of us sit down to explore any vision of the farm's future. If we had plans to teach wannabe farmers at Meadowsweet, well and good. Bob's only comment was that we would need to pay rent for the space we needed in the barn to do that.

On one occasion, when Bob and Susan and family were within an hour of leaving for a week on a family adventure to Cape Cod, he approached me with instructions about three things that needed doing: could I renew the cross fence in the six acre field where brought-in cows were grazing; the field below the compost yard needed mowing to set back noxious weeds and encourage growth of the grass; but before that I would need to grease the universal couplings on the PTO shaft of the bush hog attached to the Kubota tractor. His rapid-fire delivery allowed for no questions (how does one detach the shields on the PTO shaft? where are the fencing materials? What's the best way to open those huge field gates and drag them uphill to get the tractor through?) As it happened, I failed to perform these assigned tasks, which did nothing for the issue of trust.

He was always in a hurry, this guy, and often enough talking on his cell phone while he moved through task after task on weekends or after work. His relaxation seemed to come best when he was bouncing on the tractor seat or mowing the lawns into shape.

I pretty much confined my activities to the non-mechanical sphere, weeding and thinning cucumbers and carrots in the garden, taking care of the chickens and turkeys, tying tomato plants to their stakes and, later in the season, harvesting them by the wheelbarrow load every couple of days.

There had never been such abundance from the Meadowsweet gardens. Barbara was mainly responsible for feeling out the needs of the farm intuitively, deciding which Biodynamic preparations were best applied and when, for bringing beauty and interest to the gardens with flower plantings, beautifully shaped beds and areas dedicated to seed production. She raised the vibration of those gardens exponentially and she did that in the face of pure indifference.

Meanwhile both Barbara and I both had books to write. We were mustering up the organizational bits to flesh out Aurora Farm Family Foundation, setting up local relationships with farmers market people, goat people, alternative farming and food folks. We were neglecting all these things to try to keep the gardens and animals in good shape, and for no noticeable personal compensation. With Barbara away, when Bob and I set aside time to talk about our financial arrangements, Bob said, "We had no idea you were not going to pay rent…we have budgeted for that money…we need it." The garden work and produce, he asserted, was shared: he provided seeds and plants and labor; we provided seeds and plants and labor; he and his family were eaters and so were we. It was all a wash, Bob averred. Never mind that Woody and Barbara could have fed themselves very nicely with a garden one one-twentieth the size of the Meadowsweet enterprise. No compensation to be expected there. Anyway, he said, Barbara had been "mostly moving in" during her first month, which was incorrect and self-serving, demeaning and disrespectful, I thought.

Probably I don't need to go any further with this sad recital of the failure of another attempt at associative economics. The lesson for us? To be explicit about our intentions in that direction and to seek real agreement toward new ways of thinking about ownership and labor before embarking on such a journey.

Barbara met at a New Hampshire farmers market a couple who have lived in the Azores for many years and we decided to store our things and go there for an extended writing and resting time. Perhaps even to emigrate. The view from the south window as I write is unobstructed Atlantic Ocean, right down to Antarctica and we are happily eating local Azorean food and enjoying a Gulf Stream climate.

My Halloween notes written in my journal after a couple of days at our new home on Faial reflected the fascination I felt with the history of agriculture, written on the ground between the island's ring road and the sea. Growing out of the ground were hedges and walls of rough cut volcanic stone, the lava bubbles showing. The Azores were discovered by Portuguese mariners in the mid-1400s and settlement began, first on a single island, Santa Maria or San Miguel, I forget which; the others soon after and within a couple of decades, long before Columbus sailed for the New World, rugged homesteaders were wresting a living from small holdings on all these islands. I could see their work of 500 and 300 years ago in the village geography: the homes of rough cut stone (every householder a quarryman and mason), the walls—for windbreak and to hold livestock, retaining walls holding gardens and fruit trees against the pull of the sea; all this land wants eventually to return there. And the hedges, for windbreak and stock-holding, for firewood. These walls and hedges enclose tiny fields, most less than an acre, some plots no bigger than a small garden. These people grew all their own food, as far as I can imagine their situation, a thousand sea miles from home in Portugal. And fish. There would have been lots of fish. Some of our neighbors brought their cows down from the high pastures while we were there and put them out in small pastures near home, sometimes right next door to our winter rental home. The animals were tethered on a 20-25 foot lead rope looped through a step-on metal anchor. Often there'd be a momma cow with her calf, and a dry cow or steer and these animals would walk down the macadam road with their handlers a few minutes in the evening to the next pasture in the rotation.

So, fish, dairy, vegetables, fruit. Whatever would have been imported from the mainland would have been durable goods and live things that would multiply. Generation after generation, 500 years. Barbara caught a ride with a local who was here on business, as his real home was Gloucester, Massachusetts, where he'd been for 30 years and more. He could remember, just, the times when islanders were more or less self-reliant and minimally governed. Talking with him I would have tried to elicit some of the body memory he must still possess of the homesteader's tasks and values. Their ferocious independence. How close he was in his genes to the peasant life, to being a digger of onions and garlic, a maker of cheese. A maker of his own shelter, his own entertainment.

Afterword

"It is not a given to be welcome..." (Martin Prechtel)

What Barbara and I have run up against in the four years since leaving Aurora Farm, is that our ideals of proprietorship and stewardship have been at odds with the cultural notion of ownership and all of the baggage that goes along with that—boundaries, insurance, taxes, mortgages, worry, pride, inheritance. We are immersed in this conception of ownership, so enshrined in law and custom that it seems it couldn't be any other way. Where we have hoped to find land to have the use of, to steward, we have found owners urgently intent on the responsibilities and perquisites of possession. This is ancestral prejudice. (Also Martin Prechtel's term.) There is a vast difference between ownership and stewardship. Anyone can own land; it takes consciousness, caring, humility and a spirit of awe and wonder to be a steward. Our First Nation peoples, our indigenous brothers and sisters, were first bewildered, then enslaved, and finally nearly exterminated by white people who seized possessive, exclusive ownership of the landscape. I abjure ownership of air, water and the land just as I condemn the genocide perpetrated by my forbears.

It works the same for the seeds...

Manifesto for Seeds

We are seed users, seed eaters, seed growers...all of us. We have been wrapped in a world of seeds for eons, since long before agriculture was thought of. In hunger we ate the bird that ate the seeds; in happy accident we brewed the beer from spoiled and worthless seeds; in unwitting service to the plant we transported its seeds from place to place on our trouser cuffs. We slobber over ear corn and eat our Wheaties. It's in our language: We are of our parents' seed, our ancestors' seed. We are born into, thrive in, die in, a seed sowing, seed garnering heritage. To deny sacred status to these capsules of memory and consciousness, these enfoldments of life we call seeds, is to court foolish disaster. We have always known this.

But...now they're messing with our seeds. The power grabbing corporations and their government flunkies propose in their arrogance to irradiate...manipulate... defructify...genetically and spiritually violate, monopolize and further disrespect our ancient birthright, our real wealth, SEEDS. We are strong when we have seeds. They who would enslave us use as leverage the seeds we cherish, the seeds that nourish us. What we would pass on to the seventh generation as bridegift they seize as strategy. They would put a price on the priceless and sell it back to us. Do not let them delude you about their sophisticated seed bank in the high arctic. Seeds are not preserved by freezing them and locking them away from growers; they are not saved inside mountains and behind bank-vault doors. Hide your weapons of mass destruction there, or your bullion, if you will, but our seeds hold life which does not thrive in such places. If you would keep a seed forever and increase it—*grow it out.* Surrender it to soil and warmth and moisture; wait for the miracle of a plant; hold the hope of fruition as one seed becomes many—even millions. Then give them away.

Leave our seeds alone. Leave our seeds in the hands of the people who feed us... the family, the clan, the village group. The profession of "seedsman" was created only 130 years or so ago. Perhaps it was an aberration to try to centralize a process that had before been disbursed in clan and village gardens, homestead gardens, middens and small fields. Grandmothers and Great-uncles collected, watched over, cherished the seeds that came down to them. Grew them out with love and patience and infinite care. Grandmother's seeds... grandmother's blessing...passed from generation to generation. Reckon three generations to a century and 150 centuries in the history of agriculture and you have several hundred generations of seed gathering folk, seed saving grandcestors, passing on precious seeds to descendants. There is memory encapsulated in this line of life stretching so far back. Feelings are there too...feelings of gratitude to Gaia, of holding dear, of well wishing to the future generations, feelings of faithfulness...feminine feelings.

The memory is right there in the seed, and in our cells, in the mitochondrial DNA passed down the feminine line. When I touch my seeds I tap the memory that is there, ancestral wisdom almost lost, beaming itself into our consciousness just when it is most needed.

John Trudell said: "It's about our D N A. Descendants Now Ancestors. We are the descendants and we are the ancestors. D N A, our DNA, our blood, our flesh and our bone, is made up of the metals and the minerals and the liquids of the earth. We are the earth. We truly, literally and figuratively are the earth. Any relationship we will ever have in this world to real power--the real power, not energy systems and other artificial means of authority--but any relationship we will ever have to real power is our relationship to the earth." (1)

Seeds are concentrated wealth. Seeds are worth far more than we pay for them now, in the nursery or hardware store. You can pack in a suitcase ten thousand dollars worth of garden seeds in any variety you choose. The slavemasters and their propagandists would have us believe that money is power and, since they have plenty of money, that they are in control. They don't want us to have that suitcase, to be free to leave and plant elsewhere; or free to stay and plant many gardens, feed many people with real food.

If we are staunchly of the Earth, her power is ours to neutralize and transmute the evil work of the authority-mongers, those without conscience. We can do this with life enhancing actions. Repeat. Life-affirming actions can override and overwhelm the lifeless. Always the great stone temples of the arrogant become topsoil for living systems. It's something the corporations and governments fail to appreciate. Their authority rests on entropic processes—explosions, coercions, cultural lies. They cannot take into account the power of life, the connectedness of life. They would have us forget where we come from...so we can be entertained and exploited and addicted to their cheap dream, their gadgets and their ersatz food. If we are staunchly of the Earth we have access to the strength of the generations, the ancestory, to help us put life-affirming ideas and actions in the places where death-dealing had been. We can REMEMBER from where our power comes. Let us plant gardens. Let us plant trees. Let us tend cows.

> *Our weapons are our tools...*
> *our ammunition is our seeds...*
> *our fuel is our sacred intent to do right by the*
> *future of life on the Planet...*
> *our marching song is the thrumming of memory in our cells.*

We march in concert, but we do not march en masse. Our aim is not to dominate or overpower. Rather, our aim is service. Each of us has a plot of earth to serve, our own nature spirits and devas to consult...intuition that speaks in us...we know how to surrender to the requirements of the task, of plants and soil, in order to earn our harvest. We bow to the task in joy and service, each individual one of us mustering pure intent, a gutsy laugh, with the power of life upholding us.

Join Wendell Berry's Mad Farmers Liberation Front. No dues. No meetings. You just have to be pissed off enough to be clever. Don't be depressed, be clever. Let us be clear. There is no money in this, only sustenance. This passing forward of DNA on family or clan level is a matter of right livelihood, not of commerce.

And right livelihood brings joy. If I can feed myself, my family, a few others perhaps when surplus appears, then I have done something REAL. I am in touch with my power, and my delight. I am creating my part of the story.

JOY...What if the picture that's been drawn of peasant life as, "Nasty...Brutish... Short" is a cultural con job put out by the rationalists and the materialists, the ones who shortly would have something to sell us? What if life on a subsistence level has joys and satisfactions as well as challenges? What if people had time to laugh and sing? What if there were still people in the world who could catch the memory of this and show it to us? A friend tells me about life in the Philippines, far back on the rural islands...tells how, when two rice threshers or donkey drivers meet and begin to talk, they're laughing most of the way through the conversation. There is something boisterously entertaining about what is going on in their poverty-stricken lives.

John G. Bennett wrote of an encounter in Africa: "Following a lightly trodden path, I came upon a Basuto village. All the inhabitants were out hoeing mealies. Their ages must have ranged from seven to seventy, and they were singing and hoeing to the rhythm of their own music. As they saw me they all stopped and stood straight up in surprise. Then with one accord they began to laugh. I have never heard such laughter.

It was pure joy and friendship, without malice and without thought. I joined in, and we all laughed together for several minutes. I waved my hand and walked on, and they resumed their gravity and their hoeing.

"This was one of the unforgettable moments of my life. A lifetime's experience had convinced me that happiness is greatest where material prosperity is least. I had seldom seen a happy rich man, but I had seen many happy people among the poorest villagers of Asia Minor or Greece. I had seen happiness in Omdurman, but this happiness that I saw before my eyes was beyond all the others. Here was a village totally lacking even the smallest of the benefits of civilization. They had not even a plough or a cart. And yet they were the happiest people I had ever seen. They were without fear and without pride." (2)

They were without fear and without pride. The meek shall inherit the earth, for the meek remember who they are and where their power comes from.

"Prior to now," said Terence Mckenna, "nobody has dropped the ball. Four times the ice has ground down from the North and four times our ancestors retreated before it. They were cold and wet and miserable. They suffered more than we have ever had to." In words to this effect McKenna honors the ancestory; our people carried on the story of humans on this Earth for all those millennia. Are we going to be the ones to drop the ball? Are we going to wimp our way to our own and the Planet's destruction?

We say "NO…enough!" That dream of the would-be controllers, that our spirit could be mined to fuel their extravaganza of wastefulness and meanwhile make ourselves complicit—by acquiring all the stuff they have to sell—that dream is bankrupt and soulless. We reject it for the fraud it is.

(1) John Trudell, on the occasion of a memorial service for Earth First! Activist Judy Bari.
(2) J G Bennett, Witness Claymont Communications

Reading and Resource List for Biodynamic Agriculture

Introductory Readings

Love and its Meaning in the World, lectures by Rudolf Steiner http://www. steinerbooks.org/detail.html?id=9780880104418

Secrets of the Soil by Peter Tompkins and Christopher Bird   Many alternative techniques for natural growing, with a major emphasis on Biodynamics and Appendices on Rudolf Steiner and the Biodynamic preparations.

Culture and Horticulture: A philosophy of Gardening by Wolf Storl Comprehensive and probing coverage of all aspects of Biodynamics.

Stella*Natura [Planting Calendar] Working with Cosmic Rhythms: Inspiration & Practical Advice for Home Gardeners & Professional Growers. http://www. stellanatura.com/index.html

The Call of the Land by Steven McFadden http://www.thecall oftheland.com

Deep Gardening:Soul Lessons from 17 Gardens, a Biodynamic Memoir by Woody Wodraska http://www.soulmedicinejourney.com/Book.html

Advanced Readings

Spiritual Foundations for the Renewal of Agriculture Rudolf Steiner's seminal 1924 lectures in the Creeger/Gardner translation, 1994. Difficult and essential. Return to this time after time.

Agriculture as an Art – The Meaning of Man's Work on the Soil
The Biodnamic Spray Preparations as Sense Organs
Building Stones for Meeting the Challenges
Dying and Becoming – Man's Path to a New Communion with Nature
Growing Together – Why Should we Bother?
Tomorrow's Agriculture –Are We Meeting the Challenges

Lecture collections on Biodynamics by Manfred Klett and a few others

Resources

Aurora Farm Family Foundation www.soulmedicinejourney.com –

Josephine Porter Institute – Biodynamic Preparations, all of the above publications www.jpibiodynamics.org   276-930-2463

BDNOW! -- Email Discussion Group moderated by Allan Balliett   High volume, quirky, always interesting http://groups.yahoo.com/group/bdnow/

Agnihotra – www.agnihotra.org

Lee Valley Tools – Almost the only source for high quality Bulldog-style garden tools

Eric Sloane's Books on Early America – www.amazon.com ; for old tools and how they were used

Martin Prechtel – www.floweringmountain.com "Grief and Praise" CD-Rom

CSAs, Farmers Markets, Local food-- www.localharvest.org

ATTRA-- http://attra.ncat.org/ the latest in sustainable agriculture and organic farming news, events and funding opportunities; in-depth publications on production practices, alternative crop and livestock enterprises, innovative marketing, organic certification, and highlights of local, regional, USDA and other federal sustainable agriculture activities.

In British Columbia: Kootenay Local Agriculture Society http://www.klasociety.org

Films

The Real Dirt on Farmer John – John Peterson and Angelic Organics CSA Collective Eye Films, 2007

One Man, One Cow, One World – Peter Proctor from NZ transforms agriculture in India, 2006 www.cloudsouthfilms.co.nz

The Queen of the Sun – Bees and their plight Collective Eye Films, 2010

Acknowledgements

**This book is dedicated to
Barbara Mary Victoria Scott
whose love and loyalty uphold me.**

Fond and heartfelt appreciation to all the Missing Persons and teachers along the way. Especially in Camphill: Hubert Zipperlin, Harmtut von Jeetze, Joel Morrow, Helen Zipperlin; at Claymont, Pierre Elliot; at Kyles Hot Springs, Whitey; at Fossil, Edwin Derrick; at the B Bar Ranch, Maryann Mott, Duke and Les; in Arizona, Gabriel Cousins.

In West Virginia, many thanks to Allan Balliett and his wife Maura for faithfulness to the cause of Biodynamics and for friendship over the years.

Loving appreciation to sons Sky, William and Nathan, and to Sky's mom Ruth Aspen. And to my sister Jan Celella, who has believed in me for almost 70 years. Also, many blessings to Dominican Sister Adrian Hofsteter at St. Catharine's College in Kentucky for her ongoing encouragement.

I give thanks to have known all of you and ask to be forgiven for having rejected some of your lessons, and for having missed all together some others.

About the Author

Woody Wodraska has been a writer of non-fiction since his college days. He lives in British Columbia, Canada, with his wife Barbara Mary Victoria Scott. His 40-year gardening career has taken him to 17 gardens and another dozen agricultural endeavors in almost as many states and provinces. Always the questions arose—how to grow food, how to live in beauty and abundance with grace and in harmony and in co-creation with Devas and Nature Spirits. From backyard family gardens to a CSA enterprise feeding 100 families, Woody started from scratch or built on other gardeners' vision.